C000054297

Betrayed Ally

Betrayed Ally

China in the Great War

Frances Wood
and
Christopher Arnander

Pen & Sword
MILITARY

First published in Great Britain in 2016 by
PEN & SWORD MILITARY
An imprint of
Pen & Sword Books Ltd
47 Church Street
Barnsley
South Yorkshire
S70 2AS

Copyright © Frances Wood and Christopher Arnander, 2016

ISBN 978-1-47387-501-2

The right of Frances Wood and Christopher Arnander to be identified as the
authors of this work has been asserted by them in accordance with the Copyright,
Designs and Patents Act 1988.

A CIP catalogue record for this book is available from the British Library.

All rights reserved. No part of this book may be reproduced or transmitted in any
form or by any means, electronic or mechanical including photocopying, recording
or by any information storage and retrieval system, without permission from the
Publisher in writing.

Typeset by Concept, Huddersfield, West Yorkshire.
Printed and bound in England by CPI Group (UK) Ltd, Croydon, CR0 4YY.

Pen & Sword Books Ltd incorporates the imprints of Pen & Sword Aviation,
Pen & Sword Family History, Pen & Sword Maritime, Pen & Sword Military,
Pen & Sword Discovery, Wharncliffe Local History, Wharncliffe True Crime,
Wharncliffe Transport, Pen & Sword Select, Pen & Sword Military Classics,
Leo Cooper, The Praetorian Press, Remember When, Seaforth Publishing and
Frontline Publishing.

For a complete list of Pen & Sword titles please contact
PEN & SWORD BOOKS LIMITED
47 Church Street, Barnsley, South Yorkshire, S70 2AS, England
E-mail: enquiries@pen-and-sword.co.uk
Website: www.pen-and-sword.co.uk

Contents

Acknowledgements

We came to writing this book from different directions. Frances, author of 12 books about Chinese matters, wrote an account of the chaotic diplomacy of China in the Great War, *Picnics Prohibited*, which was published by Penguin (Australia) in 2014. Christopher's book about his grandfather, *Private Lord Crawford's Great War Diaries* (Pen & Sword, 2013), referred to the Japanese and British seizure of the German enclave in Shandong in the first weeks of the war. We had already cooperated on *Pavilions in the Air* (Stacey International, 2008), a collection of Chinese and English proverbs, with cartoons.

It seemed to us that there was room for an accessible history of China and the Great War, with plenty of illustrations, aimed at the general reader. There is, in fact, a wealth of published material about the subject, but mostly it is geared to the academic world. For example, two very fine works by Xu Guoqi, *China and the Great War* (Cambridge, 2005) and *Strangers on the Western Front* (Harvard, 2011) were published by university presses. Li Ma's *Les travailleurs chinois en France dans la Première guerre mondiale* (2012), about all aspects of the Chinese labourers' experiences, was the fruit of a scholary colloquium in 2010. These volumes are to be recommended to any of our readers who might want to delve more deeply into the subject.

Before embarking on our book, we sounded out friends and acquaintances, most of whom had only the vaguest idea of China's role in the Great War. Virtually all of them expressed great interest and curiosity. We were also encouraged by Julia Boyd, whose book *Dance with the Dragon* describes the expatriate community in China at the time. Dominiek Dendooven of the In Flanders Museum, Ypres, curated a marvellous exhibition in 2010 about the Chinese labourers in the war; we are grateful to him for his enthusiastic provision of information, images and advice. Nelson Oliver was a mine of information about the Chinese journeys across the Pacific and through Canada.

Libraries and other institutions that we found particularly helpful were the British Library, SOAS, The Library of Congress, Bibliothèque de l'Hôtel de Ville and Bibliothèque nationale de France, Paris, The National World War 1 Museum in Kansas City and UK National Archives at Kew.

We are grateful to.several descendants of diplomats who served in China during the Great War; they shared memories, illustrations and private papers with us. The archivists of three banks (Deutsche, HSBC and Barclays) provided useful information and images, for which acknowledgement is made at the appropriate place. We are indebted also to Professor Robert Bickers and Jamie Carstairs, of Historical Photographs of China/Visualising China.

We are especially grateful to our publisher, Pen & Sword; not only did they take on a title which is somewhat outside their military speciality, but they also coped marvellously with our detailed requirements. The task was made the more difficult because, while writing the book, we received many suggestions which justified some changes – the bane of any publisher. Their help has been unstinting, creative and good natured throughout the preparation of our book.

Frances Wood
Christopher Arnander

Image Credits

Plates

Taylor Archive, Barnsley, pp. 17–18, 31, 33–4, 37; Wellcome Library, London, p. 12; Tank Museum, Bovington, p. 38; *Le Petit Journal*, 6 April 1902, p. 14; Vroon BV, Breskens, p. 26;

W.R. Wheeler, *China & the World War*, 1918, pp. 28, 40–1; Mark Levitch, *Panthéon de la Guerre*, 2006, p. 52; Jeremy Rowett Johns and the Historical Photographs of China, University of Bristol, pp. 29–30; The Australian War Memorial, Canberra, p. 39; *L'Illustration*, 1919, p. 47;

Sophia McKenna Lloyd, p. 55; Sint-Andries Abbey in Zevenkerken, Bruges, pp. 42–3; In Flanders Fields Museum, Ypres, p. 20; James Brazier, pp. 35–6; Tom Cohen, p. 45; Maberley Phillips, *A History of Banks, Bankers & Banking in Northumberland, Durham and North Yorkshire*, 1894 (courtesy of Barclays Bank Archives), p. 44; John Swire & Sons Ltd Archive at School of Oriental & African Studies (SOAS), London, p. 8. Other plates from the internet.

Text inserts

Library of Congress, Washington, *Chronicling America: Historic American Newspapers*, pp. 46, 50, 68 (top), p. 82 (top), p. 130 (top & right), p. 152 (middle); *Le Petit Journal*, 3 March 1912, p. 78; *Punch*, 6 November 1918, p. 90; Taylor Archive, Barnsley, p. 86 (bottom), p. 92 (top left and top right); Honourable Artillery Company, London, Sylvester Alexander Album, p. 92 (bottom left); Historical Institute of Deutsche Bank, Frankfurt am Main, p. 54 (top & bottom); Alan Blaikley, p. 92 (bottom right), drawing by Ernest Blaikley; In Flanders Museum, Ypres, p. 92 (middle left), from *The Message from Mars*, Canadian army magazine; Barclays Bank Archives, p. 108 (top right), P.W. Matthews and A.W. Tuke, *History of Barclays Bank Limited*, 1926; University of Leeds, Special Collections, p. 90 (Major Purdon's phrase book); Municipal Archives, Weihai, p. 90 (bottom right). Other illustrations credited on the page or taken from the internet.

Introduction

'I had no idea', or 'Didn't they help with tanks and roads?' These are the sorts of responses made by otherwise well-informed friends to the question of how much they know about China in the First World War. The question provokes confessions of ignorance and surprise and few in the English-speaking world have any idea of China's participation. China was so far away from the Somme that it seems irrelevant. Yet one of the first battles of the First World War was fought on Chinese soil. How many know that China joined the Entente Allies in 1917, in the same year as America? How many know that almost 140,000 Chinese served in France, as labourers, doing essential maintenance work on roads, trenches, railways and tanks and making up for the drastic manpower shortage by working in French factories and fields?

At least 5,000, perhaps as many as 10,000 lost their lives, some at sea, most buried thousands of miles from their homes and honoured in war cemeteries in France and Belgium. A further 200,000 served in Russia, of whom many were caught up in the Russian Revolution, and whose fate is mostly unknown. At the end of the war, a Chinese delegation attended the Versailles Peace Conference in 1919 but China, no less than several other nations, felt utterly belittled and betrayed by its treatment at Versailles and did not sign the Peace Treaty.

The ensuing bitterness and riots, the May Fourth Movement of 1919, was a turning point in Chinese history. The Great War and its aftermath led directly, though slowly, to its current great power status. On the way, the Chinese people suffered the horrors of warlordism, Japanese invasion, famine, floods, world war, civil war and a reunified nation's growing pains after Mao Zedong proclaimed the foundation of the People's Republic of China in October 1949.

These events still form the background to China's sense of its place in the world. The events of 1914–1919 were of momentous significance to China in its development as a major power. At the beginning of the war, after thousands of years of imperial rule, China had been a republic for less than three years, when its territory in Shandong, formerly leased to Germany, was invaded by Japanese armed forces aided by a small British contingent. Secondly, thousands of Chinese men travelled half way across the world to work in dangerous conditions near the Western Front. And then, despite her contributions to the war, China felt humiliated and betrayed at Versailles.

Chinese territory, occupied by Germany in 1897, was handed straight to Japan as a result of 'secret agreements' made by Lloyd George and the other Allies during the war, by which Chinese territory was promised to the Japanese when Europe experienced a temporary (though desperate) need for more ships and armaments from Japan.

The secret agreements all came out at Versailles in April 1919. President Wilson himself, architect of the Fourteen Points that he proposed as the basis of peace, was sympathetic to China's cause. But he felt unable to resist the pressures of Japan and his European allies, so he agreed to abandon his policy of no secret agreements or treaties. He regretted this but it was important for him to set up his cherished scheme for a League of Nations which stood no chance if Japan opposed it. The irony is that it was killed by the US Senate in November 1919, the president having suffered a collapse of his health and with his political enemies refusing to compromise.

Japan's activities in China during the war and her eventual triumph at Versailles led inexorably to the invasion of Manchuria in 1931 and the full invasion of China in 1937. The vicious war that ensued was characterised by terrible savagery on both sides, most notoriously when the citizens of the then capital suffered the Rape of Nanjing in 1937 and the dykes of the Yellow River were deliberately broken in 1938 on Chiang Kai-shek's orders in an attempt to stem the Japanese invasion. The barbarity of the war with Japan is seen by some as having contributed to the eventual triumph of Mao Zedong and the Chinese Communist Party in 1949, since the Communists' guerrilla tactics and consistent resistance to Japan inspired the broken nation.

China today is acknowledged as one of the world's great powers and her economic dominance is watched with awe. Yet China's recent history remains a major factor in her relations with the rest of the world. Though the iniquities of the nineteenth century Opium Wars are fairly well known, the almost unknown sacrifice of Chinese lives, and the humiliation at Versailles, together with the growing threat from Japan during the First World War and after, still inform the Chinese view of her place in the world and influence current relationships and attitudes.

The details of China's role in the Great War are not well known in China itself, or elsewhere. Several academic books on the subject have appeared within the last decade but our aim is to provide a simple introduction for the general reader to a fascinating subject.

Transliteration
Chinese place names and personal names have been transliterated by Europeans in a variety of ways since the seventeenth century. The French and the Germans had their own romanisation or transliteration systems, and during the nineteenth and early twentieth centuries, most English speakers followed

the Wade-Giles system although, to complicate the matter further, the Chinese Post Office had yet another system for place names. Peking (a Jesuit Romanisation some 400 years old) survived (in correct Wade-Giles it should be Pei-ching), as did Tientsin (Wade-Giles T'ien-chin) and Canton (a southern rendering of what should be, in Wade-Giles, Kuang-chou). A major city in this account is the coastal city of Qingdao (Pinyin), which was Tsingtau to its German occupiers and Tsing-tao to the Chinese Post Office (but should be Ch'ing-tao in Wade-Giles). Today, the official convention is the Chinese Pinyin system and these cities are known as Beijing, Tianjin, Qingdao and Guangzhou, although the old names survive in certain contexts such as Peking University and the Canton Trade Fair.

We have adopted the Pinyin spellings but include the older versions in brackets on first mention.

Like place names, personal names were often rendered in non-standard versions. Sun Yat-sen would be Sun Zhongshan in pinyin, Chiang Kai-shek should be Jiang Jieshi and Wellington Koo is hard to recognise as Gu Weijun. We have used the modern standard Pinyin versions except where these non-standard versions are better known.

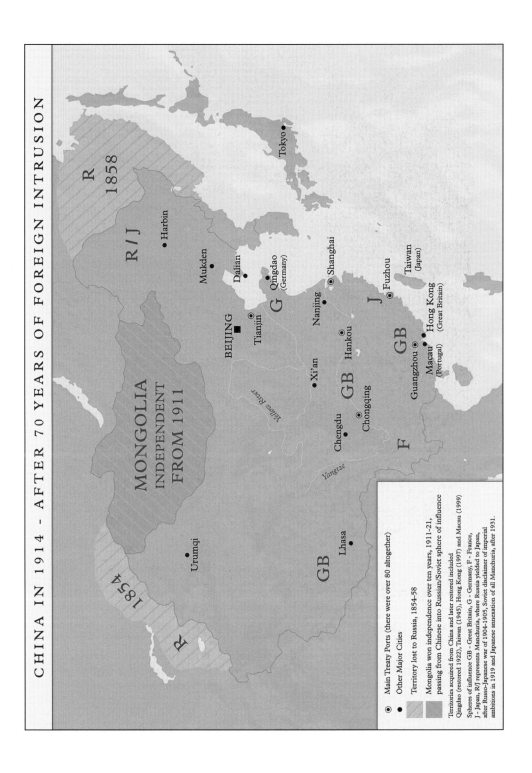

CHINA IN 1914 – AFTER 70 YEARS OF FOREIGN INTRUSION

MONGOLIA
INDEPENDENT
FROM 1911

R 1858

R / J

• Harbin

Urumqi •

Lhasa •

R 1854

GB

Chengdu •

Chongqing ◉

Yellow River

Xi'an •

Yangtze

F

GB

Hankou

Mukden •

Dalian •

Qingdao •
(Germany)

G

BEIJING ■

Tianjin ◉

Nanjing •

Shanghai ◉

J

Fuzhou ◉

Taiwan
(Japan)

Guangzhou ◉

Macau ◉
(Portugal)

Hong Kong
(Great Britain)

GB

Tokyo •

◉ Main Treaty Ports (there were over 80 altogether)

• Other Major Cities

Territory lost to Russia, 1854-58

Mongolia won independence over ten years, 1911-21,
passing from Chinese into Russian/Soviet sphere of influence

Territories acquired from China and later restored included
Qingdao (restored 1922), Taiwan (1945), Hong Kong (1997) and Macau (1999)

Spheres of influence GB - Great Britain, G - Germany, F - France,
J - Japan, R/J represents Manchuria, where Russia yielded to Japan,
after Russo-Japanese war of 1904-1905, Soviet disclaimer of imperial
ambitions in 1919 and Japanese annexation of all Manchuria, after 1931.

LE GATEAU DES ROIS ET DES EMPEREURS

Henri Meyer's cartoon, from *Le Petit Journal* of 16 January 1898, shows Britain's Queen Victoria, matriarch of the colonialists, fretting over her erratic grandson, Kaiser Wilhelm II; two months previously, he had ordered the merciless occupation of Qingdao by Germany. France's Marianne, depicted as an innocent maiden – as one might expect in a French publication – watches over her dim-witted ally, the Czar of Russia. The Japanese samurai waits pensively for the opportunity to wield his sword; he did not have to wait long, plunging it into the hearts of Russia in 1904–5 and of China and Germany in 1914, at the very start of the Great War. A Chinese official looks helplessly on the scene.

Chapter 1

Japan sees an opportunity

In the summer of 1914, Japan saw an opportunity. On 15 August, a week before officially declaring war on Germany, the German ambassador in Tokyo, Arthur Graf von Rex (who had been trying to persuade Japan to align itself with soon to be victorious Germany) was presented with a Japanese ultimatum demanding that Germany withdraw all its warships from East Asian waters and hand over the German concession in Jiaozhou Bay [Kiaochow] (Shandong province) to Japan, for 'eventual' return to China. Receiving no answer to the demands, on 23 August, Japan declared war on Germany and on 2 September 1914, 23,000 Japanese troops landed on officially neutral Chinese soil about 100 miles north of Qingdao [Tsingtao, or, in German, Tsingtau], and marched inland. Coming late to the European occupation of Chinese territory, Germany had occupied the bay in 1897 on the pretext of reprisal for the murder of two German Roman Catholic missionaries in the south of Shandong province and 'leased' 552 square kilometres of territory around the bay, which provided a fine natural harbour for the German Far East naval squadron.

The German Empire came into being in 1870, during the Franco-Prussian War; the following year, King Wilhelm I was proclaimed Emperor at Versailles. His ambitious grandson, Kaiser Wilhelm II, was determined to catch up with the other European powers such as Britain, France and Russia, which had been exploiting China for half a century. He believed in the superiority of European over Asiatic peoples whom he saw as a threat to civilisation. He coined the phrase 'Yellow Peril' (*gelbe Gefahr*) and saw himself leading Europe in a campaign to defeat it. He had a dream in which he, as St Michael, led the other European nations, all dressed as women, in this campaign. When a newly industrialized and aggressive Japan inflicted a humiliating defeat on China in 1894–5, a further rival was added to the powers in the Far East.

Foreign missionaries in China, often stationed in remote villages far from consular protection, were frequent victims of anti-foreign violence. When the two German missionaries were murdered on the evening of All Saints Day 1897, probably by members of a local peasant secret society, the event was sufficient to provoke a response from Germany which seized the fine natural bay on the north of Shandong province. The seizure and occupation of Jiaozhou Bay was achieved through yet another of the humiliating 'unequal

SHANDONG – CHINA'S KEY WAR AIM

Tsingtao was the heart of Germany's enclave in Shandong, the birthplace of Confucius. Its recovery was of great symbolic importance and was to become one of China's key war aims. Its civilian population in 1914 was about 55,000 (of which 3% were German); it has grown to the 2.7 million of Qingdao now. The construction of St Michael's Cathedral was held back by Japan's capture of Tsingtao and it was not completed until 1934. It was defaced and its clergy arrested during Mao Zedong's era, but it is now an active church again.

Railways, mostly foreign, were deeply resented, as they eliminated porterage jobs, disturbed ancestral graves, sequestered farmland and put China in hock. The Shandong Railway (SEG), founded in 1899, financed by German banks and investors, began paying dividends in 1905 (3.25%) rising to 7.5% in 1913.

The Governor of Shandong tried, unsuccessfully, to buy shares and get board representation. One of SEG's main purposes was to carry coal from the mines of another German company, SBG, needed for the East Asia Squadron, based at Tsingtao.

SCHANTUNG-EISENBAHN-GESELLSCHAFT.

Neunter Dividenden-Schein
zum Genuss-Schein № 11234

Der Inhaber dieses Dividenden-Scheines empfängt gegen Aushändigung desselben den Gewinnantheil, der nach Massgabe des Gesellschafts-Statuts auf denselben entfällt und durch den Vorstand bekannt gemacht wird. Berlin, den 31. Mai 1900.

Schantung - Eisenbahn - Gesellschaft.

SBG Coal Production (tons)

1913-14	(≈540,000)
1912-13	(≈570,000)
1911-12	(≈480,000)
1910-11	(≈420,000)
1909-10	(≈450,000)
1908-09	(≈320,000)
1907-08	(≈200,000)
1906-07	(≈180,000)
1905-06	(≈140,000)
1904-05	(≈100,000)
1903-04	(≈75,000)
1902-03	(small)

100,000 200,000 300,000 400,000 500,000 600,000

SBG's output rose steadily, but much of its production was unsuitable for bunkering and was uneconomic because of the lower costs of small Chinese competitors, which relied more on human labour than expensive machinery. Its poor financial record led to its being taken over by SEG.

Tsingtao beer (no longer branded with a swastika) is marketed in supermarkets in Europe and America – a peaceful reconquest of the former colonizing powers.

NOTES: population, SEG and SBG; *Imperialism and Chinese Nationalism* by John Schreker, Harvard UP, 1971 and *The Dragon and The Iron Horse* RW Huenemann, Harvard UP, 1984. Coal production; *Diplomatic Relations between China and Germany since 1898*, by Feng Deng Diang, published in 1913.

Tsingtao-Beer
ABSOLUTELY PURE
Brewed and Bottled by
THE TSINGTAO BREWERY

treaties' forced upon China which provoked considerable resentment and whose abolition was to be a major topic at the Versailles Peace Conference.

At the mouth of Jiaozhou Bay, stood the town of Qingdao, later described as 'one of the most fashionable watering-places of the Orient'. Originally a small fishing village, it was expanded by German occupation, into a model colonial city, redolent of towns and cities in the home country. There were familiar sounding streets, such as Friedrichstrasse, Wilhelmstrasse and Hohenloe Weg, lined with solid German-style buildings. There was a handsome Protestant church, there were schools, hospitals and a yacht club. An imposing railway station served the new Shandong Railway needed to exploit the province's mineral wealth, particularly coal to fuel the expanding German navy in its Far Eastern activities. High above the town was a magnificent residence for the governor who was a senior naval officer, underlining the naval significance of the concession.

Electrification, sewage systems and clean drinking water were installed throughout the town, a rarity in China at the time. Banks and other commercial establishments were set up and many Chinese built businesses and houses there attracted by the secure and well-managed environment. Sun Yat-sen, main architect of the Chinese Republic remarked in 1912, 'I am impressed. The city is a true model for China's future.' The Tsingtao Brewery, founded in 1903 under joint Anglo-German ownership but German management, produced a beer which is still enjoyed all over the world. Its early advertisements carried the swastika, an auspicious Buddhist symbol widely used in China before both its direction and significance were turned upside down by the Nazis.

Ships of the British Navy's Pacific squadron made 'courtesy visits' to the German East Asia naval squadron in Qingdao: in 1913, HMS *Monmouth* and her crew were welcomed there, and in 1914, HMS *Minotaur*, Admiral Jerram's flagship, called in. When the German aviator Günther Plüschow arrived in the spring of 1914, on the day of his arrival he watched a 'big football match between German sailors and their comrades from the English flag-ship *Good Hope*'.[1]

The background to Japan's engagement was complex, involving a series of crossed messages. The German Minister in Peking, Baron Ago von Maltzan later to serve as Ambassador to the United States, seems to have been trying unsuccessfully to discuss the future of Germany's concession in Shandong and its coal mines (of tremendous interest to coal-poor Japan) with the Chinese authorities and perhaps hand them back, whilst frantic messages were sent backwards and forwards between Peking, Tokyo, London and Washington.

On 3 August 1914 the American chargé d'affaires in Peking, John Van Antwerp MacMurray, reported that the Chinese Ministry of Foreign Affairs had asked the Americans to try and make the belligerent European nations undertake not to engage in hostilities on Chinese territory.[2] On the very same day, the British Ambassador in Tokyo, Sir William Conyngham Greene, reported that, with reference to the Anglo–Japanese Alliance (1902, 1905, 1911) which guaranteed mutual support in the face of threat, he had been assured that the British could 'count on Japan at once coming to the assistance of her ally with all her strength, if called upon to do so, leaving it entirely up to His Majesty's Government to formulate the reason for and the nature of assistance required'. However, the eventual Japanese landing on 2 September was entirely decided by Japan, with no reference to or consultation with His Majesty's Government.

Two days earlier, 1 August, the British Foreign Minister, Sir Edward Grey, had informed the Japanese Ambassador in London, Katsunosuke Inoue, that he 'did not see that we were likely to have to apply to Japan under our Alliance' for the British Foreign Office was narrowly preoccupied with British possessions in Asia and had no thought for German possessions in China.

> The only way in which Japan could be brought in would be if hostilities spread to the Far East, e.g. an attack on Hong Kong by the Germans, or if a rising in India were to take place … but it might be as well to warn the Japanese government that in the event of war with Germany there might be a possibility of an attack on Hong Kong or Weihaiwei when we should look to them for support.[3]

Messages were certainly crossing, for the American Ambassador in London, Walter Hines Page, reported on 11 August that, far from accepting that help was not needed, Sir Edward Grey had been informed that 'Japan finds herself unable to refrain from war with Germany…'[4] On 7 August, Britain, having declared war on Germany on 4 August, requested that 'the Japanese fleet … hunt out and destroy the armed German merchant cruisers who are now attacking our commerce.' Japan, however, saw the chance to take things further and on August 9, the Japanese Foreign Minister, Baron Katō Takaake, informed Sir William Conyngham Greene in Tokyo that: 'Once a belligerent power, Japan cannot restrict her action only to the destruction of hostile enemy cruisers' and suggested that the best way to destroy German maritime activity was to attack Qingdao as 'destroying the German naval base at Jiaozhou [Kiaochow] would provide the *casus belli* to bring the Alliance into effective operation.'

The British started to backtrack rapidly, asking that Japan 'postpone her war activities' with a further message from the British Ambassador in Japan, 'Great Britain asks Japan to limit its activities to the protection of commerce on the sea …'

German defences

The territory in question around Jiaozhou Bay was not well defended for the Germans had never anticipated a serious military challenge. However, on 4 August, after an announcement of 'the danger of war' six days earlier, the inhabitants of Qingdao learned that 'the die was cast in Europe!' but, as Günther Plüschow wrote, 'Of course, no one for a moment thought about Japan ...'

On 15 August, the Governor of Qingdao, a naval officer, Captain Alfred Meyer-Waldeck, responded to Japan's demands to 'withdraw the German warships at once from Japanese and Chinese waters' and to 'surrender the whole protectorate of Qiaozhou forthwith' by referring to 'the frivolity of the Japanese demands' which 'admit but one reply'.[5] By this time, the small number of German troops stationed elsewhere in China, including those in Tianjin and the German Legation Guard in Peking had 'quietly slipped away' and 'headed for Qingdao', to join volunteers from Shanghai in the defence of the German concession.[6] The Shanghai contingent included five musicians from Rudolf Buck's Town Band, seriously compromising Shanghai concerts. *The Times* correspondent G.E. Morrison, belittling the Japanese military achievements, scornfully referred to Qingdao as 'a weakly defended fort garrisoned by an untrained mob of German bank clerks and pot-bellied pastry-cooks.'[7]

At the outbreak of war, the armoured cruisers *Scharnhorst* and *Gneisenau* of the Far East naval squadron, commanded by Vice Admiral Count Maximilian von Spee, had, in fact, left the threatened territory in order to avoid being trapped there. Their intention was to try and reach Germany, but both were sunk by the British Navy in the Battle of the Falklands on 8 December 1914. Von Spee and his two sons were killed in the action.

A remaining light cruiser, the *Emden*, had also left Jiaozhou Bay to avoid being trapped in the harbour and was later to cause terrible devastation to Allied shipping in the Indian Ocean. She captured some two dozen merchant ships, sinking many of them before moving towards Penang where she sank a Russian ship and a French destroyer.

The remaining ships in Jiaozhou consisted of a torpedo boat, four gunboats and an elderly Austro-Hungarian cruiser, the *Kaiserin Elisabeth*, and, as far as troops were concerned, the Germans had infantry, a cavalry company of 140, military engineers in charge of machine guns and field artillery and volunteers from elsewhere in China, perhaps amounting to 183 officers and nearly 5,000 other ranks.[8]

Because it had always been assumed that any serious attack on the Shandong peninsula would come from the sea, there were a number of batteries along the coast protecting the bay and a major fort with four 280mm guns on

Mount Bismarck, facing out to sea. To the landward side where the Germans assumed there lay no serious threat from the Chinese, they nevertheless set up two defensive lines of fortifications on the hills behind Qingdao, one with forts and batteries on Moltke Hill and Iltis Hill, backed by a redoubt line with trenches, ditches and barbed wire, the other, further inland, along the Hai River to the northern side of the peninsula. These inland defences were mainly built after 1908 when a British Military Survey had declared, 'It would appear that the Germans do not intend to make Qingdao an impregnable fortress. In its present state it is probable that it would speedily fall to the attack by a land force of suitable strength, supported by a squadron of first-class armoured cruisers.'[9]

In the defence of Qingdao, the Germans had proposed to rely upon its own cruiser squadron as the first line of defence, a defence which was lost when Vice Admiral von Spee sailed away to avoid being trapped in Qingdao by the British Navy. They did, however, bring in two monoplanes for air defence but there was only one flat area on which they could land, the racecourse. This was a very restricted space and one of the monoplanes crashed in early 1914, leaving only one with a severely damaged propeller, piloted by Günther Plüschow. He used it mainly for observation and reconnaissance flights although he also pioneered aerial bombardments, making his own bombs by filling tins ('best Java coffee') with dynamite, horseshoe nails and scrap iron, which he dropped on British and Japanese positions.[10]

An unenthusiastic Britain finally involved
Politically, Anglo-Japanese relations were cordial although Sir John Jordan, the British Minister in Peking, had to smooth Sino-Japanese relations which were strained, for the Chinese government was very upset by Japan's attitude to Chinese territorial integrity. Adding the remark that 'Our thoughts are all at home nowadays – mine entirely with our little army in France whose fortunes give me constant anxiety …'. Jordan wrote from Peking on 4 September 1914, with innocent optimism about East Asian affairs:

> The Japanese Minister has expressed his warmest thanks for our co-operation. The reports that appeared in Japanese newspapers about the intentions of Japan created an atmosphere of grave mistrust here and it was with the greatest difficulty that the President was convinced of the sincerity of her motives. The Chinese went so far as to ask us to guarantee Japan's good faith in the matter. I told them that their choice lay between trusting and distrusting her. The former course would put Japan on her honour and lead to the restoration of Qiaozhou; the latter attitude would annoy her and leave her free do to as she pleased. Personally, I prefer to trust her assurances implicitly.

They showed us a number of telegrams from their Minister in Tokyo. Statements by [Japanese Foreign Minister] Baron Katō intended to be of a reassuring nature produced the very opposite effect – so little do even the Japanese understand the Chinese point of view. He told the Chinese Minister that in the event of trouble in China, the Chinese could rely on the Japanese and British stepping in to keep order. 'Save us from our friends,' was Liang Shiyi's [a leading politician of the era] comment on this statement, the far-reaching effects of which had, he said, greatly perturbed the minds of the Cabinet.

They are at last I think, really convinced that Japan means what she says, their only fear is that our participation in the Qiaozhou affair may not be sufficient to establish a claim to a voice in the eventual settlement. Their reliance on us is almost pathetic and they speculate upon what will happen if we come off worst in the European struggle and they are left to the mercies of Japan alone.

Our co-operation with the Japanese is now working most smoothly.[11]

Jordan thus revealed that the Chinese, understandably worried about Japan's intentions, were already thinking of the 'eventual settlement' after the war and hoping for justice. His emollient words about smooth co-operation did not reflect the actual situation in Shandong where the military aspect of the hastily assembled alliance was confused. On 10 August, Colonel Noel Barnardiston, commanding officer of British troops in north-east China, reported to the War Office that his force of 2,000 men in Tianjin were ready to co-operate with the Japanese, although he pointed out that 20,000 men would probably be needed. Distracted by events in Europe and still concerned with the protection of British interests, the War Office was unhelpful. Barnardiston was subsequently informed that he would have one battalion from Tianjin, the 2nd Battalion South Wales Borderers, who had arrived from service in South Africa in 1912 and were stationed in Tianjin whilst also serving in the Legation Guard in Peking and protecting the railway line at Fengtai, south of Peking. He was also offered half a second battalion, the 36th Sikhs from Hong Kong.

Despite a feeble protest from China, a second wave of a further 7,000 Japanese soldiers had landed near Qingdao on 18 September. On both occasions the Japanese landed their troops outside the area designated as the German concession and, like the Germans in Belgium, violated China's neutrality by marching an army across neutral territory. As Great Britain was unenthusiastic about the campaign, to say the least, Barnardiston's small body of men was officially sent in order to 'show co-operation' and Barnardiston was informed that he was to take orders from the Japanese. 'You will be under the control of the Japanese commander and will co-operate with him as a complete formation. Let me know the plan decided on after consulting with the Japanese general. Your force is purposely reduced to a minimum because British troops are only engaged to show that England is co-operating with Japan in this enterprise.' The Japanese, in turn, had orders to provide 'every convenience, as long as it does not impede our operations.' Further notes to the Japanese General Matsuomi Kamio stressed the importance of not firing on each other but underlined the view of Britain as the subordinate partner, 'Leaks of military intelligence tend to happen by unexpected routes. Therefore it is necessary to keep secrets even from the allied force.'[12]

Under these somewhat unpromising conditions, the 1,650 South Wales Borderers from Tianjin arrived by ship off Laoshan Bay, west of Qingdao (within the leased area and without trespassing on Chinese soil), on 22 September and the next day they disembarked, followed by 'stores, ponies, mules and carts'.[13]

One convenience was not provided, for as Lieutenant Simson reported, 'Japanese sanitation was in every way inferior to ours. They left the ground in a filthy condition when they moved. They also admit that our rations were more readily prepared for eating and the fact that we can get along on tinned meat and biscuits gives us many advantages.'

Another difference was that the Japanese soldiers looted and destroyed villages as they passed, with no concern for their Chinese inhabitants, a practice that shocked the British soldiers.

Rain poured down on the marching troops and damaged the German emplacements, and the weather continued to hamper the campaign with a typhoon on 15 October which caused widespread flooding. In late October, after the arrival of the 500 men of the 36th Sikhs, Barnardiston recorded:

> The men have been soaked through and through for as much as forty-eight hours and equipment has been buried by falls of earth, and ammunition has rusted, but in spite of all hardships and privations, the spirits and health of the troops have been excellent, and they have worked continuously at digging and the heavy fatigue work of carrying rations and ammunition and heavy beams for head cover one and a half miles to the front where wheeled traffic has been impossible – often in liquid mud halfway up to the knees.[14]

The first British casualty on 2 November was Lance Corporal James Thomas, of the South Wales Borderers, shot by a Japanese soldier who mistook him for a German. Private T. Mabbett was shot through the lungs by a Japanese patrol, also mistaking him for a German soldier. As a result of these and several other incidents, the South Wales Borderers and Sikhs had to wear a patch of white linen on top of their helmets and turbans, to distinguish them from Germans. They were soon issued with Japanese smocks or cagoules, so they looked more like the Japanese they were supposed to be helping.

In the first ever deployment of aircraft from ships, Japanese planes dropped bombs on Qingdao, and Japanese and British warships (HMS *Triumph*, *Usk* and *Kennet*), braving the mines that had been laid in the harbour by the Germans, blockaded and bombarded the city, as their soldiers inched forward, taking the water-logged German positions from the rear.

Supplies were short, 'one biscuit per man issued', but some of the British officers took matters into their own hands. On 26 September, after a 13-mile march, Major Edward Margesson,

> got hold of a butcher who said he would bring beef and pork. No arrangements made by the staff to give us a full ration; this has to be done by the Regiment. Bought 240 eggs, 18 fowls, grapes for $10. Supplies should be no difficulty now Qingdao is practically invested. The supply officer is useless and remains at Laoshan, and has no advance depot. Japanese have given us some chickens and vegetables and promised pork and beef; so they mean now to help us with supplies.[15]

British and Japanese troops dug trenches, advancing slowly in the mud and rain, under steady bombardment from the German guns.

German surrender

On 7 November, as all his ammunition had run out, the German Governor of the leased territory, Captain Alfred Meyer-Waldeck, surrendered. In the light of future events, it is notable that the document of surrender was only signed by the Germans and the Japanese, not the British (nor the Chinese). The Japanese made it clear that the territory was not going to be handed back to China, which had not been consulted or considered throughout the action, but taken over by Japan.

China was completely ignored in the conflict despite the fact that in early August, the Chinese President, Yuan Shikai, made an offer to Sir John Jordan, the British Minister in Peking, to supply 50,000 Chinese troops to assist in retaking (for China) German-occupied Qingdao. According to George Morrison, the Australian former *Times* reporter, then acting as foreign affairs advisor to President Yuan Shikai, Sir John, 'without consulting his colleagues, saw fit to advise the President to keep quiet and do nothing. It was a serious rebuff to the President. It was what the Chinese call "loss of face" for it told the Chinese who had offered to help that their help was not needed. It was a diplomatic blunder of the worst kind.'[16]

Captain Meyer-Waldeck was taken to Japan and placed under house arrest, and somewhere between 2,000 and 4,000 German prisoners were taken to prison camps in Japan from where they were released in 1920, whilst the seriously wounded prisoners were taken to Hong Kong for treatment, subsequently interned in Australia and released in March 1919. The German prisoners were treated well and respectfully at their camps in Japan. One group formed an orchestra which performed over a hundred concerts between 1917 and 1920, one of them apparently featuring the first performance in Japan of Beethoven's 9th Symphony. Their release in 1920 followed the signing of the Versailles Peace Treaty.

Brigadier General Barnardiston visited Japan in December 1914 where he was greeted as a hero and awarded the Order of the Rising Sun (2nd class) before returning to Europe to serve on the Western Front with the 39th Division. This despite Japanese reports that British soldiers 'were not good fighters and ... their officers come from good families and are therefore unfitted for the dangers and hardships of a campaign' and the 'British Army ... is cowardice itself.'[17]

The Japanese claimed 236 killed and 1,282 wounded, the British listed 12 killed and 53 wounded and the Germans, 199 dead and 504 wounded.[18] No one seems to have counted the dead or wounded Chinese inhabitants of the Chinese territory that had been seized by one foreign power from another.

Depredations of the *Emden* in the Indian Ocean

The second torpedo officer on the *Emden*, Prince Franz Joseph of Hohenzollern, left a dramatic account of the *Emden*'s raids in the Indian Ocean in his book *Emden: my experiences in SMS Emden* (London, 1928).[19] The *Emden*, a light cruiser of the Dresden class, was commissioned in 1909 and spent most of its working life stationed at Qingdao with the German Far East naval squadron. News of the events in Sarajevo reached the squadron in Qingdao in the early summer when Prince Franz Joseph and his fellow officers were enjoying swimming parties and lunch invitations. On 22 July, the Austro-Hungarian cruiser *Kaiserin Elisabeth* appeared at Qingdao and, whilst her crew was entertained with 'musical dinners' and motor excursions into the hills behind Qingdao, concern began to be felt about the possible hostility of the Russian fleet. On 30 July after Austria-Hungary declared war on Serbia, a 'council' was held aboard the *Emden* and the ship was stripped down, with all flammable items like 'curtains, carpets and wooden furniture' removed to prepare for battle.

Vice Admiral Maximilian von Spee, commanding the East Asia squadron decided that the squadron should sail away from Qingdao on 31 July, 'in order to avoid blockade by hostile warships'. Prince Franz Joseph commented with heavy sarcasm that the fleet was able to escape because 'happily, we had in the First Lord of the Admiralty, Churchill, an involuntary ally. He gave the order for the English squadron to assemble in Hong Kong though it had been poised to capture or destroy enemy ships in Qingdao.'

Vice Admiral von Spee's intention was to try to reach Germany whilst interfering as much as possible with Allied shipping. The armoured cruisers *Scharnhorst* and *Gneisenau*, together with the light cruisers *Emden*, *Leipzig* and *Nürnberg* set off across the Pacific but it was decided on 14 August that whilst the rest continued towards South America, the *Emden* would stay behind in the Indian Ocean to sink as much Allied shipping as possible and because 'conditions here would specially favour cruiser warfare and the appearance of German warships on the Indian coast would have a valuable influence for us on the morale of the Indian peoples.'

Vice Admiral von Spee's flotilla inflicted a terrible defeat on the British South Atlantic Fleet in the Battle of Coronel off the coast of Chile on 1 November 1914, when HMS *Monmouth* was sunk with all hands just over a year after her courtesy visit to Qingdao. Despite this victory, von Spee remarked gloomily, 'I am quite homeless. I cannot reach Germany ... I must plough the seas of the world and do as much mischief as I can, until my ammunition is exhausted, or a foe far superior in power succeeds in catching me.' Horrified by the worst disaster in a century, the British Navy despatched two battle cruisers, the *Invincible* and the *Inflexible* and Vice Admiral von Spee, his two sons and his flotilla, went down with their ships a month later in the Battle of the Falkland Islands on 8 December.

Whilst the doomed flotilla sailed on in early August, the *Emden* embarked on a terrible destructive spree in the Indian Ocean after first sailing northwards 'to cut the Nagasaki–Vladivostok shipping line' and capturing a Russian passenger ship which was then used as a 'commerce raider'. Commandeering *Markomannia* of the Hamburg–America line, though she did not have the characteristic large funnel, she 'was given the markings of a Blue Funnel liner' and the *Prince Eitel Friedrich* of the Norddeutscher–Lloyd shipping company took 'the markings of the more distinguished P&O' to deceive Allied shipping. The *Emden* herself was disguised by a tall funnel of sailcloth on a wooden frame so that 'from a distance we looked sufficiently like the English cruiser *Yarmouth* which was then on the East Asiatic station' and Prince Franz Joseph declared himself 'convinced that many spies were deceived by this device'.

Prince Franz Joseph frequently used hunting references to describe the *Emden*'s activities: 'hunting' around the Ryukyu Islands and, when they thought they saw the *Empress of Japan* off the coast of southern Japan, 'we were after her like a fox'. In Largini Bay, the ship's cat had four kittens and the *Emden* was lucky enough to come across the Greek ship *Protoporos*, unfortunately neutral but carrying 6,500 tons of coal from India to England which meant 'she was carrying contraband'. The coal was unloaded and soon after, the steamship *Indus* 'equipped to carry troops and horses to Europe' was relieved of her provisions (towels, linen, tinned food, fresh meat, live hens and

THE DARING GERMAN CRUISER EMDEN

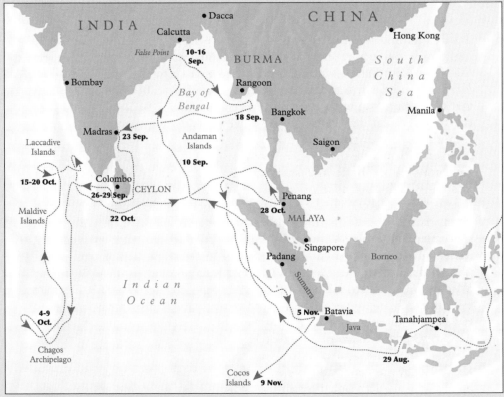

The *Emden*'s marauding exploits across the Indian Ocean became the stuff of legend. Incorrectly reported as sunk on 6 August 1914, the 'daring little German cruiser' (as *The Times* called her) had already left port at Qingdao and, for nearly three months, eluded all efforts to trace her. Apart from ships captured or sunk, she caused insurance rates to go through the roof, the Royal Navy to be embarrassed and, in one month, Indian exports to fall by 60%. The British Empire was humiliated in the eyes of the peoples of India, Ceylon and Malaya.

The ship's captain, Karl von Müller, [page 7, plate section] went out of his way to rescue survivors of sinking vessels and minimize civilian casualties. As a crowning piece of chutzpah, the *Emden* diverted suspicion by flying the Japanese flag as she approached Penang, not long before being shot to pieces in the Cocos Islands.

On his return to Germany, von Müller was showered with honours; films were made and a street named after him. The *Emden*'s name as 'Amdan' entered the Tamil language as meaning 'someone who is tough, manipulative and crafty'. (Wikipedia)

ducks, drinks, nautical instruments, charts, pencils and oilskins) and a large quantity of soap before she was sunk. They confiscated all the newspapers on the *Lovat*, sank her and took her crew and, unable to sink the British ship *Kabinga* because she was carrying piece goods, which were mostly American and would have had to be paid for, they seized the ship to carry the captured crews. They sank the English steamer *Killin*, carrying coal from Calcutta to Bombay and the *Diplomat*, also carrying coal.

In early September the *Emden* changed course, aiming for the Madras–Calcutta steamer route and sank the English collier *Trabbock* which was bound for Calcutta, and the *Clan Matheson*, loaded with goods from England destined for Calcutta, including typewriters, bicycles, locomotives and a race horse 'already entered on the list of the Calcutta racing club'. The horse was sent to the bottom with the typewriters and bicycles. The crew of the *Clan Matheson* were soon transferred to a neutral Norwegian ship and the *Emden*'s captain decided to raid Madras. On 22 September, her guns set fire to the Burmah Oil Company tanks in Madras and three days later, near Ceylon, they captured and sank the *Kingland*, having retrieved a 'splendid supply of stores, especially meat and potatoes, which were of value to us'. West of Colombo they searched the *Turmeric* for newspapers and then sank it with its 4,000 tons of sugar. The *Buresk*, loaded with 6,600 tons of the finest coal destined for Hong Kong, was kept in the convoy but the steamship *Ribera*, which yielded up 'a very complete signal book', was sunk, as was the cargo-less *Foyle*.

The *Emden* then made for the Maldives to take on coal and to haunt the Mauritius–Colombo and Australia–Suez shipping lines, the latter used by troopships from Australia and New Zealand. On 9 October, Prince Franz Joseph amused himself by telling the deputy manager of the local oil company on Diego Garcia (who had had no news from the outside world since July) that their mixed flotilla was 'taking part in "world manoeuvres" in which the united fleets of Germany, England and France had their principal base of operations in the Indian Ocean.'

The sinkings continued: on 15 October, the *Clan Grant* taking piece goods, live cattle and flour cakes from England to Colombo, and a dredger on its way to Australia, were sunk after the crews were taken off and the beer and cigarettes seized. The next day, the *Ben Mohr*, taking motors, locomotives and engines from the UK to China and Japan, was also scuttled before the *Emden* moved towards the Colombo–Bombay shipping route. There, on 18 October, the *Emden* seized the Blue Funnel line *Troilus* which was heading from Colombo to the UK loaded with copper, tin, rubber and passengers. Her captain 'blurted out the very useful information for us that the English held the safest route to be 30 miles north of the Colombo to Aden route. We could therefore await more ships with certainty on this route recommended by the English Naval staff.' Later the same day the *Emden* seized the English vessel

St Egbert which was carrying an untouchable neutral cargo but could be used as 'a dump', and in the evening the *Exford* with 5,500 tons of best Cardiff coal: 'with this supply we could work a whole year'. Next day, the English ship *Chikana* carrying piece goods and provisions to India was relieved of her 'brand new wireless installation' before being sunk, the *St Egbert* was sent to Cochin 'with captives' and the *Troilus* was sent to the bottom.

On the Kaiserin's birthday, 22 October, after saluting the colours and flying the flag, Prince Franz Joseph expressed his regret that the 'sinking of merchantmen was quite all right but it was no deed of arms for a man to be properly proud of' and it was decided to take the initiative and attack Penang harbour after a 'good breakfast of milk soup'. The attack took Penang by surprise, with those on watch 'misled by our fourth funnel' of sailcloth. Prince Franz Joseph fired his torpedoes at the Russian ship *Zemtschug* and also sank the French destroyer *Mousquet* which had been on patrol duty at the north entrance to the harbour but 'turned injudiciously, presenting us with a splendid target of her whole side'.

The *Emden*'s next objective was the shipping line from Penang to Rangoon where, on 30 October, the British ship *Newburn* was spared sinking because her cargo of salt was destined for a German firm in Singapore; instead they loaded the wounded French sailors on board and sent her off to a hospital on Sumatra. Because radio communications presented the greatest danger that the *Emden* would be found, her next target was the cable station on Direction Island in the Cocos group which relayed messages from India to Australia and Zanzibar. On 9 November the wireless mast was blown up but the British officers on Direction Island had already cabled news of the *Emden*'s arrival, and before the *Emden*'s raiding party could cut and destroy the cables, the cruiser HMAS *Sydney* appeared and, finally, the *Emden* was 'shot to pieces'.

Prince Franz Joseph, who spent the rest of the war as a prisoner on Malta (complaining at length about bed-bugs, lack of exercise space, 'it is surprising the great British Empire could not find more room for its prisoners', lack of bathing water and delays to letters), insisted that the English newspapers were wrong, technically, the *Emden* did not surrender. 'One can only surrender with weapons. As, however, our ship was a wreck and all the weapons on board had been destroyed, there could be no talk of surrender.'

The success of the *Emden* in the Indian Ocean was a source of pride to Germany. Destroying two enemy warships, sinking or capturing sixteen British steamers and one Russian merchant ship; capturing and releasing a further four British ships and taking one British and one Greek ship as colliers, she was a serious, and apparently unchallenged, menace to British shipping across 56,000 square kilometres of ocean. The *Times* correspondent G.E. Morrison, Australian by birth, was particularly concerned about the threat to New Zealand and Australia and concerned that the *Emden* went unchallenged for so long. Suspicious of Japan's motives and actions, he noted:

> the Japanese claim they were policing Australian waters. Did they do anything to stop the depredations of the *Emden*? The *Emden* sank seventeen British ships worth £2.25 million. Did it sink any Japanese ship? Did not Japanese ships traverse the water of the Indian Ocean unafraid of the *Emden*? Are we not justified in suspecting that Japanese protection to German trade in China and Japanese immunity from German submarines were in some way related?[20]

Though the most spectacular achievements of the German East Asia naval squadron were made by the *Emden*, there were some other remarkable results. A small group of fifty-three who had landed on Direction Island from the *Emden* managed to seize a derelict three-masted schooner, the *Ayesha*, and sail off to Padang where they transferred to a German freighter bound for the Yemen. From there they travelled overland to Constantinople and thence to Germany.

Another escapee was Günther Plüschow, pilot of the single air defence plane based at Qingdao. On the day before Governor Meyer-Waldeck surrendered, he ordered Plüschow to take important documents and fly away from Qingdao into neutral China. With some difficulty (pursued by Japanese spies and British officials), he took a train to the coast, sailed to San Francisco, crossed the United States, sailed for Europe on a (still-neutral) Italian ship using a false Swiss passport and was captured by the British when the ship made an unscheduled stop at Gibraltar. Transferred to Donington Hall prisoner-of-war camp in Leicestershire, ('lovely park' with charming tame deer), he escaped and got back to Germany stowing away on a neutral Dutch ship, to serve in the Baltic Sea Squadron for the rest of the war. He was the only German in either World War to escape successfully from the British Isles.

Chapter 2

New China, the 'infant republic'

The End of the Imperial System

As one of the earliest battles of the First World War was fought over Chinese soil, the new Chinese government was struggling to find its place.

In October 1911, with a five-year-old child-emperor of the Qing dynasty on the dragon throne and a number of different anti-imperial groups struggling to change China, an almost accidental uprising took place in Wuchang (part of the great industrial centre of Wuhan in central China). At that moment Dr Sun Yat-sen, leader of the main anti-imperial faction was officially exiled and away from China, raising funds in America. When he rushed back, he was made provisional President of a new Republic of China. Sun relinquished his position in early spring 1912 to Yuan Shikai, a general appointed by the Qing dynasty, to which he was loyal until he forced the abdication of the child Emperor Puyi in 1912 and assumed the office of President.

For over 2,000 years the vast territory of China had been united under imperial rule, with a succession of emperors at the apex of a huge government bureaucracy formed of men who had passed the complex, antiquated, series of examinations based on knowledge of the ancient Confucian classics. China had remained a self-sufficient entity, its relationships with smaller neighbouring countries founded upon the 'tribute' system by which they acknowledged China's cultural and political superiority. This system began to be challenged by the trading nations of Europe in the seventeenth and eighteenth centuries.

After Portuguese, Dutch and, later, British traders arrived in south China, they complained bitterly about the restrictions on trade enacted by the Chinese government. When Lord Macartney arrived in China in 1792 leading the first British embassy to China, though the magnificence of the court of the Qianlong Emperor seemed enduringly impressive, noting the lack of concern with the outside world and the conservatism of both China's institutions and technology, he wrote with prescience:

> The Empire of China is an old, crazy, First-rate man-of-war, which a fortunate succession of able and vigilant officers has contrived to keep afloat for these 150 years past, and to overawe their neighbours merely by her bulk and appearance, but whenever an insufficient man happens to have the command upon deck, adieu to the discipline and safety of the ship. She may perhaps not sink outright; she may drift some time as a

wreck, and will then be dashed to pieces on the shore; but she can never be re-built on the old bottom.[1]

Lord Macartney was right about the potential failure of leadership for the Qianlong Emperor's successors, increasingly enfeebled and corrupt, failed to resist both a series of massive and challenging internal rebellions in the nineteenth century, but also foreign onslaughts such as the two Opium Wars of 1839–1842 and 1856–1860. The treaties imposed upon China after the Opium Wars had forcibly opened China to foreign trade and established a series of Treaty Port settlements (known as 'concessions') in major cities such as Shanghai, Guangzhou [Canton], Ningbo, Fuzhou and Tianjin [Tientsin] where foreign residents could operate under their own laws in a system known as 'extraterritoriality'. The treaties were known to the Chinese as the 'unequal' treaties and were bitterly resented.

Opium Wars
The Opium Wars were the result of various factors. European traders resented China's control of trade, restricting foreigners to the southern port of Guangzhou, insisting that they trade only with officially appointed merchants, and refusing them both the right to travel to the interior and the right to reside in the city, forcing them out to the peninsula of Macau, after their ships departed.

The extraordinary demand for tea throughout Europe, with taxes on Chinese tea providing 10 per cent of the total British government revenue, created wealth for the East India Company but also created problems. The tea could only be paid for in gold and silver bullion and there was a huge trade imbalance, with British exports to China achieving only half the value of imports from China. The embassy led by Lord Macartney hoped to persuade the Chinese to allow diplomatic representation in China and to lessen the restrictions on trade but neither of these results was achieved.

The British East India Company resorted to unofficial trade in privately licensed ships carrying a product that proved massively profitable – Indian opium. With the growth in the trade, from 700 chests of opium in 1750 to 23,570 in 1852, came a reversal of the trade imbalance, with Chinese silver draining away at an alarming rate. The growth in opium addiction was also alarming, but unsuccessful attempts by the Qing government to appeal to the British opium traders evoked no response until the Opium Commissioner Lin Zexu destroyed nearly £3 million of raw opium near Guangzhou and Lord Palmerston despatched a flotilla of twenty warships and 4,000 troops which took the Zhoushan archipelago and sailed northwards to Tianjin. The subsequent Treaty of Nanjing,[2] signed in 1842, forced China to open five cities to foreign trade and residence in foreign 'concessions'.

Missionaries naturally flocked to the Treaty Ports. There had been a small number of Catholic missions in China from the very beginning of the seventeenth century, started by Jesuit pioneers (until 1773 when the mission was temporarily disbanded) but Protestant missionaries were not able to enter China proper until 1842. Even then, they were supposed to confine themselves to the foreign concession areas but they constantly chafed against this incarceration and travelled beyond the fixed boundaries, causing headaches for their consular officials. Isolated in their mission stations in the interior, they were often the targets of anti-foreign violence.

Although Britain and France were the first to benefit from the opening of the concessions, several other nations, such as the United States and Russia, soon signed their own treaties and established the principle that rights granted to one nation should be extended to others by the 'most favoured nation' clause. Not content with their concessions, European nations soon established what they called 'spheres of interest' in China: the British along the whole of the Yangtse River and the French in the extreme south, near the border of Vietnam. Germany came late to China, seizing its own concession around Qingdao on the coast of Shandong in 1897. America, with the 'Open Door policy' in 1899, proposed that China allow free trade with all nations so that American businesses could operate within the concessions but without the complication and expense of running imperial-style concessions.

In the latter half of the nineteenth century, shocked by the encroachments of foreign powers and the failure of the Qing government to resist, Chinese intellectuals and politicians responded with various solutions. Some advocated the adoption of foreign technology such as railways, arsenals and modern shipyards. The pioneers of the 'Self-strengthening Movement', Li Hongzhang and Zuo Zongtang, set up the modern Fuzhou Arsenal in 1866–67, whilst Zhang Zhidong pioneered railway construction (which involved crippling foreign loans) and modern military training. Others advocated reform of traditional examinations and the legal system, or sought spiritual 'self-strengthening' through a return to Confucian values. A few travelled to American universities but far greater numbers went to Japan to study modern technologies.

In 1900 the Boxer Rebellion, a massive uprising of famine-stricken peasants, first directed against the Qing imperial government but quickly turning against foreigners in China, massacring missionaries and destroying railway lines, culminated in the siege of the foreign Legations in Peking. The Legation quarter, an area in central Peking, was established in 1860 after the second Opium War. It was filled with foreign diplomatic buildings (the British Legations occupied a handsome ducal palace), banks and shops stocking imported items for the foreign residents, and was governed by the principle of extraterritoriality by which the inhabitants were not subject to Chinese law or control. The siege, which had lasted from 20 June to

14 August, was relieved by an eight-nation foreign force with troops from Britain, Russia, Japan, Germany, France, Austria–Hungary, America and Italy. The huge Boxer Indemnity (or reparation) demanded from China was to cripple her economy for decades.

Some changes were instituted: the traditional examination system for entry into the imperial civil service by which candidates were locked into special cells for many days to write essays on the 2,500-year-old Confucian classics, was abolished in 1905 and a Ministry of Justice set up in 1906, but these reforms came too late. In 1908 the reigning Guangxu Emperor and the powerful Dowager Empress Cixi died and two-year-old Puyi was proclaimed emperor under a regency. There have been suggestions that the death of the Guangxu Emperor one day before that of the Dowager Empress was suspicious. She had certainly treated him very badly but was already very ill herself. Some have suggested that General Yuan Shikai was responsible. Whatever the truth, the nation was effectively leaderless until the Wuchang Uprising against the forces of the Manchu Qing government in 1911 and the establishment of the Republic in 1912. Within a few months, the ancient structures of imperial rule were overthrown and China struggled to establish an entirely new form of government with a new set of institutions.

Over a hundred years after Lord Macartney had seen China as a drifting wreck, the country was in an extremely weak position. It had lost control of much of its territory to foreign predators. Backwardness had hastened the demise of the Qing dynasty. Military, industrial and political reforms had come too little and too late. The industrial revolution had not been actively pursued. The new Republic inherited large debts and was riven by factions. Some even feared that the country would be partitioned. Poverty-stricken Chinese indentured labourers were shipped around the world to work on sugar plantations, in mines and on railways. China's international status was at its nadir. In 120 years China had gone from accounting for over a third of global economic output to around 8 per cent, a devastating indicator of failure.

1911 Revolution, rebellion, uprising
There was widespread discontent throughout China which erupted almost by mistake in Hankou in October 1911. Although the bomb that set off the uprising was made by a left-wing society, 1911 saw a serious rebellion on the part of rich financiers in the south-western province of Sichuan, the result of railway financing. Most railways built in China in the early years of the twentieth century were constructed with foreign finance, but there were some local initiatives. The Sichuan–Hankou railway had been built with local finance but the debt-ridden Qing government saw a way to pay off some of its foreign creditors by effectively 'nationalising' such railways and handing them over to foreign control. In May 1911 a 'Four Power Consortium' (the British

CHINA'S ECONOMIC STAGNATION

In 1793 the Qianlong Emperor rebuffed the advances of King George III's ambassador, Lord Macartney, who had been sent to explore trade opportunities. China was then the largest empire in the world with an estimated one third share of global GDP. Its failure to embrace technology and modernisation left it vulnerable to more nimble and aggressive nations. China was invaded and carved up. A hundred years after the Qianlong Emperor's death, Europe, America and, most menacingly, neighbouring Japan were making giant economic strides and exploiting the country pitilessly. By the start of the First World War, China's share of global GDP had fallen from about one third to 9%.

During the 19th century, global economic output rose about four times, under the spur of the Industrial Revolution. Railway development was seen as a significant motor of economic progress, but in 1894, China had a mere 320 miles of track, in comparison with USA which had 175,000, though by 1914 the figure had reached 6,051.

Global GDP 1820-1913 ($bn 1990)

COUNTRY	1820	1870	1913
China	229	190	241
Europe (30 countries)	159	366	906
USA	13	98	517
Japan	21	25	72

Global GDP per caput 1820-1913 ($ 1990)

COUNTRY	1820	1870	1913
China	600	530	552
Europe (30 countries)	1,194	1,953	3,457
USA	1,254	2,445	5,301
Japan	669	737	1,387

Not only did China's failure to modernize stunt economic growth, but the middle of the nineteenth century brought an unusually savage combination of natural disasters and internal rebellions which cost tens of millions of lives and reduced the population substantially over several decades. Several countries actively industrialized: Japan's Meiji Restoration, the end of the American Civil War, the creation of the new Germany and British colonial expansion were major drivers of the global economy.

GDP per capita of Japan, Europe and America rose two, three and four times, respectively. Likewise, GDP per capita of several other industrializing, colonizing and colonized nations rose materially, while China's fell by 8%.

NOTE: figures for 1820-1913, based on the work of Professor Angus Maddison, carry an element of estimation in view of the limitations of statistics in the pre-industrial-era.
http://www.ggdc.net/maddison/Historical_Statistics/vertical-file_02-2010.xls

Hong Kong and Shanghai Banking Corporation, the German Deutsch–
Asiatische Bank, the French Banque de l'Indochine and the American group
of J.P. Morgan, Kuhn, Loeb and Company and the First National City Bank)
was bidding to build railways in Central China and when the Qing government closed down the Sichuan–Hankou railway with its many small investors,
there was a serious riot in the Sichuan provincial capital of Chengdu in
September with thirty-two protestors killed.

At the other end of the Sichuan–Hankou railway on 9 October 1911, revolutionaries in the office of the Progressive Society in the Russian Concession
in Hankou (part of the modern city of Wuhan) were preparing an anti-Qing
uprising when they accidentally set off one of their bombs. The next day some
members of the imperial New Army in Wuchang (another part of Wuhan)
mutinied. Despite the absence of Sun Yat-sen, the rebellion spread in a confused way. Foreign Office files relating to Wuhan enclose clippings from the
local papers, the *Hankow Daily News* and the *Central China Post* amongst consular reports: on 14 October, the British Consul reported that he had asked
the Admiral of the Chinese Imperial Navy, Sa Zhiye, to direct his bombardments 'in such a way to avoid all risk to the Concessions' and the *Central
China Post* of 23 October contained the headline, 'FIRE ON FRIENDS:
REPUBLICAN ARMY NEEDS BETTER FIELD GLASSES'.

The Concessions were between the Imperial army and the Republicans so
the Acting Consul General Herbert Goffe supported a request from the
General Officer commanding the Imperial army that foreigners should stay
indoors or face arrest. Shells fell close to the *Central China Post* newspaper
office and on 4 November the autumn races were cancelled. The tense situation continued into the New Year when Major Withycombe, Officer Commanding the British troops in Hankou, 'responsible to naval authorities and
responsible for sandbags' was in dispute with Mr A. Sugden of the Imperial
Chinese Customs who wanted the barricades (Major Withycombe's sandbags) removed. Bishop White wrote from Kaifeng on 1 January to report that
he was well, but he was worried about the Reverend S.J. Townsend and his
wife who were not attached to any missionary group for 'if trouble should
break out ... I think the positive disfavour with which people regard him
would make it very dangerous for him.'

Amongst the local population, many men cut off their queues (the Manchu
hairstyle for men, imposed on all Chinese since 1644) immediately the uprising began, risking the disfavour of the Governor of Henan province who,
according to the *Central China Post*, 'objects to the queueless' and reported on
2 November that 'there were many who joyfully cut off their queues, our
native employees lacking queues feared that they might be captured and given
short shrift.' One of the editors at the *Central China Post* had a house in the
Russian Concession which was 'subject to shells and bullets' and when he

returned, he discovered that he had lost six summer pongee suits (worth $20), four woollen winter suits ($22), one Italian cloth summer suit ($16) and one evening dress suit ($50). A claim for restitution was submitted to the Chinese government.[3]

Lurid tales of massacres in Hankou reached Peking from where the *Times* correspondent Morrison wrote to a friend, 'No confirmation has reached us of the massacre of women and children in Hankou. If it should be true a thrill of horror will pass through the civilised world.' Two weeks later, on 14 November, he wrote, 'Hankou stories have been greatly exaggerated. The number of killed has borne no relation to the number reported as having been killed. Similarly about Nanjing, the lurid stories sent from Shanghai appear to have little basis in fact.'[4]

In Shanghai, as O.M. Green reported:

> Nothing happened for some three weeks. Then early one morning, a handful of Nationalists crossed the river, fired a few shots in the direction of the Jiangnan Arsenal, which lies southwards of the foreign settlements and the Chinese city, and incontinently, the Arsenal threw up its hands and cried, '*Kamerad*'. The whole proceedings were really comic opera. With many other foreigners I went out to the Arsenal in the afternoon and watched the Nationalists breaking open the storehouses and serving out rifles, pistols and ammunition to practically any coolie who liked to ask. All the coolies had to do to prove their loyalty to the cause was to accept and wear a white armband, which was much easier than handling a rifle of which they knew nothing; quite a lot of them got shot through incautiously peering down the muzzle of a friend's rifle. Meanwhile, hundreds of excited youths, dressed in cheap and hideous Japanese-made foreign clothes to show their emancipation, paraded the streets, forcibly cutting off the queues of those who were too slow in shedding this badge of servitude to the Manchus, while all the shops hurriedly hoisted white flags.
>
> The last time I saw the stately old Dragon flag of the Empire was over the forts at Wusong, which held out for about a week after the Arsenal's surrender. It was a lovely flag, the purple seven-clawed dragon undulating across a yellow ground. There it floated majestically over the fort spread out by a light breeze against the cloudless blue of China's autumnal skies. Next morning, the forts had surrendered, the dragon vanished and in his place flew the five-barred flag of the Republic.'[5]

In coastal Fujian province, foreign residents were evacuated to the foreign concession area outside the city walls as 'rebel artillery was hauled up Temple Hill' and on 4 November the rebels began shelling the area in the city where the Imperial (Manchu) troops were quartered. The Imperial troops tried to storm the rebel stronghold but were defeated after a day of battle and 'doctors attached to the Anglican, Methodist and Congregationalist missions worked at four operating tables all that day and the next night'. Far away, in the interior of the province, missionaries were unable to carry out the orders of the American Consul that they make their way to the relative safety of the city of Fuzhou as brigands controlled the rivers. For three days from 13 November, they huddled in their isolated compound where tension was such that the Reverend Dr Bliss was almost shot by mistake by his next-door neighbour, Charles Storrs, also of the American Board for Foreign Missions.

In Sichuan province, Morrison reported, 'the entire foreign community of Chengdu had left there early in December' and the severed heads of the local military commander Duan Fang and his son 'had arrived at Ichang in kerosene tins whilst the northern city of Taiyuan was 'in the hands of brigands.'⁶

In Peking, there was little trouble in November 1911 although, with memories of the Boxer siege of 1900 still fresh, precautions were taken and the British Legation organised a corps of messengers ready to warn British residents and bring them to the safety of the Legation in case of danger. Arthur Stursberg of the Imperial Chinese Customs postal service volunteered, and was given a revolver and twenty-four rounds of ammunition. It was not until the abdication of the dynasty in 1912 that trouble broke out in Peking with an assassination attempt on Yuan Shikai in January and a mutiny by the troops of his Third Division (who had not been paid for months) on 4 February.

Morrison wrote:

> We thought at first it was [fire] crackers, this being a festive season, and it was not until we had … gone home that we realised rifles were being fired, not crackers … the buildings near my house were in flames … the soldiers looted from house to house.

Summoned to the safety of the British Legation, Morrison chose to stay on the street where he 'saw the systematic looting and heard the incessant fusillade.' Order was restored within a few days and the soldiers went unpunished whilst Arthur Stursberg photographed the bodies of poverty-stricken civilian looters. The 'poor wretches' were 'beheaded on the street … the head either suspended from a bamboo by the queue or nailed by the queue to a neighbouring telegraph pole'.

Such disturbances continued throughout the unstable years following, causing occasional panic to foreign residents and death and loss to local people.

Financial obligations to foreign powers

From the beginning in 1912, the new Chinese Republican government was plagued by inherited financial problems, a serious lack of expertise and

THE CHANGING MIX OF FOREIGN FINANCE

Foreign Loans to China
(excludes industrial bank loans)

	1902	1914	1930
	US $ MM	US $ MM	US $ MM
Britain	109.4	195.7	162.9
USA	4.5	7.3	50.8
France	61.0	119.9	102.7
Germany	78.3	127.1	93.6
Japan	–	27.4	373.3
Russia	26.1	45.1	–

In the years immediately before the war, leading banks of six nations formed a consortium to lend to China. At first, American banks were not included in the consortium, but President Taft used his influence to secure their inclusion. However, in 1913, the newly elected President Wilson asked US banks not to participate in the £25 million reorganisation loan, on the basis that it eroded Chinese sovereignty, being secured on government revenues – as indeed was a major part of all previous loans incurred by China. Moreover, it was declared illegal, having been arranged privately by President Yuan Shikai, outside the National Assembly. The funds were used to shore up the president's army, cover administrative costs and repay old debts, though most of it was never accounted for.

Bankers often made loans to provincial or central government politicians who might serve their ends. For example, in 1916, Heinrich Cordes, of Deutsch - Asiatische Bank, offered a loan to President Yuan Shikai in order to persuade him not to declare war on Germany, but the president died shortly thereafter and China did declare war on Germany in 1917. In 1918, Japan's loans to Duan Qirui in return for Chinese recognition of Japanese rights in Shandong fatally undermined China's negotiations at Versailles in 1919.

Main foreign investors in China and their shares

COUNTRY	1902	1914	1930
	%	%	%
Britain	33.0	37.7	36.7
USA	2.5	3.1	6.1
France	11.6	10.7	5.9
Germany	20.9	16.4	2.7
Japan	0.1	13.6	35.1
Russia	31.3	16.7	8.4

During the war, Japanese loans and investments began to grow rapidly as the other nations were preoccupied by the European theatre. Finance was part and parcel of Japan's deadly incursion into China, which was to turn into full scale war in 1937.

NOTE: statistics for foreign loans and investment in China are from C.F. Remer's *Foreign Investments in China* Macmillan, New York, 1933 political division. The destruction of foreign property (including pongee suits and evening dress suits) during the 1911 uprising led to demands from Western governments for reparation which were added to the vast sums China was forced to pay as a result of the Peking siege of the Legations by the Boxer rebels in 1900. China had to make payments of the Boxer Indemnity every month to thirteen different nations. In 1916 the monthly total was £304,100, ranging from £34,425 to Great Britain to £40 per month to Sweden, Norway, Spain and Portugal. A further indemnity charged for damage to foreign property as a result of the 1911 uprising was added to this, and the new Chinese government was also required to repay the Anglo-German loan of 1898, the Anglo-French loan of 1908, the Hukuang Railway loan of 1911 and the Crisp loan of 1912 made with various groups of British, French, German, Russian, American and Japanese banks.

The burden falling on China was to be substantially increased by the £25 million 'Reorganisation loan' of 1913 made with a similar group of banks, but excluding the Americans at the request of the newly elected President Wilson. These loans resulted from the desire of foreign countries to expand their hold over China and the Chinese government's desperate need for money; the lending-to-control syndrome was to become particularly marked with the Nishihara loans of 1917–18, which secured support from Chinese politicians for Japan's agenda at Versailles.

Willard Straight started his career in China as one of the few Americans employed in the Chinese Imperial Customs, subsequently working for Reuters during the Russo-Japanese War of 1904–5, which was fought over control of Korea and the Chinese territory of Manchuria. He served in the American Foreign Service as secretary to the Consul General in Korea and then as Consul in Mukden (Shenyang, in Manchuria) before joining the American bank, J.P. Morgan and Company. With his experience of Japanese domination in Korea and Manchuria, he wrote, 'There is one thing I want to do and that is to give people some idea of what the Japanese occupation of Korea really means. The thing that is to be done is to un-bluff the world.' He was well placed to understand the fierce rivalries of foreign powers in China. He was the leading American representative in the negotiations over railway and other loans, which involved complicated groupings of banks and governments and which the Chinese government regarded with enormous suspicion at the same time as experiencing a desperate need for money.

Writing about the proposed currency loan in January 1911, he declared:

I confess, abjectly and with more blushes than you can picture … that I am pretty darned well licked. I'm licked because the Russians … with all their subtle intrigue, bribery and misrepresentation are agin us, because there's not one man in the Chinese government who is big enough, broad enough, wise enough and honest enough, to recognize either the plight his country is in or the need for getting and taking advice to help her out, and because the American government and the American group can't deliver the goods, either politically or financially ... Perhaps we can still pull it out owing to the greed of the English, French and German bankers. That's our one hope. Through this we may secure the co-operation of the Three Powers in squelching Japan and Russia.[7]

Straight and his banker colleagues in Peking also had to face the dramatic change in the Chinese government in 1911. In the chaos of late 1911, he underestimated the slow-burning rebellion:

I must confess that at the outset I did not take the thing seriously ... the row ... seems not so much anti-dynastic as I had feared, but directed rather to securing those reforms which all friends of China desire, and which the Manchus have not inaugurated as quickly as the Young China party has wished. It looks a good deal as if our old friend Yuan, who has today been made Commander-in-Chief, has been doing a little dickering on his own account with the patriots, and the feeling is general and I think justified, that if the government gives him the powers he demands, i.e., the right to reorganize the Cabinet and create a responsible govern-ment, the Revolution in the South will fizzle out ...

Straight was mistaken about the uprising but his 'old friend' Yuan Shikai was to approach him within a month, desperate for money and Dorothy Straight wrote on 17 November:

The Chinese are so hard-pressed for money that they will offer almost any terms – terms which the bankers would not think of demanding. Yuan came to Willard with his proposal, but Willard has asked him to give the English the lead, for the Americans wish to keep in the back-ground just now and not fan the fire of jealousy with which the other Foreign Powers regard every act of the United States in the Far East.

A month later, Dorothy Straight described a meeting between Yuan Shikai and the Chinese Secretary to the American Legation, Dr Charles Tenney. Yuan Shikai's hair had 'turned white and his face had the hunted look of a man who is facing failure ... There was nothing new, only the same dis-couraging story of failing funds. Last month, his soldiers were only given half pay. He has now only sufficient money to carry on the government for two weeks longer.'[8]

And, despite Willard Straight's efforts, the American bankers were forced to withdraw from the Reorganisation Loan of 1913. The Taft administra-tion had encouraged American banks to lend to China, but when President

Wilson succeeded Taft he caused an official statement to be issued in March 1913, making it clear that it ran against Wilson's principles of self-determination, indeed, it was 'obnoxious to the principles upon which the government of our people rests' for it 'might conceivably go to the length in some unhappy contingency of forcible interference in the financial, even political, affairs of that great Oriental state, just now awakening to a consciousness of its power, and of its obligations to its people. The conditions [of the loan] include ... the administration of ... taxes by foreign agents [the Salt Administration].'

Some suggest, however, that the American banks were unable to meet their share of the loan owing to the financial state of the market at home and this statement was a face-saving ploy.

The Reorganisation Loan went ahead without American participation but the financial crises were endless. In July 1913, the Chinese navy in Shanghai, which had not been paid for two months, threatened to mutiny and join a planned attack on the arsenal by Kuomintang rebels. W.F. Tyler of the Chinese Maritime Customs was concerned and drove back from the naval dockyards in his Oldsmobile 'in a thoughtful mood'.[9] With very little time, he consulted the manager of the Hong Kong and Shanghai Bank which, as part of an international consortium 'held a considerable reserve of Chinese government money against its liabilities for loans'. Further consultations with Admiral Jerram who was supportive and the acting British Consul General (cold and unappreciative) led to his functioning as 'Treasurer', advancing money (about a million taels) to the Chinese navy which did, within the next few days, defend the arsenal.

Tyler had asked Admiral Li if money would save the situation and the arsenal and Li 'brightened up and answered, "Money would save any situation in China."' Such small financial transactions aside, many of the major loans were connected with railway construction by foreign powers. 'China is virtually being put out to auction,' said the British Minister in Peking. Loan repayments were achieved through the use of customs revenues (the Imperial Chinese Customs was managed by foreign administrators) and in 1913, the Salt gabelle (tax) was forced upon China by the Western powers, mainly to ensure that further loans would be repaid by the collection of tax on salt.[10]

On 17 September 1914, Sir John Jordan wrote of the importance (to western interests) of the establishment of the Salt tax:

The Chinese will resume payment [of the Boxer Indemnity] and there will, so far as can be foreseen, be no reason for postponing payment of either loans or indemnity. I shall never cease to look back on the appointment of a Britisher to the Salt as one of the achievements of which we ought to be proud. I wonder what would have happened if a German had held that post? The Salt has proved the salvation of China. The Chinese may curse us for opium but they will long bless us for salt.[11]

A Parliamentary system

With such western domination of the nation's finances, the new government nevertheless managed to establish a parliamentary system with 10 per cent of the (male) population entitled to vote, a proportion not achieved by Japan until 1928 and India in 1935. The Republic ratified most of the Hague Conventions (relating to the conduct of war, neutrality and dispute settlement), and joined international organisations such as the Universal Postal Union and the International Opium Commission. It improved prisons, reformed the legal system, established universities and promulgated four years of compulsory education with an entirely new and modern curriculum. The British philosopher, Goldsworthy Lowes Dickinson, visiting in 1912, spent some time at a remote village primary school on the Upper Yangtze.

> The temple ... is converted into a school. Inside the walls are hung with drawings of birds and beasts, of the human skeleton and organs, even of bacteria! The children even produce in triumph an English reading-book, though I must confess they do not seem to have profited by it much. Still they can say 'cat' when you show them a picture of the creature; which is more than I could do in Chinese ... This, remember, is a tiny village in the heart of the country, more than 1,000 miles from the coast.[12]

Of their young, missionary-trained teacher, Dickinson noted, 'One remark I remember: "China is a good place now; China a republic."'

Though extraordinary transformations were made by the new, young government, it was undermined from the beginning by the inheritance of the late-Qing regional armies with considerable local power, by damaging political divisions and by the disdain with which it was treated by the Western powers, concerned with the maintenance of their 'spheres of interest', who took some time to acknowledge the new government. Western observers laughed at the youth of many parliamentarians: 'I hear that ... at the senate the voice of the most ferocious leader of the opposition against the government has not yet broken! He must be fifteen!'[13] wrote the Italian diplomat Daniele Varè in 1913. He recorded how, on 2 January 1913, the foreign diplomats in Peking 'went today to see Yuan Shikai and to wish him a happy New Year. They chose to go on the second and not the first of the month, to mark the fact that the reception is not official, the Republican Government of China being as yet unrecognised by foreign powers.' Lack of recognition meant that 'when we [foreign diplomats] go to some official reception given by the Chinese we do not wear decorations. We pretend that we are going to a private house! Sir John Jordan forgot this important rule and arrived the other night at the Waijiaobu [Chinese Foreign Ministry] with a star and ribbon across his shirt-front. Then he saw the rest of us without decorations and took them off again, leaving them with his hat and coat in the hall.'

Recognition of the Republic of China by Great Britain was complicated by disagreements about opium and relations over Tibet, with the British 'intimating' to the Chinese in August 1912 that agreement over Tibet 'along the lines laid down by England must be a condition precedent to the recognition by Great Britain of the Chinese Republic'. With preparations for the 1914 Simla conference underway, Britain joined Japan, Germany, France, Sweden, Belgium, Russia, Portugal, Holland, Austria, Italy and Denmark and recognised the Republic on 6 October 1913 (the United States, Mexico, Cuba and Peru having done so in May).

The Republican government itself paid some attention to decorations. 'In deference to democratic views the old insignia of rank – the embroidered robes, the coloured buttons, the peacock and other feathers, the Orders of the Double Dragon – were thrown into the limbo of the past; in their place appeared Western military uniforms, frock-coats, full evening dress in the middle of the day and a batch of new Orders – the Excellent Crop (awarded to G.E. Morrison), the Striped Tiger, and others of similarly curious names,' wrote W.F. Tyler of the (ex-Imperial) Chinese Customs, a recipient of the Order of the Striped Tiger, second class.[14]

Greatly complicating China's foreign relations was the increase in internal chaos. Though a central government was finally established in Peking in 1912 with Yuan Shikai as President, it was very unstable and divided. Yuan Shikai himself shared some of Daniele Varè's contempt for his own parliament which he dissolved in 1913, before his unsuccessful attempt to install himself as a new emperor in 1916. Sir John Jordan, the British Minister in Peking, who was on friendly terms with Yuan Shikai – so friendly that Yuan, who had already invested in property in England, was threatening to buy a retirement home in England so they could be neighbours – explained:

> The one thorn in his side was the parliament in Peking which naturally objected to his concluding loans without their approval and constantly rejected his nominees for Cabinet. He was very impatient at this restraint and used to refer contemptuously to the 'puerile chattering' of its members.[15]

Sir John also reported that one of Yuan's American advisors said that 'he would rather run an ice-cream factory in hell than a republic in China.'

Yuan Shikai also complained about parliament to Paul Reinsch, the newly-arrived American minister, 'It was not a good parliament, for it was made up largely of inexperienced theorists and young politicians. They wished to meddle with government ...' Yuan continued, 'As you see, the Republic of

China is a very young baby. It must be nursed and kept from taking strong meat or potent medicines like those prescribed by foreign doctors.'[16]

The difficulty of working with an autocrat like Yuan Shikai was evident from the very first days when, having appointed Tang Shaoyi as Premier, Tang resigned after two months. Sir John Jordan met Tang Shaoyi several years later in Shanghai in 1916 when the ex-Premier 'now running an insurance company, asked me to tell Yuan Shikai that his government was an autocracy of the worst kind and that his tenure of power would be limited unless he gave the people of China some share in the management of their own affairs.[17] As for himself, he preferred to prolong the existence of his fellow creatures in his present role of an insurance agent rather than harm the people again by becoming Yuan Shikai's Prime Minister!'

Lü Zhengxiang served as Foreign Minister four times, sometimes for only a few months, resigning 'because of illness', on one occasion being succeeded by Zhao Bingjun who may or may not have been poisoned. It was common for resigning politicians to retreat the short 150 kilometres from political Peking to the protection of Treaty Port Tianjin, as the young French diplomat Alexis St Léger-Léger (the Nobel Prize-winning poet Saint John Perse) observed in 1917, 'A President of the Republic resigns and flees to Tianjin, making a public avowal of his incompetence, "Modest as the bean-pod beneath the leaf, I accuse myself of unworthiness".'[18]

Yuan Shikai banned Sun Yat-sen's majority party in parliament in 1913. The National People's Party (Kuomintang/Guomindang) was created by Sun Yat-sen and others in 1912 from the merger of various smaller anti-imperial parties including Sun's Tongmenghui, founded in exile in Tokyo in 1905. Yuan is also generally believed to have arranged the assassination of the potential Prime Minister Song Jiaoren, who was openly critical of Yuan's personal ambition, before the dissolution. Sun Yat-sen's Kuomintang party soon established a breakaway regime in the south of China and it is clear from diplomatic documents that it was hard for foreign powers to decide who was really in control. The situation was further complicated by the increasing power of local armies, originally established by the imperial house in the late nineteenth century but now acting with increasing independence; their feuding characterised the dangerous and chaotic 'warlord era' in China (1916–1945). In this, the losers were the Chinese people who suffered the burden of battling local armies.

Yuan Shikai

A key figure in the transition from imperial to republican rule and responsible for the creation of regional armies that were to ravage China in the early twentieth century, Yuan Shikai rose from humble beginnings through the military. In 1882, he accompanied an army sent to put down a rebellion in

Korea where he continued to serve in the Chinese garrison there. Success in dealing with a pro-Japanese coup in Seoul, led to his being stationed there for eight years as the Chinese Resident. In 1894 he returned to China and after a time spent helping with supplies for the Chinese army (unsuccessfully) fighting the Japanese in the Sino-Japanese War (1894–5), he took command of a new army corps, the 'Pacification Army' of 5,000 men in ten battalions which had been set up in 1894 with German instructors. It was soon expanded and re-named the 'Newly Created Army' but still modelled exclusively on German rules and regulations.

Yuan Shikai had the *Introductory Manual of the German Army* translated and distributed to his officers who were expected to recite it. German military influence in China in the second half of the nineteenth century was strong. German weapons were used and in 1885, the reformer Zhang Zhidong (pioneer of railway construction) stated that a survey of foreign armies revealed that Germany was pre-eminent. Relatively good relations with Germany, which was seen as less rapacious than France and Britain, were soured when Germany seized Jiaozhou Bay in 1897 and from 1902, China turned to Japan for armaments and military training.

Yuan Shikai's political involvement grew through his military achievements and it is probable that during the ill-fated 'Hundred Days Reform' in 1898, when the Guangxu Emperor attempted to impose modernising reforms, incurring the undying enmity of the failed reformers, Yuan Shikai revealed these plans to the Dowager Empress Cixi who placed the Emperor under house arrest until his death in 1908. Yuan Shikai was made Governor of Shandong province where, in 1900, he suppressed the local Boxer rebels and maintained stability. His action had the effect of driving the Boxers inland towards Peking where they joined with imperial forces and besieged the Foreign Legations. Because he had acted against the Boxers in Shandong, he gained foreign approval and was appointed Governor General of Zhili (the area including the capital, Peking) and placed in charge of military affairs in North China. He greatly expanded his army, now known as the Beiyang or Northern Ocean Army, with six divisions, and he set up a military training school at Baoding.

His increasing power created enemies at court and, after the death of his protector the Dowager Empress, he was ordered to retire and lived in seclusion in his villa until 1911 when rapidly spreading uprisings led the imperial regent to beg him to return. In the chaos of 1911, as the republican rebels gained ground, the imperial family accepted the necessity of abdication and asked Yuan Shikai to negotiate. Some suggest that it was Yuan himself who persuaded the imperial family to abdicate, so he was negotiating both for and against them. The young Emperor's tutor, the ex-British Colonial officer Reginald Johnston, was of this opinion: 'I believe that in all those negotiations and discussions, Yuan was working, not for the rebels and their republic, nor for the child-emperor and the dynasty, but for his own glory.'[19] Yuan himself was playing a complicated game for he 'told Sir John Jordan emphatically' that he would not accept the Presidency. 'He said that he and his ancestors had served the Manchu dynasty faithfully and he could not go down in history as a usurper ...'

Negotiations were carried out in December in Shanghai at the handsome Gordon Road home of Edward Selby Little, a former missionary who had established the pioneering mountain resort of 'Kuling', a mock Chinese place-name whose pronunciation embodied the attractions of his cool summer resort on Lu shan.[20] Britain's part in these negotiations angered Japan which favoured the establishment of a constitutional monarchy rather than a republic and she accused Britain of betraying the Anglo-Japanese Alliance by facilitating negotiations with the republicans. In London, on the other hand, it was widely believed that Japan had actively supported the rebels against Yuan Shikai.[21]

In Gordon Road, Yuan Shikai's representative was Tang Shaoyi (1862–1938) a Guangdong native, educated in the USA, who served very briefly as China's first Prime Minister in 1912, before breaking with Yuan Shikai. The Nationalist representative for Sun Yatsen was Wu Tingfang (1842–1922) born in Malacca, educated in Hong Kong, called to the Bar in London in 1876, who, like Tang Shaoyi, served very briefly as Minister of Justice in 1912. It was proposed that a National Assembly be set up in Nanjing, with Sun Yat-sen as provisional President.

Despite the arrangements agreed in the Articles of Favoured Treatment, Yuan Shikai, relying upon his military backing, was able to convince Sun Yat-sen to resign as provisional President, and compel the National Assembly to appoint himself to the post in March 1912. Sun Yat-sen told the *Manchester Guardian*'s correspondent H.C. Thomson that he had had to resign in favour of Yuan because:

> the Revolution was not sufficiently far advanced to bring about a reform of the machinery of Government or the strengthening of its economic position; that the only result of his retaining the Presidency would have been the replacement of one set of officials by another of the same kind; and that he could do better work by remaining outside the Government altogether and devoting himself to the work of revolutionary recon-struction by the education of the people and the improvement of the methods of industry, leaving the Government of the country entirely to Yuan Shikai.[22]

A more succinct version of this speech was told to W.F. Tyler of the Chinese Customs by a Chinese friend, 'I am an agitator. I have been that all my life, and it is all I am fit for. I am no administrator; and so I gladly pass things on to you.'[23]

Yuan's control of most of the military was not mentioned as a factor. Despite his duplicity, many of the western diplomats in Peking took Yuan Shikai's side, for he was a long-established and powerful political figure in the capital. They were also grateful that, where Sun and the Kuomintang had decided the new capital of the Republic of China would be in Nanjing, Yuan Shikai refused to move from Peking, his own base of power, where the foreign legations were also situated. One of his arguments was that the greatest threat to China came from the north, from Russian and Japanese encroachments in Mongolia and Manchuria and it was necessary to keep the capital in the north to better control these borders and forces.

Throughout China's history, the capital had moved from Xi'an to Luoyang and back, from Kaifeng to Hangzhou and then Peking. The first Ming Emperor chose his personal powerbase of Nanjing for the capital in 1368 but it was soon moved back to Peking, partly for the same strategic reason, the greatest threat coming from the north. For the Republicans and revolutionaries, however, Nanjing represented a clear break with the corrupt and conservative past. Yuan Shikai's trusted Third Division rebelled on 29 February, looting and burning, and similar incidents occurred in Tianjin and Baoding, 'reinforcing' Yuan's argument that the capital should not move south.

One of the ways in which Yuan Shikai became better known to western diplomats was through his appointment of the southerner Cai Tinggan (1861–1935) as his interpreter and guide in foreign affairs. Cai had been sent to school in the United States through the China Educational Mission and subsequently joined the Chinese navy. Cai corresponded frequently with the *Times* correspondent G.E. Morrison, sending him details, not just of political events and views but of more intimate events such as the day (7 December 1911) when Premier designate Tang Shaoyi (who had also studied in America through the China Educational Mission), and other members of the provisional government, had their queues cut off in Room 4 at the Wagons-Lits Hotel, marking a definitive break with the dying Manchu regime. Yuan Shikai was more prudent, waiting until a week after the abdication to make the break, but on 16 February, Cai wrote to Morrison, 'It is agreed that *I* shall clip the Premier (President's) top knot and not a barber as he feels rather awkward. *This is your scoop*. I will let you know the exact time of the act.'[24]

Other associates of Yuan Shikai were also well known to the western diplomats and businessmen. Liang Shiyi, another southerner, served as Minister of Railways from 1907 and Minister of Communications from 1911, as well as being a director of several banks. Since western interest in China in the early twentieth century involved much financial dealing as loans were pressed upon the Chinese, often for railway development, Liang Shiyi was a familiar figure, described in the *New York Times* as the 'Brains of China' (4 June 1916).

Lord Kitchener's porcelain

Liang Shiyi demonstrated his diplomatic skills during a visit to China by Lord Kitchener in 1909. The Commander-in-Chief of the British Army in India had come to add to his collection of porcelain, and his visit was described by the court official in charge of the Manchu imperial ancestral palace in Shenyang. 'He … loved porcelain to a strange degree. He is reported to have said that he regarded soldiers as his sons and porcelain as his wife.' There were tens of thousands of imperial pieces dating from the Song to the late Qing exhibited in specially built halls in the old palace. 'Foreign visitors who had visited them spread the news of their existence overseas and that was what had provoked Kitchener's saliva. If I were to let him choose the pieces himself he would no doubt have chosen the biggest and most valuable ones.' The best pieces were removed from exhibition and hidden in a storeroom but, unfortunately, Lord Kitchener had come armed with photographs of the prize pieces, placing his host in a difficult position.

Chinese traditional hospitality, which Lord Kitchener was exploiting to his advantage, implies that if a guest admires an object, it should be offered to him. When the official in charge denied all knowledge of these special pieces:

> Kitchener was very unhappy but selected two each of the smaller vases, cups and jars. They were all of the best porcelain in apple green and known as 'after shower sky azure'. He wanted still to take more of the best pieces so I stopped him saying that in the decree he was to be allowed only two pieces … Kitchener then put the jar on top of the vase saying that it was only one piece … Kitchener … put two cups in his pocket and seized one vase in each hand …

It was decided that the local Viceroy should be consulted and, fortunately, Liang Shiyi, then Minister of Railways rather than protocol, was visiting. Diplomatically he proposed that, though there was a decree limiting the number of pieces to be taken to two, they 'should not offend him because of this trifle' which at least ended the matter without further loss.

Sun Yat-sen

By contrast with the fluent and worldly politicians of Peking, Sun Yat-sen, leader of the Kuomintang party and, effectively, leader of the anti-Qing uprising (despite his absence), was relatively unknown. Born in a village in the southern tip of the southern province of Guangdong, he had attended school in Hawaii and studied medicine in Hong Kong. Associated with a series of anti-Manchu, anti-imperial movements in southern China, Hong Kong,

Japan and overseas, he narrowly escaped execution by the Qing government when he was, as his account of the events described, 'Kidnapped in London' in 1896. The *Times* correspondent G.E. Morrison described him as the 'most impossible of persons ... a fool, ... not only as mad as a hatter, but ... madder ... full of impractical schemes' although he was to be virtually canonised after his death in 1926 as the 'Father of the Nation'. In this early period, as rifts grew between Sun Yat-sen and his Kuomintang party and Yuan Shikai, western sympathies were almost entirely on Yuan's side, accusing Sun of being impractical and influenced by Germany or Japan or (after 1915) the Socialist International. Though Sun Yat-sen was a southerner and such power base as he had was in the south, where Yuan Shikai was more strongly associated with the north, with so many government ministers like Tang Shaoyi, Liang Shiyi and Cai Tinggan originating in Guangdong province, like Sun, the lines of geographical adherence were not straightforward.

Picnics and punch

Despite the confusion of governments and the growing instability due to the rise of local warlords, foreign residents in China whether diplomats or visitors, enjoyed a carefree and luxurious lifestyle against an exotic background. Despite the exoticism of their surroundings, it was possible to retain the atmosphere of home, attending Anglican services on Sundays in Peking when Bishop Norris preached and 'Aglen (afterwards Sir Francis Aglen, Inspector-general of Chinese Customs) sang more heartily than anyone else; and Barton (afterwards Sir Sidney Barton, HM Minister in Abyssinia), then student-interpreter, passed the plate around; Tours, who afterwards was HM Consul General in Mukden, played the harmonium'.

The Dutch diplomat Sir William Oudendyk described the new Dutch legation building:

> a copy on a smaller scale of the well-known country house, 'Middachten', near Arnhem, belonging to the Bentinck family ... in the big hall of the legation I installed a mantelpiece in carved teak wood, adapted from the design of an old English one which I saw in *Country Life*. An old Chinese carpenter ... perfectly apprehended the idea of the acanthus in the capitals of the fluted Corinthian columns, and the royal coat of arms in the central panel no Italian artist could have executed better.[25]

When not trying to replicate life in distant Europe, foreign residents made the most of what exotic China had to offer, picnicking in temples, enjoying horse-racing at the race course surrounded by willows and 'situated in picturesque surroundings near a pretty lotus lake', fancy dress balls and dancing. On 11 February 1913 Daniele Varè attended a ball at the Russian Legation with 'the usual floods of champagne, mounds of fresh caviar in hollowed blocks of ice, and giant sturgeons from the River Amur'.[26] 'We all danced the mazurka, directed by Grawe who is Court Chamberlain' and 'gave orders in a voice like a train going over a bridge.'

Brooke Astor (who lived in Peking as a child between 1909 and 1913 when her father was a military attaché in the American Legation) described a literary society called The Purple Cows whose members were expected to produce a paper for each meeting.[27] It was:

> composed of the French Minister and Madame de Margerie (she was the sister of Edmond Rostand …), the Americans Mr and Mrs Daniel de Menocal, Mr and Mrs Willard Straight (she was Dorothy Whitney of New York), the French banker Casenave … The idea of calling the Society the Purple Cows emanated from Mr Straight. Monsieur Casenave sent to Paris for purple Charvet dressing gowns with orange collars and cuffs that members wore over their suits at meetings, with impressive effect.

Little Brooke Astor enjoyed endless fancy-dress parties and the 'British Legation was a great centre for these parties. I remember one occasion when all girls came dressed as flowers and all the boys as insects … Harrison Hatch, aged six, three years my junior, was dressed as a ladybug and kept buzzing around me, sticking his tongue out.' Fancy dress was not just for children for her mother 'had Tailor working night and day turning her into a Columbine, a Madame de Pompadour, a Reynolds painting and once, when she danced the cakewalk with Willard Straight, into a black-faced mammy.'

William Oudendyk also recalled the prominence of the British Legation in the social round:

> I shall never forget the Christmas night in the British Legation in Peking when the whole staff and myself were entertained by Sir Claude and Lady MacDonald. I can still see Sir Claude with an Indian turban on his head, a drum-major's mace of his highland regiment in one hand and a recipe book in the other, standing on a stool. Punch had to be brewed. Sir Claude read an ingredient out of the book: 'One pint of Curacao!' A wild roar of approval arose from the audience standing around. W.P. Ker (afterwards HM Consul-General in Tientsin) uncorked a bottle and solemnly poured out the contents into the bowl. 'Six bottles of white wine!' sounded Sir Claude's stentorian voice. 'Hurrah for the white wine!' responded the rest of the company vociferously. So it went on; the excitement grew with every new ingredient, suddenly Sir Claude announced, 'One kettleful of boiling water!' Loud sounds of discontent …[28]

New Year's Eve was celebrated in 1910 with a large party in the residence of the Inspector-General of Customs in Peking. As Sir Robert Hart was away on home leave, the party was organised by Lady Bredon, wife of his deputy. Arthur Stursberg of the Chinese Posts (part of the Customs administration) described the 'paper cotillion':[29]

> Lady Bredon had assembled a collection of paper fans, sunhats, and paper lanterns in the shape of birds or animals, all the wonderful paper objects that the Chinese made, which the gentlemen would present to their partners ... the male guests stood behind a curtain so that only their shoes showed, and the women picked their partners by their feet. The male wallflowers pelted the ladies with confetti and paper ribbons (there were never enough women to go around ...). Champagne flowed, a sumptuous repast was served, 'Auld Lang Syne' was sung and the party ended at 2.30am.

Riding to school every day on her little Mongolian horse Ginger, Brooke Astor once saw a dead body and another time the aftermath of a mass execution, with bodies and severed heads, but life was mostly carefree.

> The thing I liked best of all were the picnics, and the best picnics were the winter ones, which were really delicious. My favourite place was the Princess tombs. We used to skate out on the frozen canals, arriving at the tombs in time for lunch ... The boys had come out early in the morning, long before we were up, and brought with them a trestle table, benches, linen, silver, food and wine. The table was set just as prettily as at home and the food was all piping hot. To keep warm we had fur rugs over our legs and charcoal braziers between every two people.[30]

One summer, instead of going to the beach resort of Pei-tai-ho (Beidaihe) 'a sort of little Deauville, filled with Western-style villas, bordering a broad beach', which remains a favourite seaside spot (visited by Mao Zedong and Deng Xiaoping and other leaders), Brooke Astor's parents rented a temple in the Western Hills where they decamped with all their servants and a shower rigged up by the Marines from a 'perforated gasoline can'. Many foreigners summered in temples in the Western Hills and Daniele Varè recalled climbing uphill from 'his' temple with an important telegram for Sir John Jordan. 'I walked in unannounced. He was dining in one of the courtyards. And though he was all alone, on a hot summer evening in a Chinese temple, he was correctly dressed in a dinner jacket with black tie.'[31]

Sir William Oudendyk, who served in China for many years between 1894 and 1931, remembered his summertime conversations of 1895 with Henry Cockburn, a British diplomat:

> lying on long chairs on the uppermost terrace of that reposeful Buddhist temple ... the Hall of the Dragon King ... We had been talking of many things ... and finally landed on European politics and the general

chances which the different armies would have should a general war break out. And I can still hear him say, 'Well, should we ever have to fight against the German army, I should fix all my hope on the Kaiser, he will be sure to make a mess of things for the Germans.' Afterwards, when the French-English rivalries of those days had made way for an entente, I often thought of those words, and when war had broken out, they were constantly on my mind.[32]

In the treaty port of Shanghai, less grand than Peking with its diplomatic grandeur, the city shut down twice a year for the horse races on the race club's ground in the centre of the city. Although there were amateur dramatic clubs and music provided by Rudolf Beck's orchestra, sport was of considerable importance in Shanghai, with teams of cricketers and footballers drawn from such businesses as British American Tobacco and local institutions such as the Shanghai Municipal Police Force. For a lack of foxes, keen riders followed paper chases across the countryside outside the city. Edward Ward recalled being chased by an enraged peasant 'wielding a formidable thornbush', probably reasonably enraged at the damage to his crops, and charged by an angry water buffalo. In the early summer of 1914, as war threatened, the Shanghai Rowing Club held its annual regatta (at a site outside the city which they renamed 'Hen-li') and, characteristic of the mixed but still cohesive cosmopolitan foreign community of Shanghai, German teams took all the prizes.[33]

Despite the dominance of sport in Shanghai, it was also the headquarters of such academic institutions as the Royal Asiatic Society Shanghai Branch, where local residents could improve their minds, or indulge in nostalgia for home, by attending lectures. On 23 December 1911, the Reverend C.E. Darwent who had published an immensely popular guide to Shanghai, *A Handbook for Visitors and Residents*, in 1904, lectured on a very different subject, 'Rambles in Sussex'. As the *North China Herald* reported:

> A large and keenly appreciative audience assembled in Union Church Hall on Wednesday evening to hear the Reverend C.E. Darwent tell of his holiday at home among the antiquities and unchanging joys of one of England's loveliest counties … Unfortunately, after Mr Darwent had been speaking for rather more than an hour, some difficulty occurred with the 'transformer' in the electrical apparatus of the machine. A coolie, with more zeal than discretion, came to the rescue with a bucket of water and short-circuited the whole electrical system. The lecture had, perforce, to be abandoned.

In the same paper, it was reported proudly that Sir Ernest Shackleton had taken Manchurian ponies with him to the South Pole, chosen for their 'pluck, grit and determination'.

Chapter 3

Japan: not playing straight

After the restoration of imperial rule in 1868 (the Meiji Restoration), Japan underwent huge changes in its political and social structure. The country rapidly modernised and industrialised at a speed that left most of its neighbours behind, particularly China. Some Chinese looked with admiration at Japan and in the last decade of the nineteenth century and the beginning of the twentieth century, many went to study in Japan. It was not long before Japan's ambitions extended beyond her territory.

Japanese expansion in the Far East began with the Sino-Japanese War of 1894–5 over the control of Korea. Victorious Japan occupied the island of Taiwan and seized the Liaodong Peninsula (in south-western Manchuria) in 1895. At the end of the war, the Treaty of Shimonoseki between China and Japan acknowledged Japan's occupation of Liaodong, which included the port of Lushun, or Port Arthur (so called by Europeans after Royal Navy Lieutenant William C. Arthur who surveyed it from HMS *Algerine* in 1860 during the Second Opium War). The Treaty of Shimonoseki was signed on 17 April 1895 but almost immediately, the Triple Intervention of 23 April forced Japan to withdraw from Liaodong. The Triple Intervention involved Russia, Germany and France. Britain and the United States were invited to join in, but refused. Japan was unable to resist the military might of the three great powers and, when she was forced to withdraw from Liaodong, Russia immediately moved in to seize Port Arthur, a port Russia coveted because the port of Vladivostok, at the end of the Trans-Siberian railway, was only accessible during the summer, whilst Port Arthur was ice-free all the year round.

These alignments and re-alignments of European powers over China reflect the extraordinary shifting and slipping of alliances in the period leading up to the First World War. In 1882 Germany, Austria-Hungary and Italy joined in the 'Triple Alliance' and to counter that, France and Russia signed the Dual Alliance treaty in 1892 to unite in trying to counteract German influence. Despite the apparent drawing of lines, the Triple Intervention was forced on Japan by France and Russia, in this instance, allied with Germany. Alliances were different when they involved seizing parts of China: both Russia and Germany wanted ports on China's coast. Russia moved in to Port Arthur, forcing a twenty-five year lease from China in 1897 (which also included significant railway rights through the Liaodong peninsula to link up with the Trans-Siberian railway then under construction) and Germany acquired Jiaozhou Bay from China in 1898. Only France was not seeking a port on China's eastern seaboard as she was fully engaged in her own 'sphere of influence' in south-western China adjoining 'French Indochina' and Guangzhou Bay.

Despite the recent war, Japan and Russia signed agreements in 1907. The public agreement offered a general acknowledgement of the independence and integrity of Chinese territory and upheld the principle of equal opportunity on trade and industry in China. The secret agreement, which was not published until October 1917 when Leon Trotsky, newly appointed Foreign Minister in Russia, made public all the secret agreements signed by the Tsarist regime, recognised Japan's 'special interests' in Korea and (the Chinese territory of) Southern Manchuria and Russia's equally 'special interests' in Outer Mongolia and Northern Manchuria. In 1910, Russia and Japan signed a further agreement. This was provoked by the proposal by the American Secretary of State, Philander C. Knox, that the railways in Manchuria should be made commercially neutral, for he wanted to facilitate the investment of American capital in them.

In 1909, an Anglo-American financial group, supported by the then Governor of Manchuria's Fengtian province, Tang Shaoyi, (who later served as China's first Premier in 1912 until he quarrelled with Yuan Shikai) proposed an American financed, British built railway across Manchuria. This never materialised for it was firmly opposed by both Russia and Japan who wanted to maintain control of the area and its railways, and their public agreement declared their determination to maintain the status quo and promote 'friendly agreement' in improving railways in Manchuria. The private agreement included an acknowledgement by Russia of Japan's 'special interest' in Korea which Japan formally annexed in 1910.[1]

By the secret agreements, Russia and Japan effectively divided Manchuria into Japanese and Russian 'spheres of interest'.[2] Sir John Pratt, who served as British Consul in the capital of Shandong, Ji'nan, during the Japanese seizure of Qingdao (when he described British participation in the expedition as 'a complete farce') saw the situation in Manchuria as one of Japanese domination: 'with the silent and ruthless efficiency that has marked their every step in their career of aggression and which is in marked contrast with the haphazard and vacillating methods of Russia, they set about establishing a political and economic stranglehold over south Manchuria ...'[3]

The newly appointed US Consul-General in Mukden (now known as Shenyang, the capital of Dongbei or Manchuria), Willard Straight, wrote in 1906, 'it's at Mukden that the biggest game in the East, save Peking itself, is being played. Lord knows that Qingdao is a summer's day compared to the incipient cyclone that is hovering over North China.' In the lead-up to the

Russo-Japanese Agreements, he referred to Japan's determination to achieve 'a dominating position in Manchuria which China and the other Powers had refused to accept'. Straight was the originator of proposals that alarmed Russia and, especially, Japan, for American investment in Manchurian railways and, in his promotion of their interests, he 'detected and reported Japanese treaty infringements which were very disturbing to Peking and Washington'. Such activities included an attempted assault on Straight by a Japanese postman who had been barred from entry to the Consulate and returned with 'four pals ... entered the compound, even going into my bedroom, pulled the servants by the hair and made generally bad mess.'[4]

With American railway plans, advanced on the principle of 'the open door' but threatening Russian and Japanese plans for control of both territory and railways in Manchuria, the situation was complicated by yet another, earlier, treaty arrangement in place, this time between Britain and Japan. This had been prompted by fears of the extension of Russian interests in the Far East with the construction of the Trans-Siberian railway and the development of Vladivostok. Britain and Japan signed the first Anglo-Japanese Alliance in 1902 and it was further ratified in 1905 and 1911. The terms of this Alliance were to be of major significance in the course of events in China during the First World War. The Alliance was primarily regarded by the British as a naval alliance and negotiations over the 1911 ratifications reflected anxiety about the relative strength of the German naval forces in the East China Sea, and Germany's naval building in Europe.[5]

The first clause of the Anglo-Japanese Alliance, like the Russo-Japanese Agreements, began with characteristic hypocrisy:

> The High Contracting parties having mutually recognised the independence of China and Korea, declare themselves to be entirely uninfluenced by aggressive tendencies in either country, having in view, however, their special interests, of which those of Great Britain relate principally to China, whilst Japan, in addition to the interests which she possesses in China, is interested in a peculiar degree, politically as well as commercially and industrially, in Korea. The High Contracting parties recognise that it will be admissible for either of them to take such measures as may be indispensable in order to safeguard those interests if threatened either by the aggressive action of any other Power, or by disturbance arising in China or Korea, and necessitating the intervention of either of the High Contracting parties for the protection of the lives and properties of its subjects.

Nowhere was there genuine recognition of the 'independence of China and Korea'.

Clause three proposed 'the promise of support if either signatory becomes involved in war with more than one Power' whilst by signing clause five, both sides 'promise to communicate frankly and fully with one another when any of the interests affected by this treaty are in jeopardy.'

Commenting on Japan's seizure of Qingdao, the American Secretary of State, Robert Lansing wrote that, 'though not compelled by the terms of the existing Anglo-Japanese Alliance to take part in the conflict against the Germans, the Japanese government seized upon that agreement as a pretext ... to gain a new foothold on Chinese territory which would advance its political influence and economic control over the Republic.'[6] The Anglo-Japanese Treaty was always regarded with suspicion by America and Canada whose relations with Japan had become strained after the Russo-Japanese war, to the point that in 1907, the officer commanding US troops in the Philippines was warned of a possible attack by Japan and in March 1908, Sir Edward Grey had to 'assure the Canadian government that in the event of trouble with Japan Canada would have Great Britain's support regardless of the Anglo-Japanese Treaty'.[7]

With their concessions, railways and spheres of influence, Western powers had sought to dominate and dictate in China from the middle of the nineteenth century and at the very beginning of the Republic, with Japan's annexation of Korea, China was now subject to even more acute pressure from Japan. In late 1911 an American newspaper reported that Britain, with Japan's support, was 'using its influence for a monarchical [imperial] government for China'. Willard Staight's diary records that G.E. Morrison told him that the report was erroneous and probably resulted from Japan's failure to explain its views and activities to its ally, Britain, thereby causing considerable embarrassment:[8]

> Sir John Jordan, the British Minister and Ijuin, the Japanese Minister, acted under explicit orders from their chiefs to co-operate. They both separately so informed Yuan. Ijuin, however, without telling Jordan, advised Yuan that Japan would never recognise a republic and would interfere with force, if necessary, to prevent its establishment. In view of what both Jordan and Ijuin had said about co-operation, Yuan took this as meaning that Great Britain agreed with this attitude. He therefore wired Tang Shaoyi (who was negotiating in Shanghai) that Japan and another power would not consent to a republic. Tang told Morrison (then also in Shanghai) that England and Japan would not consent. Morrison wired to *The Times* and the Foreign Office wired Sir John Jordan, asking for an explanation. Sir John ran it down. He informed Yuan that Great Britain had done her best to bring the contending factions together but cared not a damn whether there was a republic or a

monarchy. This was sent to Tokyo. Jordan asked Ijuin to correct his statement made to Yuan. Ijuin had to get instructions. They came. On Wednesday Ijuin also said that Japan would be neutral.

As well as recording such 'mischief-making', Willard Straight reported Japanese treaty infringements and the secret Russo-Japanese Agreements made it clear that Japan and Russia had divided Manchuria between them without consulting or informing allies. In April 1914, the Japanese government proposed the construction of a railway between Jiujiang and Nanchang, running through the Yangtse area that Britain considered its own 'sphere'. The British Ambassador in Tokyo, Sir Conyngham Green complained that, 'while they will never let us onto their spheres, they are trying to steal a march into ours, and this is not cricket between Allies.'[9] The journalist Putnam Weale wrote, 'Japan was vastly active behind the scenes in China long before the outbreak of the European war gave her the longed-for opportunity.' Throughout the war, Japan continued to make use of her 'opportunity', her position, in her view, reinforced by the Anglo-Japanese Alliance.

Writing on 26 August 1914, whilst worrying about the Battle of Mons, 'we are awaiting with breathless anxiety for further news of the great battle which is now going on,' Sir John Jordan reflected, 'Japan is now taking the leading part in the game out here ... I am not an admirer of Baron Katō's methods, some of which recently have been of a rather brusque nature, but of course it was Japan's opportunity and she was bound to seize it.'[10]

With considerably misplaced complacency, he continued:

For some time past, Japan has realised that our influence in China enables us to do a great many things she cannot do and she hopes that the restoration of Qiaozhou to China will place her on a moral pinnacle as high as ours. Of course the rendition will be accompanied by conditions but they will not obscure the outstanding service rendered to China ...

With Qingdao and the surrounding areas of Jiaozhou Bay in Japanese hands by early November 1914, the Japanese Prime Minister, Okuma Shigenobu, issued a reassuring, though grossly inaccurate, statement to the effect that 'Japan has no territorial ambitions, her warlike operations will not extend beyond the defence of her own legitimate interests. Japan has no ulterior motive, no thought of depriving China or other peoples of anything which they now possess.'[11]

In September 1914 Britain asked for a division of the Japanese battle fleet to be sent to the Mediterranean, and offered to pay the costs involved. The request was turned down. On 3 November, another request for naval help was made, this time over a project to enter the Baltic. The request was, once again, refused. Japan had other priorities.[12]

Japan's 'Twenty-one Demands'

On 18 January 1915 the Japanese made their interests in China more explicit. The Japanese Ambassador handed the 'Twenty-one Demands' to President Yuan Shikai, insisting upon secrecy, breaching the spirit, if not the letter, of the Anglo-Japanese Alliance and Japan's relations with her other allies. The American journalist Carl Crow, who was shown a copy by the Russian Ambassador to Tokyo, despite the Japanese insistence on secrecy, described them as 'revelations of the sordidness and ruthlessness of Japanese diplomacy and the value that can be placed on Japanese pledges, even when given by her highest and most renowned officials . . .'[13] The Demands were in five sections and preceded by the usual hypocritical and meaningless preamble, 'The Japanese government and the Chinese government, being desirous of maintaining the general peace of eastern Asia and further strengthening the friendly relations and good neighbourhood existing between the two nations agree to the following articles . . .'

The first section related to German concessions in Shandong province, now in Japanese hands, 'The Chinese government engages to give full assent in all matters upon which the Japanese government may hereafter agree with the German government relating to the disposition of all rights, interests and concessions which, by virtue of treaties or otherwise, Germany now possess in relation to the province of Shandong.' China was not to lease land anywhere in the whole of Shandong province to any other nation, to agree to open more cities in Shandong to trade and allow Japan to build a railway there.

In section two, 'since the Chinese government has always recognised the special position enjoyed by Japan in South Manchuria and eastern inner Mongolia', she was to hand over control of the railways and all mining rights in the area and allow the Japanese free access to trade and the right to settle.

Section three related to the Han-yeh-ping Coal and Iron Company, a major industrial resource in Wuhan. This was particularly attractive to resource-poor Japan which sought control as a 'joint concern', restricting any Chinese actions over the company and its significant associated mines, whilst section four forbade the Chinese to 'cede or lease to a third power any harbour, bay or island along the coast of China'. By way of persuasion, the Japanese generously offered to restore Jiaozhou Bay to China 'at an opportune time and subject to certain conditions' (an offer that it transpired Japan had no intention of carrying out in a hurry) if China signed up.[14]

After much negotiation (what Sir John Jordan called 'a typical Oriental fencing match' noting 'there is no reasoning with a highwayman well-armed and Japan's action towards China is worse than that of Germany in the case of Belgium') but with few modifications, Prime Minister Cao Rulin finally signed sections one to four on 25 May 1915, effectively conceding South Manchuria to Japan and giving her far greater power over Shandong than

Germany had enjoyed. The fifth section was 'postponed for later negotiation' and sometimes described by the Japanese as 'desiderata' or 'wishes' rather than 'demands'.

Section five, which Carl Crow declared would have made China 'Japan's slave' revealed quite clearly that Japan was looking to establish a form of protectorate over the whole country, and was unconcerned about trespassing on 'rights' already conceded for it included a demand that Japan be allowed to construct railways in the Yangtse valley, a concession already granted to Great Britain which considered the Yangtse valley to be 'British' territory, and not just as far as railways were concerned.

Sir John Jordan reported, 'The Chinese are especially surprised at the bare-faced attempt to appropriate our Yangtse railway concessions'.[15] It also proposed to extend Japanese influence into the province of Fujian (opposite Japanese-held Taiwan) and demanded that either China 'shall purchase from Japan a fixed amount of munitions' or else establish a jointly-worked arsenal which would purchase Japanese material and employ Japanese experts (and presumably require China to purchase the munitions with ruinous Japanese loans).

The motive behind stipulations in section five that 'the Chinese government shall employ influential Japanese as advisers in political, financial and military affairs' and that in order to prevent troublesome disputes between Chinese and Japanese, 'police departments in important places in China shall be jointly administered by Japanese and Chinese, or that the Chinese police departments of those places shall employ numerous Japanese …'[16] was obvious and, despite the fact that this last section was not agreed, subsequent Japanese activity revealed a determination to achieve such control.

On 18 March 1915, a boycott of Japanese goods was organised in Shanghai; in a weak position *vis à vis* the Japanese, Yuan Shikai banned the boycott on 25 March.

In May 1915, after repeated unsuccessful requests for Japanese troops for the Western Front (and an understandable reluctance to ask, for the third time, for naval assistance), Lord Kitchener, Secretary of State for War, asked Japan for 200,000 rifles with ammunition, saying, 'This would be a graceful acknowledgement of our good offices.'[17] He was refused.

The British Foreign Minister declared that the presentation of the Demands 'without previous communication with us was indefensible' and 'the concealment of Chapter V (the British had eventually been offered an edited version of the Demands) was something worse'. More in sorrow than anger, Sir John Jordan reflected on the deviousness of Britain's ally. 'The idea that they were not continuing to play straight never seems to have been shaken until the full text of the Demands' proved 'a rude awakening'.[18] With considerable understatement, he added, 'I hope I am not unduly prejudiced

JAPAN FLEXES ITS MUSCLES

MAGAZINE SECTION — THE SUNDAY TELEGRAM — SPECIAL FEATURES

THIRD SECTION — CLARKSBURG, W. VA., SUNDAY, MAY 9, 1915. — EIGHT PAGES

TWISTING THE CHINESE PIGTAIL

Will the Great War Leave Japan
In Virtual Control of the Destinies
of the Celestial Empire?

MIKADO YOSHIHITO OF JAPAN

PRESIDENT YUAN-SHIH-KAI OF CHINA

So weak was China that President Yuan Shikai had to agree to the bulk of Japan's Twenty-one Demands issued in January 1915. The images and article, from *The Sunday Telegram* of Clarksburg, West Virgina of 9 May 1915, demonstrate a typical American view of China's weakness and Japan's promise. The Japanese emperor Yoshihito is portrayed as a strong and vigorous leader, but, in fact, he had to be kept out of the public's sight as much as possible, because of neurological problems which prevented him from carrying out his functions. Yuan, on the other hand, though humiliated by Japan's Twenty-one Demands, was a tough and ruthless operator, who had assumed nearly dictatorial powers; at least, he succeeded in evading eight of the Twenty-one Demands.

The brutality of Japan's demands shocked Britain, America and her other allies. The demands confirmed Japan's seizure of Shandong and her rights there, enhanced her role in Manchuria and Inner Mongolia, gave Japan control of Han Yeh Ping Coal & Iron Company – which was already under Japanese influence by virtue of shareholdings and loans – and barred China from giving any coastal or island concessions except to Japan. On top of these demands, Japan was to be entitled to appoint advisors to the police and military, to establish Buddhist schools and temples in China and to take control of Fujian. In the end, this last group was not insisted on, but China was forced to accept thirteen of the Twenty-one Demands. The humiliation gave rise to riots and protests throughout China and brought disgrace to the official, Cao Rulin, who signed the aggreement. [Illustration of the agreement in Chinese can be found through this link http://en.wikipedia.org/wiki/Twenty-One_Demands which is on the Wikipedia page for Twenty-One Demands]

Not to be outdone, Russia issued its own set of demands, twenty-two in number – perhaps in a spirit of one-upmanship as well as imperialist rivalry – mainly centred on Outer Mongolia, which had broken away from China on the demise of the Qing dynasty and was beginning its inexorable journey to becoming a Soviet satellite in the 1920s.

NOTE: Russian demands *Wilson and China* by Bruce Elleman, Routledge, 2002.

but the whole game seems to me one which is hard to characterise in terms suitable to the role of an ally.'

Sir Arthur Nicolson, Permanent Under Secretary to the Foreign Office commented that 'the Japanese were 'the most unaccommodating allies which it is possible to conceive'. Continuing to wield a crooked bat, Japan rebuked the British government during the long-drawn out negotiations that took place before China finally declared war on Germany, on 14 August 1917. Ignoring the secrecy and failure to inform Allies about the Demands, the Japanese Minister for Foreign Affairs 'expressed the further hope that His Majesty's Government would adhere to the precedent hitherto observed of consulting Japan in the first instance in all questions concerning China as agreed in the Anglo-Japanese Treaty of Alliance ...'[19]

The Zhengjiadun Incident, August 1916

George Morrison was concerned with Japan's activities at home, noting that 'Japan is acting in regard to Germany as a neutral power and not an enemy power. Germans have every freedom to trade in Japan.'[20] He was also concerned that the preamble to the fifth section of the 'Twenty-one Demands' offered Japan the chance to declare herself a 'Protector', as in Korea. 'She can foment disturbance', and he noted, 'in the past the Japanese have admittedly taken a very active part in promoting and fostering internal disturbance' and, having fomented disturbance, 'by virtue of this Clause, come into China and suppress the disturbance and in that case, judging by the past history of Korea, she would remain in possession after the suppression.'

Morrison's fears were borne out by a dispute in Zhengjiadun, a town in Manchuria near the Mongolian border (Manchuria and Mongolia being areas in which Japan claimed 'special interests') which led to a serious fight between Chinese and Japanese soldiers. There were conflicting views as to how the dispute started – was it a completely unprovoked attack upon an innocent Japanese, or was it a dispute over prices between a Japanese and a Chinese boy selling fish? However it started, it provided yet another 'opportunity' for the Japanese who demanded that Chinese police forces in Southern Manchuria and eastern Inner Mongolia should have Japanese officers and advisors and that Chinese troops should similarly be advised by Japanese military officers. Reporting to the Foreign Office in London on the 'collision of Japanese and Chinese troops', British diplomats in Peking offered yet another explanation of the cause of the disturbance, that a Japanese tradesman had refused to move when the Chinese army was trying to remove all foreigners to a place of safety.

A note in the Foreign Office file read, 'the suggestion that the Chinese army should be disbanded is perfectly sound – it is a useless machine for anything but providing incidents of this kind', but a slightly more measured report referred back to Japan's 'Demands' and persistent pressure on China, often involving ambiguities of interpretation:

> This appears to be a repetition of the old story of the 'demands' and 'wishes'. Coupled with the appointment of General Aoki Nobuzumi as military advisor [to the Chinese government], it evidently means the beginning of a comprehensive attempt to control the Chinese army. Incidentally, Baodingfu has the largest military school and we shall no doubt find that Japanese instructors have been appointed there also.

The Japanese Minister of Foreign Affairs told the British Ambassador in Tokyo that 'these privileges [military appointments to the Chinese army] had been put forward as desired in order that the Chinese government might offer them spontaneously. They would not be treated as demands unless the Chinese government refused ...'

Writing on 18 September 1916 to the British Foreign Minister, Sir John Jordan reported that:

> Since the presentation of the Twenty-one Demands in January 1915, no incident has occurred in China which has excited so much agitation ... that the object of this ... is to obtain control of the Chinese army can hardly be open to doubt.
>
> [There was] in China no enthusiasm for Japanese rule. On the other hand, China feels herself isolated at present and the new generation may think it better policy to throw in their lot temporarily with the Japanese than to base their hopes of a continued so-called independence upon the support of the White powers which the present European war has shown to be an uncertain quality. A sympathetic attitude towards China and the good government of our Indian empire and of our Asiatic Dominions generally are, I venture to think, likely to prove in the long run the best means of counteracting all the influences which have been awakened by the War.

The British military attaché, Lieutenant Colonel W.S. Robertson, demonstrating the unthinking conviction that British imperial rule was good for everyone and that Britain had the right to dictate, commented on the state of the Chinese army and its increasing control by Japanese officers:

> The Chinese army contains much excellent material but the weak point is the Chinese officer and there seems little hope of an officer class of the right type coming into existence in the near future. The Chinese army as at present constituted can hardly be taken seriously as an instrument for aggression outside China. But if it could be reorganised and stiffened by Japanese as appears to have been done to some extent by the Germans with the Turkish army, it might become a very formidable instrument for

offensive purposes. This could hardly fail to affect our position at Hong Kong, on the Burmese border and in Tibet and for this reason alone Great Britain would apparently be entitled to have a voice in any proposal for the reorganisation by foreigners of the Chinese army ...[21]

It is however very uncertain whether in the long run the task of forming a strong army in China is within the power of Japan. It is a big task and Japan has yet to show that she is capable of doing with alien races what the Anglo-Saxon has shown can be done in the case of India ...[22]

The Lansing–Ishii Agreement

Verbal niceties, such as the Japanese presenting effective 'demands' as 'desiderata' so that the Chinese government could offer 'spontaneous' agreement, continued in the negotiations that took place between Japan and America before the signing of the Lansing-Ishii agreement on 2 November 1917. Unaware of the textual minefield that lay ahead, the American Secretary of State, Robert Lansing, mindful of the restrictive nature of the Demands, and some complications on the home front, wrote:

> Three or four days after these unconscionable [Twenty-one] demands were made upon the Chinese President, the Department of State was advised of them and the importance of defeating Japan's aggressive designs became the subject of consideration by the President ... The situation was a difficult one because while there were ample grounds for protest by the United States, for the Demands were in certain particulars an invasion of the treaty rights of American citizens, the acute state of the controversy growing out of the pending California land laws as well as of the proposed Anti-Japanese legislation in Oregon and Idaho and the inability of the United States to use coercive measures to force Japan to retreat from her program ... made a direct issue inadvisable.

A formal letter was sent to Japan stating that the United States could not agree to anything that impaired the treaty rights of Americans, the political or territorial integrity of China or the 'Open Door Policy' which America, with no territorial concessions in China, supported enthusiastically in the name of free trade. Negotiations between the Americans and Japan's special envoy, Ishii Kikujirō, involved the question of Japan's supply of shipping to support the Allies, a demand for her support for the Open Door Policy, and an attempt to agree questions of Japanese spheres of influence in China.

Over the question of shipping, Japan proved extremely tricky and difficult. In early June 1917, when ships were urgently needed, the British Ambassador in Tokyo was instructed to 'remind Japan of the secret arrangement concluded in 1907 whereby Great Britain undertook to lend Japan 140,000 tons of shipping for transport work in the event of war, also to point out that

AN ASIATIC MONROE DOCTRINE

The headlines of *The Sun* newspaper of New York on 18 April 1915 reflected the American belief that Japan was trying to secure control of Asia through its own version of America's Monroe Doctrine.

Asia for the Asiatics Declared to Mean the End of the Open Door Policy in China

Capture of Tsing-tao Called a Big Step in Nippon's Scheme of Aggrandizement

The policy, that came to be known as The Monroe Doctrine, was promulgated by President James Monroe in 1823 in his State of the Union Address. This was soon after several Latin American countries had liberated themselves and was designed to prevent any further European colonization in the Americas and for the United States to take a fatherly interest in the nations to its south. In this *New York Herald* cartoon of 1902, Uncle Sam tells the Europeans "That's a live wire, gentlemen!", discouraging them from intervention in Venezuela.

In 1915, the old colonial powers were bleeding to death in Europe and the United States was content to rely on the 'Open Door' policy, proposed in 1899 by the American Secretary of State John Hay, under which all foreign nations were to have equal access to China.

It was a great opportunity for Japan to assert itself and embark on its policy of dominating Asia. Much as many in the West (and even in China) admired Japan's recent progress, there was considerable shock at the brutal manner of Japan's imposition of the Twenty-one Demands, which looked likely to lead to China becoming a vassal of Japan.

Japan's shipping interests have derived no small benefit from the war'. He was to ask the Japanese government 'to bear their part in the Allies' common burden of sacrifice' and to point out that Britain and America could 'apply pressure by withholding supplies of steel and other materials ...'

Later in the month Great Britain asked for 'four more destroyers for European waters', to which the Japanese responded by demanding the lifting of the embargo on steel. Britain replied that she needed all the steel she had and suggested that Japan apply to the United States. In July, Japan said she had no ships available but proposed to 'release vessels in the course of construction or about to be laid down, and this on the condition that they are supplied with all the materials requisite for building them'[23] – a challenge to the threat to withhold steel supplies – and the British-Japanese saga continued with threat and counter-threat, Japanese complaints about the scarcity of haematite and pig-iron and reports from British diplomats in Sweden that Japanese agents were buying all the steel that they could find. Morrison commented, 'I am confident that the Japanese appeal for the removal of the ban on the export of steel was a blind. Japan has got stocks of steel ...'[24]

Lansing's desire to have more ships built by the Japanese was met with the same objection, namely that the ship-building was held up by the iron and steel embargo. His main intent, however, was to establish an agreement by which Japan would respect the Open Door Policy in order to facilitate American trade opportunities. This required recognition by the United States of Japan's 'special interests' in parts of China and the standard pious introduction stressing the 'territorial sovereignty of China' which was undermined by the rest of the text. Unlike the Anglo-Japanese Alliance in which both sides had 'special interests' in different parts of China, the United States could only one-sidedly recognise Japan's special interests in China:

> particularly to the part to which her possessions are contiguous. The territorial sovereignty of China, nevertheless, remains unimpaired and the Government of the United States has every confidence in the repeated assurances of the Imperial Japanese Government that while geographical proximity gives Japan such special interests they have no desire to discriminate against the trade of other nations ... The Governments declare ... that they always adhere to the principles of the so-called Open Door ... they mutually declare that they are opposed to the acquisition by any government of any special rights or privileges ... that would deny to the subjects or citizens of any country the full enjoyment of equal opportunity in the commerce and industry of China.[25]

Despite the inherent contradictions (where was China's territorial integrity in these areas of 'special interest'?) and the unlikely chance of success, it was decided that the agreement would be published simultaneously in both countries on 6 November 1917. Lansing was appalled to find that a 'deliberate perversion of the language' had taken place in the version handed by Japan to the Chinese government as the Japanese had placed upon the words 'special interests' the objectionable interpretation of 'paramount interests' and 'special influence'. He concluded that it was done 'with the evident intent to create the impression at Peking that the United States had abandoned China to the scheme of her aggressive neighbour and to sow in Chinese minds distrust of the genuineness of American friendship ...'

Wellington Koo (Gu Weijun), a Chinese diplomat who had obtained a PhD in international law at Columbia University before being appointed China's Minister to the USA in 1915 at the age of 27, and who was to impress world leaders at the Versailles Peace Conference when Japan's territorial acquisitions, unimpaired by pious references to China's 'territorial integrity' were acknowledged, wondered, did contiguity also refer to Russia and confer yet more 'special interests'?

Koo, who had to present China's case at Versailles, was wrong-footed there by one of the most damaging agreements signed between China and Japan, the Sino-Japanese Military Alliance of 16 May 1918. This granted Japan the right to station troops in Shandong province, construct and manage railways on the area and provide Japanese instructors for the local police. In the exchange of notes relating to this agreement, which was made so that the Chinese government could obtain a 20 million yen loan, the Chinese Ambassador to Tokyo reported that 'the Chinese government was pleased to agree ...'[26] That the Chinese had agreed to accept most of the Twenty-One Demands, acknowledging Japan's interest in China, was bad enough but this second agreement, signed in secret and not disclosed to the Chinese delegation at Versailles, badly undermined China's position there when trying to wrest back control of Qingdao and Shandong from Japan.

Sir John Jordan, back in Peking in the autumn of 1917 after a long leave, mused in his private correspondence about the future of China, about which he was fairly sanguine as long as the subjection of Japan, which he referred to as 'the Power of Evil', could be achieved.[27]

Chapter 4

China in wartime, 1914–1916

In the autumn of 1913, most of the European powers finally made a formal recognition of the Chinese republican government, although recognition involved some confusion. Some six months earlier, Sir John Jordan had narrowly avoided another diplomatic *faux pas* by arriving at an eighteen-course dinner ('I repeat, eighteen' wrote Daniele Varè in his diary[1]) wearing 'the great ribbon of the Indian Empire' when the Italian Minister, Count Sforza was, as protocol demanded, without decorations. 'I told you so!' exclaimed Lady Jordan, whereupon the British minister took off his tailcoat and removed his waistcoat in the hall, and, in his shirt and trousers, took off his decorations. Countess Stirum, wife of the Dutch Minister, attending her first official Chinese dinner, watched in astonishment. Official recognition meant that decorations could be worn but for the Norwegians, this privilege was delayed for the British chargé d'affaires, Beilby Alston, who was supposed to represent Norway, had 'completely forgot that he was their representative' and failed to attend the appropriate meeting.[2] Britain had tried to impose conditions upon recognition, wanting China to accede to the British position over Tibet. America recognised the Republic in May 1913 and Britain, Russia, Japan and other powers followed in October the same year (although China would walk out of the Simla Conference over Tibet the following year).

Official recognition meant that when war broke out, China could officially declare itself neutral, despite the rather non-neutral offer of Chinese troops to assist in taking Qingdao from Germany. Neutrality in a time of war and distance from the battlefields of Europe meant that for many, life continued as before. A young American, Ellen Lamotte, who had spent two years as a nurse in France, arrived in Peking in 1916 and reported that 'in China there is no sympathy for the Allies. The atmosphere is not at all pro-German, however.' She was not surprised by 'this atmosphere of total indifference to the outcome and objects of the war'. She had been struck, as an innocent American, 'that China has suffered at the hands of the great powers, has suffered at the hands of England, Russia, France and Germany' and 'with 79 per cent of her territory under foreign control, China can hardly believe in the disinterested motives of the fighting nations.'[3]

IN THE HANDS OF THE BANKS

Bankers had a large measure of control over the late Qing dynasty and the early Republic of China. Bank loans and bond issues were a potent instrument of colonization, being often secured by railway, customs, salt and other governmental revenues. Bankers imposed foreigners to run or advise on these activities. Splendid offices were built and magnificent bank notes issued – an erosion of Chinese independence. With a fluid political scene, the risk of default was high. Banks earned large fees and passed the risk on to other investors; in the £25MM reorganisation loan of 1913, the fees were 6%. The banks also profited from mandatory compensating deposits and foreign exchange transactions. When China defaulted, investors – not the banks – were the big losers. Today a £100 certificate is worth more than its face value as an investment – perfect for wallpaper.

The Han Yeh Ping Coal & Iron Company, Hankou needed modernization; Japan needed iron ore and coal. Soon after its overwhelming defeat of China in 1894-5, The Yokohama Specie Bank made loans of $40MM and Japanese acquired shares in the company. It then entered into a contract to supply Japan on unfavourable terms and paid dividends which starved the company of working capital. Japanese gradually acquired effective control, which increased its influence in the Yangtse valley, which Britain regarded as its own special sphere of influence. One of Japan's Twenty-one Demands in January 1915 was to acquire an even greater measure of control than it already had.

汉阳铁厂，前临汉江，后靠龟山。由清末翔广 总督张之洞创办。1893 年建成投产，有大小十个分厂。是当时亚洲第一大钢铁联合企业。图为 1894 年 7 月 3 日张之洞视察汉阳铁厂。

In 1889, Deutsch-Asiatische Bank was formed by 13 leading German groups, soon after Germany acquired its colony in Shandong. It rapidly became an active lender in China. It helped form and finance the Shandong Railway Company and Shandong Mining Company, both instruments of Germany's colonial strategy at the time. When China declared war on Germany in August 1917, British attempts to put the bank into liquidation were hampered by Chinese desires not to upset Germany, in case it won the war; moreover, there were legal niceties, insisted on by Frans Beelaerts van Blokland, Minister of the Netherlands, which was neutral in the war.

'A Social Hell'

Whilst many Chinese may have been cynical, the declaration of war caused significant upset amongst China's foreign inhabitants. Many, such as Sir John Jordan who had two sons and a son-in-law fighting in France, felt the distance keenly. On 26 August 1914 as the Battle of Mons was being fought, he wrote, 'We are awaiting with breathless anxiety for further news of the great battle which is now going on ... one feels heartbroken at the thought of our tiny force and the task before it'; but on 26 January 1915, 'We heard yesterday of the sinking of the *Blücher* and an involuntary hurrah escaped me ...'[4]

At the beginning of the war, the Scandinavian countries were neutral, as were Holland, Spain, Italy (until 1915), Portugal (until 1916) and America (until 1917). Even the representatives of neutral countries felt the change as the Danish minister wrote in 1914, 'I suppose Peking was the most international spot on earth and all the nationalities got on together as in the Garden of Eden. Today it is more like a social hell, people who fought together as brothers on the barricades in 1900 are now cutting each other in the streets.'[5]

Sir John Jordan described the 'final call' of the German chargé d'affaires on the day before war was declared, who, 'in the course of conversation, said with emphasis that the Kaiser would have lost his throne if he had failed to bow to the will of the German people. I meet him frequently in the course of my afternoon walks but do not venture to ask him now what he thinks of the Emperor's chances of retaining the throne.' He did not exactly 'cut' the Germans for he described how on his afternoon walks on the high wall surrounding the Legation quarter, 'I meet Maltzan [German chargé d'affaires] and Rosthorn [Austro-Hungarian Minister] occasionally on the wall and the exchange of bows is the only form of relation that exists between us.'[6]

A senior Customs official in Peking, Cecil Bowra (father of Sir Maurice Bowra, classical scholar and Vice Chancellor of Oxford University), attended a memorial service at St Michael's Church on 7 July 1914, 'for the Archduke Franz Ferdinand and his wife who were assassinated at Sarajevo a week ago'[7] but a couple of months later 'was surprised at the aggressive bellicosity of Peking's German community and rather shocked when an esteemed friend, Herr Cordes, the manager of the Deutsch-Asiatische Bank said, "I tell you, if the Kaiser does not want to fight, the German people will make him!"' just as the German chargé d'affaires had warned Sir John Jordan. Heinrich Cordes[8] had formerly led his bank into a significant and friendly partnership with Willard Straight (leading American banking interests), Maurice Casenave representing the Banque de l'Indochine, and Guy Hillier of the Hong Kong and Shanghai Bank set up in the last years of the Qing to finance a railway loan which failed, largely because of Japanese opposition.

As the senior (longest serving) minister in China, Jordan used to preside over regular meetings of the entire (foreign) diplomatic body in Peking, held in his house and interrupted by his parrot. Now he had to fight off the challenges of the new situation. He wrote to Alston who was in the Foreign Office in London,

> You ask me how diplomatic meetings are carried on these days. The answer is simple. They are not carried on at all. The Swedish Minister, Wallenberg, with his usual tactlessness, made the amusing suggestion the other day at the instigation of one or two of the belligerent colleagues. After a vast amount of preliminary apologies, he asked me if I did not think it better to resume Diplomatic meetings and meet together in a neutral Legation under the presidency of a non-belligerent colleague. As he is next senior to me, the object of the gentle insinuation was obvious enough but he received a reply which is not likely to encourage him to make further overtures of the kind.[9]

And he explained:

> I do everything by circular, propose a certain course of action which is sometimes accepted in its entirety, sometimes with modification. Fortunately there have not been many controversial questions and the French Minister, who used to be in opposition, is now arrayed on our side. So far the system has worked wonderfully well as I can always command a good majority composed of the Japanese, Russian, French, Belgian, American and some other representatives.

He described the varying attitudes of the different ministers to the war, 'The attitude of the different Legations is a study at present. The Allied representatives [Britain, Russia, France, Italy and Japan] see a great deal of each other but nothing of the enemy. The American Minister holds a watching brief but is very suspicious of Japanese doings, American opinion in China being, as always, distinctly anti-Japanese. Dr Reinsch, being of German parentage, is naturally very circumspect and cultivates friendly relations with us.' Reinsch was a distinguished scholar of international relations with a special interest in China. The fact that his parents had emigrated from Germany to Wisconsin was a constant reference, together with the completely unfounded assertion made by several diplomats that, not only was he German, but he was also Jewish.

Of the other Legations, Jordan said:

> The Dutch Legation, whilst scrupulously neutral, has an undoubted bias in our favour. The Italian and Danish Legations are divided amongst themselves by marriage ties. The Italian Minister, Count Sforza, while always professing a great admiration for Sir Edward Grey [British Foreign Minister] was a supporter of the Triple Alliance [between

Germany, Austria-Hungary and Italy, dissolved at the beginning of the war], while his wife, who is the daughter of the late Belgian Minister at Vienna, feels keenly the wrongs done to her native country.

The Danish Minister, Count Ahlefeldt, is entirely pro-British but carries no weight. His wife, who is Russian and a person of more character, is an out and out champion of the Allied cause. The only concession she makes to neutrality claims is to have two reception days, one for the Allies and one for enemy representatives!'[10]

The question of diplomatic entertainment in a world that was divided by war was one that affected all the neutral powers. The American Secretary of State Robert Lansing described how the American President's customary annual dinner at the White House had to be held twice because 'the diplomats of the Allied powers and those of the Central powers could not sit together at the same table, even if it was the President's'.[11] The solution was for the President to host 'one dinner with the Entente [Allies] and another with the diplomats of Germany, Austria-Hungary and Bulgaria present' with 'all the rest of the diplomatic corps representing the neutral group ... invited to both dinners.' The American Minister in Peking, Dr Paul Reinsch, followed his President's lead: 'Dinners had to be given in two sets, one for the Entente Allies, the other for the Central Powers' and, because neutral diplomats were invited to both, diplomats in Peking were, 'if anything, more socially busy than at other times.'[12]

News from Europe affected social life as Daniele Varè reported:

The first telegrams that arrived in Peking about the Battle of Jutland announced what appeared to be a German victory. The garden party at the British Legation on 3 June 1916 – King George's birthday – was steeped in Cimmerian gloom, whereas the Germans celebrated the news with so much enthusiasm that they set fire to the petty-officers' barracks in their Legation Guard compound, under the Tartar Wall. From the top of that wall we watched after dinner, the strange spectacle of German soldiers in uniform, and the soldiers and sailors of the Allied Powers, united for once in their efforts to fight the flames.

We could not see much ... the heat and smoke kept us at a distance. I myself was busy watching the efforts of my own Legation Guard (we had a new Fiat fire-engine of which we were inordinately proud) to spray the straw matting roof of the houses in the Belgian Legation, next door to the German barracks ... The Commander of the Belgian Guard had asked us to help him keep the fire from spreading. But owing to the darkness, the hose of our fire-engine was not lowered into a well as we had supposed, but into a cesspool. The results can be better imagined than described.[13]

Joining up

Whilst Count Sforza, the Italian Minister, gloomily contemplated being trapped in Peking in a war that might last decades, many younger men working in China thought of returning to Europe to fight. Volunteers from Shanghai – 110 of them – sailed away into the wake of the *Emden* and at least sixteen died whilst many others were horribly wounded, Albert Grimble losing both legs, Frank Reuter losing one at Mametz Wood and a dozen men receiving such terrible wounds they could no longer continue fighting.

In Peking on 1 November 1915, Douglas Gray, Medical Officer to the British Legation, wrote a formal letter to Sir John Jordan asking him to 'forward my offer of my services for a temporary commission in the Royal Army Medical Corps for as long as the War lasts', stressing his 'special experience in military surgery'.[14] Gray later ran the hospital for the Chinese Labour Corps at Noyelles-sur-Mer where he insisted that the treatment of his Chinese patients should be exactly the same as any British patient.

H. Porter, from the Consulate at Yantai, was at home on leave at the outbreak of war and asked to join up but, as the Foreign Office, not sharing Count Sforza's gloom, thought at the time that the war would be finished before his nine-month leave was over, he was refused permission. Other diplomats were not to be spared for the armed forces as it was thought to be a waste of their long years of training in diplomacy though young men in the (junior) Consular Service were eventually allowed to join up. Even Sir John Jordan, in his sixties, wrote, 'I sometimes wish I were younger and able to make munitions or do something useful instead of spinning ropes of sand in China.'[15]

It was easy enough for the Foreign Office to prevent young diplomats from joining up, but British firms in China could not do the same; it was unnerving when they were asked by consuls to identify potential candidates for military service. Jack Swire, chairman of the shipping and trading Swire group, pointed out to the War Office that 'the Japanese are doing their utmost to secure dominance in trade in the East' and that British firms risked being weakened by the withdrawl of men who could not be replaced. From time to time 'recruiting fever', as a local Swire manager, G.T. Edkins called it, broke out and lots of young men yearned to go to the front in Europe. So many of the staff handed in their notice that it was a struggle to keep Swire's business operating efficiently.[16]

A.H. Rasmussen, a Norwegian working in China for the trading firm Arnhold Karberg & Co., originally German-owned but in 1914 'liquidated' and transformed into Arnhold Bros, registered in Hong Kong as a British firm, made two attempts to join up. In 1915 he was in London on leave, when he realised he had 'done nothing about myself in relation to the war'.[17]

> There were men in khaki everywhere … I saw the Red Cross trains, too, and ambulances with their tragic burdens … I suddenly felt very small

and rather ashamed. I registered as an alien at Brixton police station, where the sergeant, rather rudely, asked what I was doing in England, having a holiday in war-time. A recruiting sergeant asked, equally rudely, why the hell I thought I could join the British Army. I was a neutral and this was their war, not Norway's. It was no use my trying as they were not anxious to take on any neutrals. It was clearly a gentleman's war, and the rules were being strictly observed.

As Rasmussen tried to join up in London, Sir John Jordan made one of his rare references to the war, referring somewhat inaccurately to the attack on the Dardanelles in March 1915, 'The Turk is, I expect, beginning to find out that he has made a huge blunder. Poor Tyrrel has lost his boy in the trenches after less than a month at the front …'[18] Lord Tyrrell, later head of the Foreign Office, was to lose two sons in the war. Shortly after, Jordan reported, 'We live here on the telegrams and follow the fortunes of our expeditionary forces with breathless interest and anxiety. A British Tommy who goes through this ordeal has done more for his country than all we poor civilians can hope to do in a lifetime, and all honour to our soldiers and sailors.'

Rasmussen did not give up. During the winter of 1917, he reported: 'I shot fourteen boars and worried the life out of the British Military Attaché in Peking to be allowed to join up. It was the spring of 1918 when at last I succeeded. I sold the bungalow and all I had. We went back to England via the Pacific and Canada. But I arrived too late, the war was nearly over.'

The situation was slightly different in the Chinese Imperial Customs Service, officially a Chinese government body but traditionally headed by a British subject (usually an Ulsterman) and employing a wide variety of nationalities. Apparently retaining loyalty to their country of origin, many young men volunteered for military service, causing some concern that the international balance might be upset (in favour of Japan) and that traditional British numerical superiority would be hard to maintain. One (controversial) Customs official, Paul King, feared that Japan would take advantage of multiple vacancies:

The international features of the service would have been obscured by a too great preponderance of recruits of neither Chinese nor Western provenance and the valuable balance of East and West in its ranks might have been irrevocably lost. Luckily, however, it was early recognised in the right quarter that there were British trenches, impalpable and invisible, but still real, to be held elsewhere than on the actual battlefront.

At the Customs Language School in Mukden in Manchuria, C.H. Brewitt-Taylor asked for advice, and struggled to maintain numbers after the British Consul had invited all British subjects of military age to consider volunteering for action. Brewitt-Taylor's own younger son, Captain Raymond Brewitt-Taylor MC, had joined the Royal Army Medical Corps in August 1914 and been mentioned in despatches for 'joining with the stretcher bearers to bring in the wounded under fire at the Battle of Ypres that same year'. After service in Mesopotamia from where he was sent home with malaria, he rejoined the RAMC and died of his wounds at Thiepval in August 1918. Morrison wrote a letter of condolence to Brewitt-Taylor who replied simply, 'Yes, my son had gone the way of thousands of young men.'[19]

Numbers of recruits in the Mukden Language School dwindled to the point that there was only one student in a class. Sir John Jordan reported in October 1914:

> Nearly all the unmarried men in the outdoor staff of the Customs Service have applied to go and if all the applications were granted, the working of the Customs would come to a standstill. Aglen [Commissioner of Customs] is most anxious to do all he can to meet the call and probably all men who have had military training will be allowed to go. But it is a difficult and somewhat risky experiment as the Chinese want to fill up all the vacancies with their own people …[20]

Picnics and shopping

Whilst young men dithered between attending double the usual number of dinners and frostily cutting the representatives of enemy nations, diplomats and their guests and the wealthy inhabitants of Peking in wartime continued to shop for curios in antique shops and at temple fairs, such as that at the Longfu temple in the east of the city. Here stalls offered 'everything made in China or ever made in China, today or in the remote past – porcelain, bronzes, jade, lacquer, silks, clothing, toys, fruit, curios, dogs and cats. Three times a month, everything of every description finds its way to the Longfu temple, and three times a month, all foreign Peking, to say nothing of native Peking, finds its way to the temple grounds to look for bargains.'[21]

They would board the special train to take them out to the races at Paomachang: 'all the ministers and secretaries of the legations with their family and guests, and all the foreign residents of the Legation Quarter … Americans, English, French Danes, Russians, Swedes; only the Germans were absent' came to watch races between 'little Mongolian ponies with short, clipped hair'.[22] On the day Ellen LaMotte went to the races, there was a sudden spring dust storm, producing 'invisible races' before tiffin. She had time to note that whilst Japanese were eligible to join the race club, there were none present and, of course, 'no Chinese, no matter how high in rank, is admitted to membership'. As Brooke Astor remembered, the favourite pastime of foreign residents in Peking was picnicking in the deserted tombs and Buddhist temples in the cool Western Hills.

Ellen LaMotte was invited to join a group led by the American Minister on a picnic excursion to a temple, setting off by train where Dr Reinsch's two servants were on hand to buy the tickets and to carry large and imposing lunch baskets.[23] The transfer to the donkeys which were to take them up to a temple, was 'pandemonium' with dozens of donkey drivers fighting for their custom. Finally mounted on 'a square seat, about as wide and unyielding as a table top … an astonishingly wide seat … with stirrups dangling somewhere out of reach … behind each donkey ran its owner, flicking its heels with a long-lashed whip, urging it to a speed likely to tip one off at any moment.' They ate at a large table in the central courtyard of the temple, watched by silent Buddhist monks and stray dogs, sheltered from the rain by large overhanging trees and looked out at the other temples on the hills. 'Over yonder was Mr So-and-So's temple; beyond, on that hilltop, was Mrs So-and-So's, all occupied during the summer months by foreigners who escape from Peking in the hot weather.'

Food parcels and sewing circles

Across China, though social life for the Allies continued almost uninter-rupted, groups were set up to collect for the war effort. In Tianjin, H.G. Woodhead reported. 'On the initiative, or mainly the result of the support of the *Peking and Tientsin Times*, a military aeroplane was presented to the British Government at a cost of £1,500 in October, 1915.

> During the magnificent resistance of the French at Verdun in 1916 I proposed that the British community should show their appreciation by a gift of a motor ambulance. Allied and neutral sympathizers insisted on sending in contributions, and eventually we presented two motor-ambulances – one all-British and the other the gift of Allies and Neutrals.
>
> The most successful of the local funds, however, was that organized for the supply of food parcels to British prisoners of war. The idea originated with the wife of the British Consul-General, who invoked my aid and called a meeting of a few residents of both sexes during the Christmas season of 1915. It was agreed to form a nominated committee, of which I was appointed Hon. Secretary and the British Vice-Consul Hon. Treasurer. Donations and monthly subscriptions were invited by a public appeal. From previous experience I knew how such funds dwindled if left to individual subscribers to forward their remittances monthly, or if 'shroffs' (Chinese collectors) waited upon them at their residences and offices. I therefore arranged with the foreign banks to accept a form of bank-order from their clients, authorizing payment of so and so many dollars by the debiting of current accounts, on the fifth of each month. And this arrangement continued until the end of the war.

As far as I remember, the committee never met after its inauguration. The hon. treasurer's duties were confined to checking the pass-books, forwarding remittances monthly to Berne, and soliciting support from new arrivals. I compiled a monthly report, consisting mainly of extracts from the letters we received from the Berne administration. Stacks of postcards acknowledging the receipt of parcels by British prisoners reached me, and a selection of these was sent with the printed report to each subscriber. I tried to pick out the more interesting of these pathetic receipts. By the end of the war, over £11,000 had been remitted to Berne, and nearly a thousand prisoners were receiving regular parcels of food and other comforts from North China subscribers.[24]

In Shanghai, Annie de Sausmarez, wife of the British Supreme Court judge, was an early organizer of voluntary support. On 25 September 1914, she announced a scheme to supply garments and bandages to British troops. A British Women's Work Association sent its first packages to Queen Mary's Needlework Guild in November.[25]

Trade almost as usual in Shanghai

In Shanghai, which had developed into a much more cosmopolitan society, the mood was more complicated. The British Consul-General, Sir Everard Fraser was concerned when British naval forces were withdrawn to Hong Kong. There were 'restless Chinese troops' in the vicinity. Twenty men responded to the German Consul-General's mobilisation order and took the train north to join the garrison at Qingdao, but in October 110 British citizens sailed for service in Europe. They arrived in Penang to find dead Russian sailors floating in the harbour, for 'they had arrived the day after the German cruiser *Emden*, whose marines had marched along the [Shanghai] Bund back in January, had dashed through the harbour at dawn and in disguise – "the colossal cheek of it all!" – torpedoed the Russian cruiser *Zhemchug* – also familiar from Shanghai – and a French destroyer and then successfully escaped.'[26]

When John B. Powell arrived in Shanghai in February 1917, he wrote:

I was surprised to find that the Germans went about the city in complete freedom and safety, despite the fact that they were involved in war with both the British and the French who occupied a dominating position in the city ... it was interesting, at noon-time, to see the British and German businessmen passing each other on the Bund without a nod of recognition, each headed for his club for luncheon, where the chief subject of conversation was the war. Each club had a large mounted map of the Western Front, but the thumb tacks were on opposite sides of the line.[27]

As in Peking, there was some social ostracism in Shanghai, and the Statistical Secretary of the Chinese Customs wrote to George Morrison, 'Feeling here against the Germans is now suddenly running very high, and they are being elbowed out of all the clubs. Matters may go further as there is actually talk of driving them out of Shanghai! All this is in consequence of the *Lusitania* incident.'[28]

Yet Sir John Jordan reported in January 1916:

> Shanghai at the present moment is a unique specimen of an international community. A large Volunteer Force, amounting almost to a little army, and composed of British, German and all other nationalities, musters weekly under the command of a British Colonel ... the only difference that the war in Europe appears to have made is that instead of toasting the Sovereign and Rulers of their respective countries they now drink on occasions of ceremony, the health of the Chairman of the Municipal Council![29]

At the very beginning of the war, though the chairmanship of the Shanghai Municipal Council had traditionally alternated between Britain and Germany, an attempt was made by the British Consul General to replace the German candidate by a Japanese as a 'just and graceful concession' to an ally that had driven the Germans out of Qingdao.[30] The attempt was only half successful for whilst the German was placed at the bottom of the list of candidates by the (narrow) group allowed to vote, the Japanese candidate also failed to get on to the council.

Sir Everard Fraser, the British Consul-General in Shanghai was concerned to protect British commercial interests against those of Germany but this was not simple. He wrote to Sir John Jordan:

> This place is full of greedy rascals, chiefly German and American, with a fair number of British 'merchants' whose loyalty is a very feeble defence against probable traffic with the enemy and some others who retain the original Shanghailander point of view that resented any interference with their accustomed cosmopolitan dealing.[31]

The complexity of trading arrangements meant that British attempts to forbid trading with the enemy could actually harm British business for 'many Manchester firms, for example, relied exclusively on German agents in China'. The enormously successful Anglo-German Brewery Company (with its headquarters in Shanghai and brewery in Qingdao) proved difficult to disentangle but the British Legation deemed it largely German so it was wound up and sold to a Japanese company.[32] And the country that did best out of trading in Shanghai during the war was Japan whose percentage of the total trade rose from 19.4 per cent in 1912 to 45.5 per cent in 1918.[33]

NEW PATTERNS OF TRADE & INDUSTRY

Distribution of China's Trade

	1906	1913	1919	1927
Imports from	%	%	%	%
UK & Hong Kong	52.2	45.8	32.1	27.9
Japan & Taiwan	14.3	20.4	36.3	28.4
USA	10.4	6.0	16.2	16.1
Russia	0.1	3.8	2.1	2.2
Germany	4.0	4.8	0.0	0.4
France	1.0	0.9	0.5	1.4
Others	18.0	18.3	12.8	20.2
Total	100.0	100.0	100.0	100.0
Exports to				
UK & Hong Kong	40.6	33.0	29.9	24.8
Japan & Taiwan	14.0	16.2	30.9	22.7
USA	10.9	9.3	16.0	13.3
Russia	7.9	11.1	3.4	8.4
Germany	2.4	4.2	0.0	2.2
France	10.7	10.1	5.4	5.6
Others	13.4	16.0	14.4	23.0
Total	100.0	100.0	100.0	100.0

It was not only in Shanghai that Japan did best in wartime trading. Because all attention was on the battlefield of Europe, the leading European powers and the United States left an opportunity for Japan to step in and increase its share of trade with China. Japan's success in increasing its share of China's trade matched its increased share of foreign loans and investments. After the war, Japan's trade dominance was slightly checked, as Europe, America and others rebuilt their trade with China.

Growth of Industry in China

	1913/14	1919/20
FACTORY TYPE	Number	Number
Textile	231	475
Food processing	105	280
Printing	25	51
Machinery	101	252
Chemical	153	383
Coal Production (MM tons)	12.8	20.1
Iron Production (MM tons)	1.0	1.8
Steamship tonnage	141,024	236,622

While the war enabled Japan to increase its share of Chinese finance and trade, it also provided a great opportunity for indigenous industries to grow. A new class of entrepreneurs came into being who would play a part in China's nationalist movement and did not depend on foreign capital. Major growth across many industries took place in the war, but China was to be in turmoil over several decades and remain extremely impoverished before being able to approach its economic potential in the early 1980s.

NOTE: *Cambridge History of China, Volume 12* – Hong Kong was a British Crown Colony. Japan occupied Taiwan.

Sir John Jordan encountered irritating problems with companies trading in China. The German-owned trading company Arnhold Karberg & Co., for which the young Norwegian A.H. Rasmussen worked, transformed itself in 1914 into Arnhold Bros., registered in Hong Kong as a British firm. Sir John Jordan was not entirely convinced, writing in 1915 when one of the Arnhold Brothers was to visit Peking:

> From your last telegram I see that you are prepared on certain conditions to let him have a run for a certain time so that the new firm may have the opportunity of showing whether they are really a bonafide British business or only a cloak for Arnhold Karberg & Co. I have no wish to see the German firm kept alive and there have been many suspicious circumstances connected with the dealings of the Arnhold Brothers, but as it was originally decided to allow them two months to show their good faith I confess I am not sorry that you have taken this line, though I have little doubt it will cause some gnashing of teeth in China. We find great difficulties in getting to the bottom of their real liabilities to the Banks but are inclined to believe that unless time is allowed to clear these off the Banks must be losers. I have personally been a good deal harassed by C. Arnhold who is, of course, a Jew, but as far as I can see, not a German. I take all his assurances '*cum grano*' but he continually declares that all his brother has done has been done with the knowledge of our Consular officers.[34]

As China was officially neutral, the British could do nothing about German commercial activities in China but very early on in the war, in October 1914, Sir John Jordan defended the Chinese government's actions against accusations from London that 'China had entirely failed in her duties as a neutral ... There are British, German and French vessels interned at some half a dozen or more ports and there are sixty-one German belligerents confined at Nanking. Of course there has been a good deal of laxity but we have bene-fitted by that far more than the enemy.'[35]

Chinese reactions

John Powell, newly arrived in Shanghai as a newspaperman in early 1917, reported that 'the largest English-reading group of all was the younger gener-ation of Chinese, the intellectuals, graduates and undergraduates of mission and municipal schools who were just beginning to take an interest in outside world affairs. They were tremendously concerned by the World War and, like everybody else, were deeply anxious to find out what America was going to do about the war and a number of other things.'[36]

There are a number of autobiographical accounts by such educated young Chinese although many, in fact, spent the years of change abroad in the new enthusiasm for foreign education. Many reacted positively to the new Republic. F.T. Cheng, who served as Chinese Minister to London from 1946–1950, studying at the Bar in London in 1911, wrote of 'the beginning of a new regime, based on popular will, everyone was hopeful and every form of business prospered. Some of my friends, most of whom were now much better off, said to me if I had not been abroad I would have made a fortune.'[37]

Song Qingling (who later married Sun Yat-sen) was a student in America and published an article in the magazine of Wesleyan College, Georgia, describing the foundation of the Republic as 'The Greatest Event of the Twentieth Century'.[38] The European war did not have the same effect on all Chinese students. F.T. Cheng was back in London by 1914, so he experienced London in wartime, rather than China. Similarly, Mai-mai Sze, whose father, Alfred Sze (Shi Zhaoji 1877–1958) was Chinese Minister in London from 1913–1919 (when he went to Versailles for the Peace Conference) also lived through the war in England. She travelled to England with her mother and brothers in 1914 and 'it was not until we had proceeded through the Suez Canal and into the Mediterranean Sea that we encountered any signs of war. Somewhere in the blue waters of the Mediterranean, the *Nippon Yusen Kaisha* was ordered to retrace her previous day's course, and to carry a contingent of British sailors. Their destination must have been Gallipoli. Not speaking a word of English, we children had a wonderful time with the soldiers who fed us Nestlé's milk chocolate in bars wrapped in crackly silver paper.'[39]

Much more important to Chinese students at the time was Japanese activity in China. A significant intellectual figure in Chinese higher education and a patriot who was later to challenge successfully the right of foreign explorers to remove artefacts from Chinese sites, William Hung (1893–1980)[40] was a student at the Methodist Anglo-Chinese College in Fuzhou in November 1914 when students in Tokyo (apparently led by Li Dazhao, later co-founder of the Chinese Communist Party) sent an inflammatory message about the secret Twenty-one Demands Japan had just presented to China. Students of the Anglo-Chinese College printed out thousands of copies of the letter and distributed them around the city until the authorities arrested as many as they could find. William Hung spent much time and effort pleading for their release from jail, claiming that they had been led astray by the radicalised Chinese students in Japan. From his experience and that of many others, it is clear that Japanese activities and intentions were of the greatest concern to students in China, more than the distant European war, one small part of which had been fought on Chinese soil where it ended in a Japanese victory.

The future premier Zhou Enlai[41] was a student in the progressive Nankai Middle School in the Treaty Port of Tianjin during the war, but only participated in one demonstration in 1915, a mass rally against Japan's

Twenty-one Demands. The seventeen-year-old made a speech in which he argued that China's problem was economic weakness and that China should no longer depend on foreign loans. He proposed that every Chinese donate one yuan to a national salvation fund to resolve China's economic situation. He also seems to have demonstrated considerable opposition to Japan's growing influence, perhaps partly as a result of spending three years before he moved to Tianjin, staying with relatives in Manchuria where the Japanese were extending their influence inexorably and with some brutality. This did not stop him travelling to Japan to study in 1917 (although this was largely because it was the nearest and cheapest place to study abroad). He returned in 1919, in the wake of the Versailles Treaty and his real commitment to political activity began then, in the reaction of China's humiliation at Versailles.

Chinese students in Japan were radical and increasingly radicalised by Japan's treatment of China and Manchuria. Those at home, far from Shandong or the major cities, like Mao Zedong, were affected more or less by the founding of the Republic. Mao cut off his queue even before the Hankou uprising, indicating his radicalism, and he spent a few months in the revolutionary Hunan Army in 1912. Although he left to continue his studies and intended to become a teacher, he too, said little about the European war, not mentioning it at all in his 1935 conversations with the American journalist Edgar Snow. He was appalled by Japanese activities and wrote of Yuan Shikai's craven acceptance of most of Japan's Twenty-one Demands, 'The 7th of May dishonours our motherland. How can we students take revenge? With our very lives!'[42]

Yuan Shikai proclaims himself Emperor

Yuan Shikai complicated international relations and seriously affected the maintenance of law and order in an increasingly divided nation, when it became known that he planned to proclaim himself emperor in 1916 which, he decreed on 31 December 1915, would be the first year of the Hongxian reign, a designation he explained to the American Minister, Dr Reinsch, that meant 'Grand Constitutional Era'. He announced that the practice of using eunuchs as palace servants would not be revived and he ordered 40,000 pieces of porcelain for his palace, all to be marked with the Hongxian reign-mark. His imperial robes were said to have cost 800,000 yuan, the jade seal of office 120,000 yuan, with the total budget of the proposed enthronement reaching 30 million yuan. New silver dollars were issued with a portrait of Yuan Shikai in a feathered helmet and a dragon on the reverse, and new stamps were designed.

This was all proposed at a moment when the national budget for 1916 showed a deficit of 88 million yuan. Part of the problem, according to

YUAN'S ROAD TO RUIN

SON OF HEAVEN NOW, WHAT HONOR NEXT FOR YUAN SHI KAI?

Chinese President's Assumption of Spiritual as Well as Temporal Prerogatives of Emperor Leads Many to Declare Him Tyrant and Usurper. ஃ ஃ ஃ ஃ ஃ

YUAN SHI-KAI

In September 1914, President Yuan Shikai announced his plan to resume worship of Confucius – a practice that had lapsed over the previous decade. In December of the same year, having procured overwhelming parliamentary support, he reintroduced other rituals from the imperial era. Heaven was blessed by him in Beijing and by local officials throughout China. He fasted for three days, changed into special robes and supervised the offering of sacrificial items to Heaven.

A forerunner of his forthcoming monarchy, it provoked much apprehension and mockery. The *Washington Herald* devoted a full page to the occasion on 24 January 1915, remarking acidly that Yuan '*not entirely satisfied with the democratic honors of his earthly position, now seeks a foothold in heaven*'. Later he introduced stamps, bank notes and coins as part of his imperial project.

When he died in June 1916, generals of provincial armies, mostly appointed by him, fought each other for supremacy in the era of the warlords which lasted until 1928 when it was partly tamed by Chiang Kai–shek. The losers were the Chinese people.

Morrison, was the increase in corruption of a time-honoured sort. Writing on 21 May 1915, refusing to write an article on China's finances, he explained:

> The new Minister [of Finance] Zhou Xuexi, although not an old man – he is not much above 40 – has reverted to the old-time methods of the Chinese mandarin and is removing from office one by one the men who had acquired knowledge and experience under the previous minister, and is filling up the vacancies with his own henchmen and fellow-provincials. He has removed the highly competent head of the Salt Gabelle, Zhang Hu, he has removed the head of the Bank, Sa Fuma, who was bringing the Bank to quite a marked state of efficiency, and he has removed the best financial commissioner in the provinces of China, Zhang Yuquan, who has been bravely fighting for the Central Government against much opposition in Wuhu. To the posts vacated by these three men, the new Minister has appointed highly incompetent officials whose only claim is that they are from the same province of Anhui.[43]

Yuan's imperial ambitions aroused fierce opposition at home. His former colleague Tang Shaoyi wrote (addressing him as 'Mr Yuan'), '... people consider this the most shameful action, unprecedented in the history of China and of every other country'. The great reformer of the nineteenth century, Kang Youwei, wrote, 'From the point of view of the Manchu Imperial House, you are a usurper, and from the Republic's point of view, you are a traitor.'[44]

Though Britain, France, Russia, Italy and Japan declared their opposition to Yuan's bid for the throne, their unity was severely challenged by Japan's continuing admonitions which Sir John Jordan noted, 'have been making themselves [the Japanese] and us ridiculous by all these repeated representations which have produced no effect except antagonizing the Chinese and driving them into the hands of the Germans ... we all feel that we are so many puppets pulled by Japanese strings.' Morrison, serving as an advisor to Yuan, ('the Emperor-Elect will receive you this afternoon at 3.30') was against the proposal, but wrote that Yuan was 'evidently worried by the mess he is making of things and wishes to do something theatrical to retrieve his prestige'.

Most serious was the effect on the generals in charge of the regional armies who rebelled and starting infighting in the south-western provinces of Yunnan, Sichuan and Guizhou. In 1916, in the middle of the chaos caused by the 'monarchical crisis', British Consul Meyrick Hewlett[45] and his wife were exploring a cave near Yichang when their boatman, 'who had gone ahead with flares, ran back, calling out, "There's a dragon!"' and they examined 'what appeared to be either a number of dragons made in stone or actual fossils.' Having reported the find, the local authorities, conscious of the fact that in traditional belief, dragons were symbols of the emperor, sent photographs to Peking, 'no doubt in the hope that the district of Yichang in which the Divine Dragon had appeared would come at once into imperial favour. The discovery was reported to the Emperor-Elect ...'

The Emperor-Elect 'made an exceedingly sensible reply: From the very beginning, the only thing which can ensure the rise of any dynasty has been the effort put forward by the Government for the improvement of administration and popular enlightenment ... No improvement will be made in the Government when the people begin to talk freely of signs of Heaven ... such as "spiritual birds", "yellow dragons" etc.' The Emperor-Elect ordered scientific investigation which revealed that the potential divine portents were a natural rock formation.

In the face of opposition from many in China, including powerful military leaders, from the western powers and Japan, Yuan Shikai cancelled his imperial inauguration on 22 March 1916 and died of uraemia [kidney failure] and despair on 6 June 1916, as warring generals continued to fight in the south-west.

Chapter 5

The Chinese Labour Corps: Yellow 'eathens are 'elping out in France

This remark, missing the aitches, 'Yellow 'eathens are 'elping out in France',[1] was made by a ship's carpenter repairing the bunks used by workers of the Chinese Labour Corps on their long, dangerous and uncomfortable voyage to Europe. The Allies had effectively ignored Yuan Shikai's offer of Chinese troops to help recapture Jiaozhou Bay from the Germans in August 1914 but as the war progressed, the frightful death toll on the battlefields intensified the shortage of manpower and a Chinese proposal to provide labourers for Europe was regarded with more favour. French factories and farms were drastically short of manpower and the British Army required a massive input of labour to supply the front line, dig trenches, build railways for transport and maintain tanks and other equipment.

There was a well-established precedent for Chinese 'coolie' labour (the term derived from the Chinese 'kuli' which means hard labour) had been used from the beginning of the nineteenth century in the sugar-cane fields of the British West Indies and Cuba and in mines and railway construction in the USA, Peru, Canada and Australia.[2] It was not without its problems, based on racial fears. Despite the usefulness of coolie labour in the construction of the Pacific railroad, American prejudice and opposition to Chinese settlement resulted in the Chinese Exclusion Act of 1882 (extended in 1892, made permanent in 1902 and only finally repealed in 1943, when China and America were allies in the Second World War). In 1904, Britain transported 64,000 indentured labourers from China to work in the South African gold mines, but they were repatriated in 1910 after violent opposition from local people who feared that they might become 'threatening competitors to the whites in commercial and mechanical operations'.

Liang Shiyi's proposal
In June 1915, Yuan Shikai's Finance Minister Liang Shiyi first proposed to the British that China send 300,000 'military labourers' armed with 100,000 rifles, to France. Liang Shiyi was an effective finance minister (and amassed a huge personal fortune) and a close confidant and advisor, especially on foreign affairs. His proposal technically violated China's neutrality but it would have served Liang's purpose which was to demonstrate China's willingness to fight

CHINESE EMIGRATION

Traditionally, the Chinese preferred to stay in their villages, close to ancestral graves, but economic necessity drove many, particularly from the South Eastern coastal provinces of Fujian and Guangdong, to seek their fortunes elsewhere, especially in South East Asia, where they formed 'Chinatowns'. Emigration was officially discouraged and to 'desert the Celestial Kingdom' became a capital offence under the Qing dynasty.

When slavery was abolished in 1833, the British Empire needed new sources of labour for its development. In 1858 Britain and France were able to force a change in Chinese policy and recruit coolies, as was the United States. Recruitment was facilitated by several calamities, whose impact was heightened by the weak authority of the Qing dynasty:

1849	Major famine	13,750,000 deaths
1854-6	Taiping rebellion	20,000,000 deaths
1877-78	Major famine	9,000,000 deaths

ANTI-CHINESE

MASS MEETING

Under the Auspices of the

Tacoma Trades Council

Wednesday Eve., March 26, 1902

These and other smaller such events, coupled with coolie emigration, caused China's population to fall from 391 million in 1842 to 314 million in 1882.

Despite their important contribution to railways, mines, agriculture and industry, coolies were often reviled and mistreated in the Americas, South Africa and Australia. Considerable efforts were made to deny permanent residence to the coolies, but Chinese communities flourish today wherever the coolies went.

NOTE: calamity and population figures from Ta Chen, *Chinese Migrations with Special Reference to Labor Conditions*, US Government Printing Office, Washington 1923. Cartoon from Frank Leslie's illustrated newspaper, 1882.

THE ONLY ONE BARRED OUT.
ENLIGHTENED AMERICAN STATESMAN. "We must draw the line *somewhere*, you know."

alongside the Allies in the war, with the eventual aim of gaining a seat at the peace conference and achieving the return of Shandong. Although the British military attaché in Peking, Lieutenant Colonel David S. Robertson, was keen on the plan, it was not immediately taken up by the British Government. Meanwhile, the Russians (who eventually took well over 200,000 Chinese labourers) and the French, who had been arguing about the possibility of using Chinese labour to make up their shortfall since March 1915, were keen to accept Liang Shiyi's proposal when it was made in June.

Now conscious of the need to appear to uphold China's neutrality to prevent repercussions from Germany, Liang Shiyi had dropped the idea of 'military' labourers in favour of straightforward labourers. He was also keen to establish the fiction that the matter originated in France and to stress that the system was one of indentured labour, not government service. This did not stop the Germans led by the German Minister in Peking, Admiral von Hintze (who succeeded Baron Ago von Maltzan in 1917) from issuing repeated complaints on the basis that one foreign worker was the equivalent of one Allied soldier.

In January 1916 a retired lieutenant colonel in the French army, Georges Truptil, officially described as an agricultural engineer, was sent to Peking to begin recruitment. Although he worked under the auspices of the French Ministry of War, his mission was officially unofficial. The fiction was continued by the establishment in May 1916 of the Huimin Company by Liang Shiyi and the director of the Chinese Industrial Bank, Wang Kemin. The Huimin Company was to handle recruitment and signed a contract with the French which stipulated that the workers were not to be used for direct military action, that they should be treated like French workers with their living and working conditions checked by Chinese government officials. Truptil worked mainly in north China, although he signed an agreement with another Chinese company to hire skilled workers from Shanghai. Another recruiting mission under Louis Grillet set off to enlist workers in the south-western provinces of Yunnan and Sichuan.

The French recruiting missions encountered obstacles such as a shortage of transportation and the jealous opposition of the French Minister in Peking, Alexandre-Robert Conty, who disapproved both of War Ministry control and of the existence of two separate missions. French efforts were further hampered by the Laoxikai Incident of 20 October 1916 when the French *chargé d'affaires* ordered the seizure by force of an area of land in Tianjin that the French had long coveted in order to expand the area of their concession. The French eventually retreated from Laoxikai and recruitment was resumed. Recruitment for the French by the Huimin Company in Hong Kong (3,221 recruits), Pukou, near Nanjing (18,950), in Qingdao, Shandong (4,413), added together with others from Shanghai (some specialists) and southern China, amounted to a total of about 40,000.[3]

Opposition to recruitment

From May 1916 the German Legation in Peking began to issue warnings to the Chinese government about the recruitment of Chinese labourers, saying that it was the equivalent of sending soldiers to fight (because the CLC were freeing up French and British manpower). Although China maintained that it was a private arrangement and that Chinese workers were entitled to find work overseas, the Germans continued to protest. They posted leaflets in Chinese in the areas of recruitment and (with some truth) warned prospective recruits that they would find themselves in war zones. With reference to the traditional Chinese fear of dying far from home with no relatives to care for the wandering soul, they threatened:

> You will suffer the worst atrocities in the world and become the spirits wandering on the field of battle. You will never find your way home and can never be buried in your native land.

In both France and Britain, local workers' organisations and Trades Unions strongly opposed the use of Chinese labour (which may explain why Lloyd George wanted to call it the Chinese 'auxiliary' rather than 'labour' corps). However, the death toll on the Somme was such that in the summer of 1916, Lloyd George was overheard saying he feared that the war would be lost unless supplementary labourers could be found to replace the huge number of casualties.

On 24 July 1916, Hansard records that Winston Churchill argued in the House of Commons for the expansion of the search for labour resources, noting that the Germans had a large pool of prisoners of war they could use, and criticising the India Office for its failure to make use of 'the manpower of India and India's great resources effectively. The India Office attitude is one of general apathy and obstruction.'[4] He broadened his search for manpower beyond India and Africa:

> I am now coming to something which I hope will not strike unnecessary prejudice, but I hope my right honourable friend will not hesitate to use African and Asiatic labour behind the lines for all purposes of carrying material and strengthening our fortifications. There must be great resources there and in this matter I would not even shrink from the word Chinese for the purpose of carrying on the War. These are not times when people ought in the least to be afraid of prejudices. At any rate there are great resources of labour in Africa and Asia which, under proper discipline, might be the means of saving thousands of British lives

and of enormously facilitating the whole progress and conduct of the War.

There was no further discussion of the subject in Parliament that day and Lloyd George concealed from the public the fact that Chinese labourers were being recruited, twice refusing to answer direct questions on the subject in the House of Commons in November 1916. Urgent discussions on the use of overseas labour at the Front were, however, continuing. In his *War Memoirs*, published in 1933, Lloyd George attributed China Labour Corps recruitment to Sir Eric Geddes (former General Manager of the North-Eastern Railway who had been brought in to solve urgent transport problems):

> Closely connected with the transport developments was the recruitment of the Chinese Auxiliary Corps by Sir Eric Geddes who sent an officer to China to recruit 15,000 Chinese labourers for France, out of whom some 6,000 were required for work on the railways and 1,000 for inland water transport, the others being employed at various tasks on the road, rail-head, dumps etc.

In a report to the War Office, it was noted that the climate of northern France was not suitable for labourers from British India or Africa but that northern Chinese were 'inured to hardship and almost indifferent to the weather'. The War Office and the India Office expressed varying and inconsistent views on the physical and political suitability of troops and labourers from across the Empire and beyond. The Indian Army was mobilised and the Indian Expeditionary Force sent to Europe in the autumn of 1914, still wearing thin tropical uniforms and carrying out-of-date rifles. Preparations for their nourishment had been made more carefully with the calculation that they would run out of French goat meat within weeks and arrangements made to import goats from neutral Spain and Corsica. It was impossible to maintain such thoughtful arrangements on the Western Front and their experience was not improved by the fact that the winter of 1914–15 was one of record cold. All soldiers suffered but those that were not equipped with winter clothing, suffered most and the myth grew that, as Conan Doyle put it, 'these children of the sun' found the conditions incapacitating.[5]

British recruitment (kept secret from Parliament by Lloyd George throughout 1916) began when Thomas J. Bourne, with nearly thirty years' experience in China, ending up as engineer-in-chief of the Beijing–Hankou railway, assisted by an accountant and G.S. Moss from the Consular Service, arrived in the British 'leased territory' of Weihaiwei in Shandong in November 1916, and by late April had sent 35,000 Chinese workers to France, far more than those recruited thus far by the French. The British had originally planned to use Hong Kong as a convenient British recruiting post but the Governor of the territory, Sir Henry May wrote on 16 October 1916 that northern Chinese would be better than southerners as the War Office had already suggested, because 'They are inured to cold … They eat farinaceous food … They are more amenable to discipline … They are not impregnated with malaria.'[6]

By putting up announcements in front of temples and at fairgrounds which designated a local tea house where potential recruits could gather and learn the terms of employment before (if agreeable) being sent to Weihaiwei in groups, between January 1917 and March 1918, the British team had recruited 94,458 workers in Weihaiwei.[7] In November 1917 the Army Council proposed a further recruitment of 150,000, partly because there was a planned repatriation of Egyptian and South African labourers, who, it was feared, might cause problems in the colonies if they stayed much longer in France: the labourers might return 'disabused of the respect they should bear for the white race … ideas above his station'.[8] The replacement of these workers by Chinese seemed the obvious solution but it became impossible owing to the shortage of shipping and on 30 April 1918, in a communication between the Treasury and Bertram Blakiston Cubitt of the War Office, it was stated that 'owing to the impossibility of providing transport both now and in the near future, it has been found necessary definitely to close the recruiting of Chinese coolies for labour in France and to cancel the contracts of those coolies already enrolled and awaiting embarkation in the depot at Weihaiwei.'[9]

Contracts

Both those recruited by the French and British were hired with written contracts. The French contracts for unskilled workers were for five years, with all the same holidays as French workers plus an extra day for Chinese National Day. Medical treatment was to be provided and each worker hired by the French received 'two blue cotton shirts, two pairs of blue cotton trousers, one pair of cloth shoes, one hat, two pairs of Chinese socks, one padded garment, one pair of padded trousers, one padded quilt … cooking utensils, one travelling bed, one pair of woollen lined trousers and one straw mat.'[10] In France they were supposed to get a daily minimum of 100 grammes of rice and daily pay at a rate that was more generous than the British 1 franc per day.

No lists were provided of the clothing allocated to British recruits but they were certainly supplied with army issue underwear (which they did not like) and their 'approved clothing' which had to be worn whenever on duty, must have been centrally issued. However, one observer with the Royal Artillery noted that:

> they would be handed whatever kind of clothes were available at that time. They had very little idea of how we used clothes, so they just put

everything on in the order in which it was received, so it was no uncommon thing to see a man with his pants on top of his trousers and a flannel body belt on top of his pants, his padded jacket on top of that, and other pullovers and shirts he had been given on top of that.[11]

As the French were punctilious in listing all garments provided to recruits whilst the British handed out whatever they happened to have around at the time, it is interesting to compare the different contracts made with CLC recruits. A British contract made with Liu Yongxiang on 24 August 1917 is short and simple.

By the terms of this contract, I the undersigned coolie recruited by the Weihaiwei Labour Bureau, declare myself to be a willing labourer under the following conditions, conditions which have been explained and made clear to me by Weihaiwei Labour Bureau, viz:

- Nature of Employment: work on railways, roads, etc., and in factories, mines, dockyards, fields, forests, etc. Not to be employed in military operations.
- Rates of pay: Daily abroad: Labour 1 franc, Ganger (60 men) 1.5 francs. Monthly in China (to family etc): Labour 10 dollars, Ganger 15 dollars. Bonus on embarkation: 20 dollars (additional to pay).
- Compensation to family in case of accident: Death or total disablement: 150 dollars. Partial disablement: up to 75 dollars.
- Additional: Free passage to and from China under all circumstances. Free food, clothing, housing, fuel, light and medical attendance.
- Duration of employment: Three years, with liberty for employer to terminate contract at any time after one year on giving six months notice, or at any time for misconduct or inefficiency on the part of the labourer. Free passage to be given back to Weihaiwei or a Port North of Woosung.
- Deductions: No daily pay abroad during sickness, but food given. Monthly pay in China continues up to six weeks sickness. After six weeks sickness, no monthly pay in China. No daily pay abroad for time lost owing to misconduct. In case of offences involving loss of pay for 28 days or more, deductions of monthly pay in China will be made.
- Hours of work: Obligation to work ten hours daily, but a lesser or longer period may by fixed by the Labour Control on a daily average basis of ten hours. Liability to work seven days a week but consideration will be given to Chinese festivals, as to which the Labour Control will decide.

By contrast, the French contract, for workers, many of whom would be working alongside French workers in fields and factories, is extremely detailed.[12]

THE QUEUE – SYMBOL OF SUBMISSION

Le Petit Journal

ADMINISTRATION
61, RUE LAFAYETTE, 61
Les manuscrits ne sont pas rendus
On s'abonne sans frais
dans tous les bureaux de poste

5 CENT. SUPPLÉMENT ILLUSTRÉ 5 CENT.

27ᵐᵉ Année Numéro 1.111

DIMANCHE 3 MARS 1912

ABONNEMENTS

SEINE et SEINE-ET-OISE.. 2 fr. 4 fr. 00
DÉPARTEMENTS........ 2 fr. 4 fr. 0
ÉTRANGER............. 2.50 5 fr. 0

The queue was introduced by the Qing dynasty when it took control of China in 1644, expelling the last of the Mings. The Qing rulers were Manchus from the north; their alien character helped provoke numerous rebellions, until the final one which unseated them in 1912. From the start of their rule, the Qing insisted on the Chinese wearing their hair, Manchu-style, in the form of a queue as a symbol of loyalty, on pain of death. When China was formally declared a republic in 1912, the queue was eagerly dispensed with, President Yuan Shikai leading the way. Civil servants were required to do likewise.

YUAN-SHI-KAI FAIT COUPER SA NATTE

The queue was a means of humiliation and mockery for the many Chinese around the world who left China to work in mines, ships and factories. However, old habits die hard and some Chinese continued to wear their hair in the form of a queue, most notably in July 1917 when Zhang Xun ('the pigtail general') led an army so coiffed, in a vain attempt to restore the monarchy. Because of the incompatibility of the queue with military labour, the recruits to the Chinese Labour Corps as a rule had them removed before leaving home, but some grew them again when they reached France or Belgium.

It ran for five years and the financial arrangements were more complex, although the family in China only received a single payment of 30 dollars on embarkation 'as a consolation'.

- Rates of pay per working day while abroad: 5 francs. Workers receiving board shall get 3.25 francs a day, those receiving both board and lodging shall get 3 francs a day. The labourer must give from his daily wage 25 centimes for clothing and shoes, and 25 centimes for expenses in case of sickness and insurance against death.
- Clothing: apart from the long list of clothing issued on embarkation, 'upon reaching France, each labourer shall receive the following: one pair of leather shoes, one hat according to the season. Six months after the labourer's arrival in France, and in every six months thereafter during the period of this contract, he shall receive clothing as follows: two blue shirts and trousers, one pair of leather shoes, one hat, one padded coat, one pair of padded trousers, one pair of socks. In addition, one padded coat and one pair of trousers will be given him annually, at the end of September or each year.'
- Food allocation: for each labourer this was detailed in grams of rice, wheat, meat, salt or fresh fish, beans, fresh vegetables, tea, lard or vegetable oil and salt.
- Recreation: labourers were to enjoy 'all the liberties, especially religious liberty, as guaranteed by French laws to its citizens' as well as the 'same opportunities for rest and vacation as enjoyed by French workers employed in the same establishments'.

The contract listed compensation in case of deaths of all sorts, complicated by the French law of April 1898 respecting accidents which did not allow indemnities to be paid to the non-resident family of a foreign worker, which had to be overruled in this case, and ends with M. Truptil reserving the right to 'sublet' a worker's contract to 'any responsible factory owner'.

Most, though not all, of the labourers recruited by the British in Weihaiwei were from Shandong province. Most were poor farmers from the interior (many had never seen a ship or the sea) hoping simply to earn a better living. Quite a few were skilled, including carpenters and blacksmiths, and even one teacher who was interested in seeing the world and who told a YMCA official that the pay was better than his salary as a teacher.[13]

Medical examination
There was an initial medical examination, the same as that used for British recruits, in which many potential recruits were turned down through ill-health, with as many as 60 per cent of the potential recruits rejected, often because of the eye disease trachoma or dental problems. Successful recruits

had their long queues or pigtails cut off. Daryl Klein, a second lieutenant in the Chinese Labour Corps, who in 1919 published a useful and informative description of his service, *With The Chinks*, (not a title acceptable today) was surprised that so few seemed regretful, 'to lose so intimate a thing, picking it up after it had been sheared, handling it fondly and examining the careful plaits'.

The Manchu form of hairstyle, with the front of the head shaved and the hair at the back worn long and plaited, had been imposed upon the Chinese from the Manchu conquest in 1644. In 1912 with the foundation of the Chinese Republic, many men, especially intellectuals and most city-dwellers, cut off their queue as sign of progress, but farmers in the countryside had been unaffected by the modern fashion. Next they were washed in a great vat of hot water:

> On the edge of the vat stood a Chinese official who relentlessly pushed his victims into the water, first daubing their heads with liquid soap. This vat itself was a welter of human bodies, getting clean each after his own manner. Then a brisk rub with a towel after which the skin would show a glistening polish, like the surface of a stone washed by the sea for many years. It was a study for Michael Angelo.

The new recruits were medically examined, drilled, inoculated against small-pox, given zinc sulphate eye drops against trachoma, and drilled again for several weeks before embarkation (a process that was frequently delayed for lack of shipping). Their details were meticulously recorded, names and addresses and fingerprints taken, and a number assigned to each man, written on a wooden tag tied to his raincoat and stamped on a metal bracelet that was riveted around his wrist. One Chinese recruit described the physical examination to a YMCA worker, expressing his puzzlement that the doctor only took the pulse in his left hand, failing to examine the right one (as a doctor of traditional Chinese medicine would do, using both pulses as a significant means of diagnosis). 'Even my eyelids he turned up. I confess I was glad when this gentleman moved on to the next fellow in the line for I had not the slightest idea what he might have in his head to try next. It was the strangest examination I ever saw. I was not asked to write a single character.'[14]

The journey to France

The system of recruitment was long and complex. Klein described the entire process from health examination and drill training in Weihaiwei, to the long and extremely uncomfortable journey to France across both Pacific and Atlantic Oceans. The first 8,000 recruits sailed via the Cape of Good Hope, on a journey that took three months and led to complaints about the short-age of fresh vegetables so this route was abandoned. Klein and his labour force embarked on a Blue Funnel Line ship for Vancouver and quarantine, then they boarded the *Empress of Asia* and travelled south, sailed through the Panama Canal, crossing the Atlantic to England and then France, arriving five months after embarkation.[15]

Transportation of the Chinese workers was, at the beginning, almost entirely by sea, around the Cape or though the Suez Canal and the Mediterranean, but the first major sacrifice of the Chinese Labour Corps took place on 17 February 1917, when the French transport ship *Athos* was sunk by a German submarine off Malta with the loss of 543 Chinese workers (and 209 Chinese sailors) in that one disaster. The French, nevertheless, continued to use the dangerous route but British recruiters elected to follow a longer sea route, usually via Canada, where most contingents of Chinese workers were sent across the country from Vancouver to Halifax in sealed trains, rather than sailing through the Panama Canal.

Concealed from Canadians
In the recruitment and training camps in China, the labourers were housed in long, low buildings with bunks where they slept 'on wooden shelves – like books in a public library'. When they were finally handed their kitbags and marched onto the steamer, they were forced to sleep, packed below deck, on hastily erected tiers of bunks which had a tendency to collapse. The ship's carpenter, called upon to re-build these 'sleeping shelves' buckling under the weight of thirty bodies, though not a natural liberal, was moved to think that these 'yellow 'eathens were 'elping out in France'.[16] Arriving in Canada, the Chinese workers were hurried onto trains with darkened windows and rushed across the country in secrecy, with newspapers officially forbidden to report their passage. After a period in a (closely guarded) quarantine camp, on the other side of Canada on Victoria Island near Vancouver, they were packed onto the *Empress of Asia*, *Empress of Russia* or other chartered passenger liners for the voyage to Europe. Even in these voyages, secrecy meant that some ships' manifests listed them as tourists and Canadian officials sometimes referred to them as Japanese in official correspondence.

There were numerous reasons for attempting to conceal the passage of thousands of Chinese workers across Canada. There was the need to protect Chinese neutrality, there were fears of sabotage for Sun Yat-sen's anti-war Kuomintang party had considerable support amongst the small number of Chinese resident in Canada, and any leak of information could add to the dangers already faced by British shipping from German submarine attack in the Atlantic. There was also the problem of the Canadian Government, which imposed a heavy immigration tax to deter would-be Chinese settlers and did not want any Chinese to escape from the trains. The Canadians agreed to waive their 'head tax' in the case of the Labour Corps, but only on condition

UNRESTRICTED SUBMARINE WARFARE

The New York Times.

"All the News That's Fit to Print."

EXTRA
8:30 A.M.

VOL. LXIV NO. 20,929 ..... NEW YORK, SATURDAY, MAY 8, 1915.—TWENTY-FOUR PAGES. ONE CENT

LUSITANIA SUNK BY A SUBMARINE, PROBABLY 1,260 DEAD;
TWICE TORPEDOED OFF IRISH COAST; SINKS IN 15 MINUTES;
CAPT. TURNER SAVED, FROHMAN AND VANDERBILT MISSING;
WASHINGTON BELIEVES THAT A GRAVE CRISIS IS AT HAND

In February 1915, Germany began an economic blockade of Britain by threatening to sink any ship (even if neutral) trading with Britain. In May, the passenger ship, *Lusitania*, was sunk by a U-boat with loss of many American lives.

Germany then applied the policy rather fitfully, anxious not to provoke a still neutral America, until in February 1917, it announced unrestricted submarine warfare; this decision soon brought America into the war and, a few months later, China.

An early victim of the German submarine policy was the *Athos*. In its report on 24 February, *The Times* reported the ship as carrying the Chinese mail, but makes no reference to carrying Chinese labourers and sailors, 752 of whom lost their lives. This was not untypical of the attitudes of the advanced nations of the era. The Chinese were constantly belittled, ignored or treated as non-persons. The memory of their humiliation was to be a powerful driver in the creation of modern China.

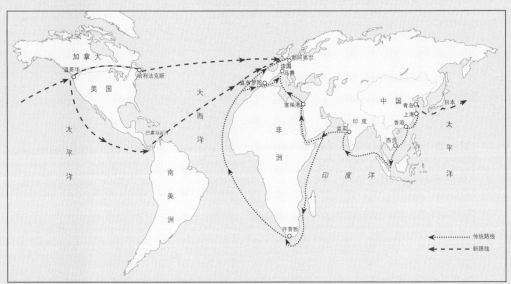

A Chinese map shows the routes that the labourers took to reach Europe; after the early tragedy of the *Athos* most went via Canada.

NOTE: *New York Times*, 8 May 1915. Map *Convergence de deux civilisations*, Xu Guoqi, 2007.

that the workers be locked into the trains. There was a complete ban on reporting the transport of Chinese labourers in the Canadian press but it could not be enforced in America where a newspaper reported that twenty-five Chinese had died of cold on a train passing through Maine.[17] This was denied by the Canadian authorities.

From the quarantine camp at William Head on Vancouver Island (established in 1893 mainly to deal with cases of smallpox on ocean liners and the odd leper), Joe Hwei Chun, a Christian from Shandong province, wrote to his parents-in-law in April 1917,

> Your son-in-law left on 5th month, 3rd day. We went aboard ship and started on our journey and travelled till the 24th. We have arrived in English Canada from where we take a train and in about 16 days we will arrive in France. My journey has been one of peace and tranquility under the protection of the Heavenly Father and I have met with no dangers or hardships. Every day we have all we want, our eatables, clothing and everything we want are excellent.[18]

A total of 84,473 Chinese labourers passed through the William Head Quarantine Station on their way to France and Joe Hwei Chun was one of a group of 2,057 who arrived on 18 April 1917. When they were all examined on arrival, one was found to have smallpox so they were all automatically detained for fourteen days. Ships continued to arrive with thousands of Chinese labourers on board, all destined for quarantine in a camp that had been constructed to deal with a couple of hundred people at most (with space for fifty-four first class passengers from infected ships in a separate group of huts). Bell tents were set up but conditions deteriorated as rain set in during October. Desperate to keep dry in their tents, the Chinese labourers 'helped themselves to anything which would keep them off the wet ground, including doors of buildings and entire walls and roof of the blacksmith's shop.' A local farmer complained about the 'Chinese soldiers' who took rail fences for firewood and stole vegetables.

Although they were officially confined to barracks and disciplined by the 5th British Columbia Company of the Royal Canadian Garrison Artillery, a few attempted to escape. One immensely tall man from Shandong was easily found in Fantan Alley in Victoria's Chinatown where he towered above the others. He was returned to the camp and sent off by the next ship via Panama to Britain.

Spending weeks in the quarantine camp, the Chinese labourers were organised into gangs to do the laundry, dig the flower and vegetable plots, repair station facilities and in the evening they practised digging trenches and dugouts. They amused themselves by making 'dioramas', which sound rather like the pictorial pavements found in grand Chinese gardens and temple grounds. One child of one of the camp staff reported:

> They spent hours making what they termed 'pictures', they would build a platform of rock and earth about 8 feet by 10 feet, level the top and construct the picture. It was meant to represent a story or a play, and they made it by using pebbles, bits of coloured glass, flower blossoms and tiny shrubs. The children were delighted with their handicraft.[19]

The ladies of Victoria were invited to the camp to buy handicrafts, some 'supplying silks and embroidery threads' and putting in 'orders for cushion covers or etched brass shells'.

After quarantine, some of the labourers were sent back by rail, in the same locked trains with covered windows, from Vancouver to Halifax, to take ships to Southampton. Others boarded ships like the *Empress of Asia* which sailed to Liverpool through the Panama Canal. They were sent across the Channel to Dunkirk. In September 1917, Germans attacked and twenty-seven labourers were killed on the beach at Dunkirk.

Conditions in France

When they finally arrived, conditions for the Chinese Labour Corps in France were very varied. The French recruits were spread across the country, either working in agriculture or in factories, some of which were making munitions. A list details eighty-seven places of employment (as of 16 October 1918) including munitions factories in practically every *département* throughout France, ports, road-building enterprises, steel and iron works, two paper mills, the Société de Gaz[20] de Paris (where the CLC workers went on strike in April 1920 demanding higher wages and threatening Paris with a blackout), the Société Chimique des Usines, the Société Chimique du Rhône, the Blériot aviation works and glass works of the Usines de Saint-Gobain.

CLC labourers under French contract had Sunday off and all the public holidays enjoyed by the French and, though their movements were restricted for they were not allowed to travel by train without special permission, they enjoyed comparative freedom in the nearby towns and villages. One of the YMCA interpreters reported that Chinese labourers were happier with the French, not just because of their working conditions but because the French officers were less race conscious.[21] 'They were more democratic in their manners. The British stood on their dignity as officers, and perhaps as white men, most of the time.' In 1917, 11,500 of the French-recruited workers were transferred to American army control, which they were not at all happy about for they came under military discipline like the British contingent, locked into camps, losing their Sunday off and working seven days a week. The

Americans returned their 'borrowed' labourers to the French immediately after the Armistice.

The British-recruited Chinese lived in barracks and camps, behind barbed wire and often dangerously close to the Front. In this proximity and, despite their contract specifying no military work, they dug trenches, some 6,000 worked on the military railways, 1,000 worked on inland water transport, the others being employed at various tasks on the road, railheads, dumps etc.[22] A British officer also praised their trench work, reporting that they dug an average of 200 cubic feet a day whilst his Indian labourers managed 160 and the British Tommies only 140. They made duck boards with speed and skill, one group producing the allotted number some hours before the end of their stipulated 12-hour days, so they downed tools and smoked and refused all encouragement and threats to work overtime. They moved great weights with ingenuity, lifting a huge naval gun weighing several tons with carefully placed wedges and beams, according to the officer in charge.

A draft history of the Tank Corps recorded the invaluable work of 500 Chinese 'artificers' from the 51st Company, Chinese Labour Corps, repairing tanks when, with training, they 'picked up the class of work which was required … undertook any type of job with the greatest ease', requiring practically no supervision. Apart from repairing and maintaining tanks, they made massive, heavy fascine bundles of tightly-packed brushwood which enabled tanks to cross trenches 15-feet wide. Lloyd George wrote, 'They are immensely powerful fellows, and it was no uncommon sight to see one of the Chinese pick up a balk of timber or a bundle of corrugated iron sheets weighing 3 or 4 hundredweight and walk off with it as calmly as if it weighed only as many stone!'[23] He noted that with aerial bombing or long-distance shelling, 'they were far less nervous under fire than the British West Indian Auxiliaries.'

A Canadian artillery platoon commander digging gun pits near Arras offered a different picture. As he and his men settled down for the night in the gun pit, 'Just as we were spreading our blankets one night, in through our only entrance barged half a dozen Chinese, some of whom had been at the William Head quarantine station … It was quite evident they had "the wind up" and were astonished at the violence of the exploding shells above them.'[24]

Lloyd George's only complaint was that 'if they suffered any fatal casualties, they would all break off work to attend the funeral, and neither threats nor cajolery had the least effect on them, nor would bombing or shelling by the enemy scatter their cortège, until the obsequies had been duly completed.' A memoir of service at Montreuil-sur-Mer by a British officer stated that the Chinese Labour Corps released men to fight at the Front which 'was of notable help to the British Army' although he, too, noticed the complicating

BIG ENDS, SPROCKETS AND RIVETS

Britain and France developed the tank to break the deadlock of trench warfare; Germany was slow to do the same. Its utility in battle was dented by its complexity and vulnerability to enemy gunfire. There were large losses and constant maintenance and replacement was needed. For the Shandong peasant – no less than for the traditional British soldier – the tank was a bizarre invention; across one inventor's proposal, an official had scrawled 'this man is mad'. Translating 'tank' into Chinese, some mimicked the English sound with 'tang ke', literally 'soup' and 'overcome'. Another description was (in five characters from right to left in the drawing) Iron Scaled Mo-Tuo (=motor) Vehicle. The interpreters had a hard time; how many would have known the Chinese word for 'big end', 'sprocket' or 'rivet'?

The problem of crossing the trenches was solved by making fascines, binding up to 100 of them tightly together in bundles and dropping them in the trenches, so that the tanks could pass over them without totally falling in. More than 1,000 Chinese labourers worked at the tank workshops in Teneur, Pas de Calais. Some soon became highly skilled at riveting, replacing engines and sprocketing. Others were engaged in immense physical labour of cutting, assembling and moving very heavy fascine bundles. Their work earned golden opinions; it was 'beyond all praise'. Field Marshal Ludendorff became demoralized, lamenting the inexhaustible pool of enemy tanks. It was a key contribution to the war effort by the Chinese.

NOTE: Chinese work on tanks from *Tank Workshops Report in World War 1*, The Tank Museum, Bovington, UK.

significance of burial and referred to an army leaflet entitled 'How to bury a Chinaman properly'.[25]

Lloyd George's reference is a reminder of the dangers of CLC work and the constant possibility of fatal casualties. He also paid tribute to their hard work but he concluded that, overall, compared to that of Serbia or Belgium, China's contribution to the war had been insignificant.

Language skills

Corporal A.W. Paton, a gunner, recalled passing a CLC camp in Reninghelst in Belgium where there was a large notice reading 'Do Not Speak to the Chinese'.[26] Beneath this, in equally large letters, some wag had chalked, 'Who the hell can?' A major problem in the lives of the Chinese Labour Corps was the dire shortage of interpreters who could sort out quarrels and disputes which sometimes became violent. With camps holding, for example, 800 labourers and only two interpreters, misunderstandings could lead to tragedy and heap misunderstanding upon misunderstanding. Suicide was, apparently, not unusual:

> One night as the Bosche drove us to our dugout we found suspended at the entrance a dead coolie. This coolie had nursed a grudge against the captain and had decided to show his displeasure in this distasteful manner. Next morning the captain spoke to the company on parade. The coolies expected their captain to be deeply moved over the affair, even remorseful, though the original difference with the coolie had been of the pettiest. But no. The captain was too astute, he did not even deign to speak directly to the coolies, though he knew their language well. 'Tell the coolies', he said to the interpreter, 'that last night one of them hung himself in the officers' dugout. Tell them if any more of them must hang themselves to be so good as to do it in their own dugouts. We don't like such a mess in ours.'[27]

The captain may have known their language but he clearly knew little of their culture. For more than 2,000 years, assigning blame by committing suicide in the house of the wrong-doer has been an acknowledged part of the Chinese legal code: the coolie was accusing his captain, as the other coolies would have understood. There were some twenty-five strikes and riots in the CLC between 8 November 1916 and 24 July 1917, many of which could have been avoided with more and better interpretation and understanding.[28]

Missionaries who had served in China were recruited as interpreters and officers, and students studying in Europe were brought in for their language skills. Eventually in June 1918, Chinese students studying in America came over through the YMCA. A possibly apocryphal story relates that the Chinese workers were upset by the translation of the order to march, 'Zou!

[走 Let's go!]' which sounded much like the word for dog (狗 gou) and they found it insulting.[29] There are many reports of officers in charge of the CLC finding that lack of interpreters made their work more difficult. In response, Major R.J. Purdon of the 91st Company, Chinese Labour Corps, produced *A Chinese phrasebook for Chinese labour*, listing in English, Romanised Chinese (Wade-Giles) and Chinese characters, all the words and sentences that 'are absolutely necessary to the performance of labour'.[30]

Major Purdon made 'diffident' claims for his handbook, 'Written in the theatre of war, with many interruptions, under trying circumstances and without any reference books.' Though his phrasebook was written 'in simple language, as spoken by the Chinese coolie', he noted the difficulties arising from the variety of dialects spoken in the CLC. 'As a single instance, the first word in the book, 'man', may be pronounced in four different ways, all of which are correct.'

Purdon stressed the importance of correct relationships and their significance in achieving the desired results:

> The Chinese 'ganger' is the most important link between the officer and the labourers, and his position should be clearly defined and upheld. The responsibility and use of the Chinese ganger should begin from the day of arrival at the depot in France and his 'face' carefully considered. Nagging at gangers always leads to bad work and distrust and a ganger who calls for this should be dispensed with. The best work is always accomplished by giving definite tasks to the Chinese ganger and making him directly responsible for the carrying out of the work. Details as to the moment to prise up, lift, shoulder and move off with the baulks, rails etc., should be left to the Chinese ganger. The same applies to the simultaneous lowering of heavy loads carried by the gangs. A heavy bodily strain is imposed during these operations, which are not expedited, but rather retarded, when every movement is directed by the European in charge. Possible subsequent strain and injury to the workers may be laid by them to the charge of the white man ordering details of movement.
>
> Constant supervision is essential ... supervision should be as unmilitary as is compatible with efficiency. Whenever possible, the Chinese should be employed by themselves, and not where they are in a position to judge or criticise the same class of work performed by white men ...

Purdon stressed that continuity was important to the 'conservative' and 'clannish' Chinese. He also suggested that 'Officers who are not fluent Chinese speakers should avoid, as much as possible, giving orders or directions to working parties or units which are not under their direct command.' It would be difficult to achieve fluency through Purdon's *Phrasebook*, although it might have been a useful reminder for those who had some Chinese. The first few chapters, which he recommended be learnt parrot-fashion consist of vocabulary: 'Come here quickly!' 'Bring it here', 'This one', 'That one' or lists: 'water, wait, eat, food, speak, have, have not, many, few', whilst later sections incorporate sequences of questions and answers, some more positive than others. The question, 'Have you begun work?' is followed by the answer, 'No', and the conversation continues with, 'Why not?' to which the answer is, 'We have not had our food', a problem which one hopes was easily resolved.

Other sequences illustrate the problems encountered in many phrase books where a simple question may elicit an incomprehensible response: 'Why does the carpenter need so much wood?', 'Have you anything to say for your-self?' A couple of suggested responses will be familiar to Chinese speakers, although the translations are quaint. *Bu xing* – 'it won't do, or it won't work' is taken rather further in Purdon's translation, 'That won't do, the game is up' and the very common phrase, familiar to any Chinese speaker, *mei you fazi* – 'it can't be done', 'no way', is dramatically translated as 'there is no help for it, or Kismet'!

Chapter XI of Purdon's phrasebook reveals that many Chinese labourers seem to have been employed as batmen or personal servants, hardly the con-tribution to the war effort envisaged by Liang Shiyi. 'Bring some soap and a towel', 'Bring some water for washing. I want to wash.' 'Go and wash your hands.' 'You must have a bath tomorrow.' 'This basin is dirty: wash it.' 'Bring me a glass of water.' 'Bring me some hot water: I want to shave.' 'Brush my clothes', 'When you have cleaned my boots, put them under the bed.'

Entertainment and education

Medical care for the CLC was detailed in their contract of employment although, despite the clause specifying non-military work, labourers were frequently required to work very close to the front line and at least 3,000 died in France from bombing and shell-fire. The sick and injured were, however, cared for with compassion and skill by Dr Douglas Gray, former medical officer to the British Legation in Peking, who had volunteered for active service. In his CLC hospital at Noyelles-sur-Mer, he insisted that his Chinese patients receive exactly the same standard of treatment as a British soldier and he procured a canary for each ward, knowing the enthusiasm for pet birds that was so widespread in China.

With very little spare time and very limited provision for entertainment, as in the quarantine camp on Vancouver Island, in France and Belgium, the Chinese Labour Corps continued to decorate the ground around their tents with sand and pebbles and pieces of broken glass forming pictures and patterns. In some camps they built mess halls and painted them with trees, dragons, constellations and fearsome beasts. In the CLC Hospital they built a pagoda. They played all sorts of games and entertained others with stilt

COMMUNICATION DIFFICULTIES

N.C.O. "Don't yer know yer own bloomin' number – yet?"
Chinaman (proudly) "One-seven-six"

There was always a shortage of interpreters. Allied officers were often imbued with a sense of superiority towards Chinese, whom they saw as an inferior race; one British officer complained that they 'all looked alike'. However, those in immediate contact with their work were almost always very complimentary. Many had similar names; in the autumn of 1918, some 12% of the Chinese in British service were called Wang and 10% Chang. Identification was aided by the use of thumb prints and the use of personal numbers for each worker.

The awkwardness of translating simple English into Chinese can be imagined from Major Purdon's phrase book. Interpretation would have made more difficult by linguistic differences in different parts of China and by the importance of pitch in correct pronunciation. Would it have been any use in a complicated dialogue, such as in some of these below?

He spoke for a very long time, and even then I did not understand.
他 說 了 半 天 我 還 是 不 明 白。
He spoke half day I still am not understand
T'a shuo la pan t'ien wo hai shih pu ming pai

Incinerator.
燒 糞 爐
Burn manure stove
Shao fên lu

Isolation hospital.
傳 染 醫 院
Transmit infect hospital
Ch'uan jan i yüan

N.C.O.s' wash-house.
英 工 頭 洗 臉 房
British overseers wash face house
Ying kung t'ou hsi lien fang

Notice board.
告 白 板 子
Inform clear board
Kao pai pan tzŭ

CLC officer and interpreter at Weihaiwei

NOTE: Similar names *The Chinese Labour Corps* by Gregory James Bayview Educational, 2013.

dances and *yangge* (a popular North Chinese peasant dance, rather like the conga). Daryl Klein described a cacophonous concert with Chinese musical instruments and also how one man created beautiful paper flowers. They played the Chinese form of badminton where a light ball with feathers is kept in the air by the players simply kicking it; they celebrated (when allowed) festivals with stilt dancing and acrobatics. At the end of the war when the remaining workers were salvaging live and dead ammunition, they continued the tradition of 'trench art' in their own way, decorating shell cases with engraved lotuses, lilies, birds and flowers reminiscent of the designs on blue and white porcelain.[31]

Some of the special skills of the CLC were put on display when King George V paid a visit to his troops in November 1918 and it was arranged that he should have a quiet lunch at the camp of the 58th Company, Chinese Labour Corps. The labourers drilled and practised perfect salutes, and used their own money to buy brightly coloured cloth for bunting and to decorate the doorway of the mess. They put up a proper Chinese triumphal arch for the king and practised shouting 'Hao! Hao! Hao!' (Good! Good! Good!) which sounded sufficiently close to 'hooray' to please the king.[32]

When he left, apparently very satisfied with his visit, the labourers were allowed to eat the remains of the cheese and beef sandwiches prepared for the royal party. 'One lad took a morsel and tried to conjure some special flavour into it. "Hmm, it has a taste of king," he said.

Though much has been made of the efforts of the Young Men's Christian Association (YMCA) to entertain and educate members of the CLC, it came very late, for it was not until after America joined the war, in June 1918, that the YMCA began to promote educational work. It set up ninety clubs, with canteens, shops selling Chinese goods (providing profits for Overseas Chinese shop-keepers resident in France), sports and games, concerts and cinema shows, as well as evening classes in language, hygiene and general knowledge. It published the *Jidujiao qingnianhui zhufa huagong zhoubao* (*French YMCA Chinese Labourer's Weekly*) for those that could read. It recruited young Chinese studying at American universities who travelled to France to help with interpreting and education amongst the workers, from basic literacy programmes to lectures on health and international affairs. Though their interpreting work was invaluable for there was a terrible shortage of linguistic skills amongst the military in charge of the Chinese, the effect of the well-meant educational programmes in the small number of clubs was limited.

More significant from the beginning of the war and of considerable influence on China's later history was the educational work promoted by a group of prominent Chinese intellectuals who were in France in the early years of the twentieth century. Li Shizeng (1881–1973) from a wealthy background in Hebei province, arrived in France in 1902 to study chemistry and biology

RECREATIONS

The Chinese labourers, despite their great workload, found time to entertain themselves and others in a variety of ways.

Trench art flourished among the Chinese men; here, a man shows off one of his model ships.

Religious rites

A Canadian army magazine illustrates the child-like enthusiasm that many of the coolies had for different sorts of headgear.

Première Année. — N° 11. — Prix : 25 centimes. — 10 Août 1917.

HA - KON - TSA - TCHEU

Revue chinoise populaire, publiée par le groupe d'éducation populaire

SOUS LE PATRONAGE DE LA SOCIÉTÉ FRANCO-CHINOISE D'ÉDUCATION

8, rue Bugeaud, Paris.

Paraissant le 10 et 25.   Le Gérant : Arthur Pardoux.

Groups of student workers had been coming from China to France since the end of the Qing dynasty, as part of China's opening to the outside world and France's desire to increase its influence in China. They had their own newspaper which awaited the labourers when they started arriving in 1917.

The extraordinary strength of the Chinese labourers, particularly those from the north of the country, has often been cited; some paid great attention to physical fitness and competitive sports.

and, in 1912, set up a soya bean factory making various soya products. An early anarchist, he joined the Tongmenghui, a forerunner of Sun Yat-sen's Kuomintang and was keen to promote study in France to raise educational standards and political awareness amongst Chinese students.

He was associated with other Chinese studying in France who later rose to prominence: Wu Zhihui (1865–1953), a philosopher and linguist, Wang Jingwei (1883–1944), a prominent Kuomintang activist but condemned in the 1930s for his collaboration with the Japanese, and Cai Yuanpei (1868–1940) an educationalist who became head of Peking University and the Academia Sinica. They founded a magazine for the Chinese workers of the CLC, *Huagong zazhi* (*Chinese Labourers' Journal*) and Cai Yuanpei also published educational booklets designed especially for them. He invented a scheme for teaching literacy through phonetics and a limited vocabulary of 600 characters which was remarkably successful and literacy classes were the most popular of those offered by the YMCA. It was reported that 20 per cent of the labourers were illiterate on arrival in France but this was claimed to have risen to 38 per cent in 1921, a figure that some dispute.[33]

A few of these publications and associations, most notably the Association for Frugal Study in France, continued to support Chinese who came to France after the war on work-study programmes. These students included future prominent Communist Party leaders such as Zhou Enlai and Deng Xiaoping, who worked in a Renault tractor factory on a work-study programme and as a shoe mender once sacked for refusing to work. Mao Zedong thought seriously about studying in France but was put off by his lack of language skills.[34] Their experience of Europe and of working conditions in factories, as well as the clubs and societies set up for their support, all increased their camaraderie and developing socialist ideas.

Discipline

The lack of interpreters and the lack of understanding of Chinese culture contributed to occasional violence. Chen Ta listed twenty-five riots and strikes by CLC workers between November 1916 and July 1917.[35] These included strikes after particularly devastating German air-raids such as that on 2 September 1917 near Dunkirk. Such dangerous raids, not unnaturally, terrified the Chinese, often provoking them to escape the camps and several were killed or injured during attempts to round them up. There was a riot in the Poudrerie Nationale involving the entire CLC group there; a strike by workers transferred from an aircraft factory to an iron and steel works which resulted in a lowering of their wages; a strike at Caen over the lowering of the bread ration, and a strike by workers in the Paris Gas company, again over lowered wages.

There were also problems over the substitution of horsemeat for beef and a failure to issue raincoats. Strikes and riots often ended with shootings by armed guards and the British executed ten members of the CLC, one for murdering his British officer, the others for killing fellow CLC members in fights that sometimes broke out over gambling tables. There are several versions of a story of Chinese aggression when, after a Chinese camp near Calais was bombed and several men killed, the survivors turned on a group of German prisoners-of-war and killed them. In their defence, as they were not themselves soldiers, they had not been trained in the conventions of warfare.

Reconstruction
When the war ended, about 3,000 of those recruited by the French stayed behind in France, marrying French wives (against some initial discouragement by both the Chinese and French governments) and establishing Chinatowns.

Some CLC workers recruited by the British were sent back to China straight away after the Armistice, this time travelling openly through Canada, their presence recorded in the local newspapers. As many had not yet served out their three-year contracts, they were kept behind in France and Belgium on reconstruction work. They filled trenches, re-built roads, removed barbed wire and, most dangerously, collected unexploded bombs and other munitions. The task they disliked the most was that of collecting corpses for burial. They had paid great attention to the burial of their own comrades because in traditional Chinese belief, it is a tragedy to die and be buried far from home, but the repatriation of the bodies of CLC casualties was not permitted. In China, annual ceremonies honouring ancestors, feeding and nourishing their souls, take place in family graveyards but the soul of a person who died far away from home and family would forever wander unhappily, as German propagandists had pointed out in 1916.[36]

The retrieval of dead bodies was a particularly distasteful task to the Chinese but other post-war activities were positively dangerous, particularly clearing battlefields, pockmarked with live ammunition, and the removal and disposal of the ammunition gathered. Wang Yushan extinguished a fire in an ammunition dump and Yan Dengfeng similarly prevented an ammunition store from exploding by drenching it with water. Both received the Meritorious Service Medal, but many others were killed and injured by unstable or carelessly handled armaments.

During the war, the attitude of many, whether in charge of the CLC or inhabitants of the regions where they worked, was generally neutral, if not exactly favourable. In many accounts, the CLC workers are described as infantile or child-like, oddly dressed (a description of a man who liked to wear three hats occurs often) but unthreatening. Accounts by local people occasionally demonstrated sympathy for these hard-working strangers, far from home, unable to communicate with the locals, and some recounted acts of kindness as when one CLC labourer brought bags of oranges to a sick woman.

Sadly, in the years after the war, when the CLC was engaged in reconstruction work, clearing battlefields and devastated towns and villages, relations worsened. One of the first guidebooks to the battlefields, published in Flemish in 1919 warned, 'Do not travel alone and do not go out at night in the southern part of western Flanders because you risk meeting many Chinese coolies who have made this region dangerous. If you meet them, do not show fear but move away without provoking them.'[37] With fewer British officers to supervise them, they were able to wander more freely from their camps and the Chinese were accused of stealing firewood and looting and worse. Questions were asked about the CLC in the Belgian parliament with appeals to the British to exercise more control over them. Though there was some evidence that an armed attack in late September 1919, on a bar, L'Étoile, set up in a hut not far from Ypres was carried out by members of the 101st Company, CLC, since one (No. 46564), was shot dead on the spot by the barman and another corpse was found soon after, many other armed attacks were attributed to the Chinese without any evidence at all. Indeed, in some robberies and murders, it would seem that the perpetrators disguised themselves as Chinese, to escape justice themselves and cast blame on the Chinese in France 'and the development of their socialist ideals'. To prevent further trouble, 101st Company was sent home at the beginning of October 1919.

Throughout 1919, CLC labourers were gradually repatriated although in October, there were still 54,000 of the British recruits in France and Belgium. That month, the French Minister of Reconstruction called a meeting to sort out problems 'created by the Chinese' and organise the 'immediate repatriation of this undesirable labour force'. General Gibb, representing the British Army in France and Belgium, stated that most of the crimes attributed to Chinese labourers were committed by those in French control who were badly supervised and 'spoilt'. The French accused the British of preferring to recover usable armaments from the battlefields rather than destroy dangerous weaponry. General Gibb said that since he no longer had access to German PoWs for the work, he was forced to use the Chinese, though they were less effective. It was decided that repatriation should be hurried along and the British started sending back 15,000 a month. The last of the British CLC recruits arrived back in Qingdao on 13 September 1920.[38]

Perhaps the worst fate of all was that of the 200,000 workers sent to Russia. Russia had been using cheap Chinese labour, particularly on its railway construction and in mines in the Arctic Circle and the newly acquired territory of Siberia since the mid-nineteenth century. During the war more were recruited to keep railways, mines and factories going. Although they, like those recruited by the British and French, had initially been recruited under contract, as conditions, already dire, worsened in Russia, they were reduced to near starvation and lacked protection from the cold. In 1917 a few joined the Red Army (one becoming a personal bodyguard to Lenin), some joined the Whites, but some 40,000 were repatriated by the new Bolshevik government in 1919. Some sixty were rescued from the Arctic ports by British naval vessels in 1918, and returned to China via England, some were participants in the Allied invasion of Siberia (in an attempt to prop up a White Russian regime there) but in 1926, there were still 100,000 Chinese in Russia.[39]

Aftermath

Most of the Chinese workers who travelled to France were semi- or completely illiterate. Even if a few learnt Cai Yuanpei's 600 characters, very few were able to write home or compose any written record of their experience. Apart from a few accounts taken down by YMCA workers, little or nothing is known about their lives and very few were able to write home. Returning labourers went back to their villages and their village life between 1918 and 1920, carrying little of Europe with them, and although many had saved enough to buy land, it was reported that 3,001 were penniless when they returned to China. There were no victory parades for them, and even today there is little recognition of either their contribution or their sacrifice in China or elsewhere.

Of the 140,000 labourers sent to France, up to 10,000 died, their sacrifice dismissed by Lloyd George and Balfour. An element of the dismissal was the view that they were simply part of the widespread use of Chinese 'coolie' labour on railways and in mines throughout the world. They had been recruited 'privately' (because, despite the desperate need for their help, the recruiting system had to be invented to uphold China's neutrality) and therefore, could be dismissed as non-combatants. The stigma of 'coolie' labour may be one reason that they have not yet been accorded much recognition in China today, although it is apparent that younger Chinese, especially those who study abroad in Belgium where the In Flanders Fields Museum, Ypres, commemorates the CLC, are beginning to make annual pilgrimages to the cemeteries at the Qingming festival (fifteen days after the Spring equinox, 4/5 April each year). Qingming is a Chinese national holiday when people go to family graves, tidy them and make offerings of incense, paper money and food to feed the ancestral spirits. Moved by these graves of Chinese who died far from home, with no relatives nearby, the students take offerings of tangerines and wine to each grave.

Those who died in Western Europe, from bombs, injuries or sickness, are buried in forty neatly tended war cemeteries established and maintained by the Commonwealth War Graves Commission. The largest, at Noyelles-sur-Mer, has a Chinese style stone gateway and 838 graves, each with an inscription and the name of the deceased in Chinese, made possible by the complex record-keeping of the recruiting officers.

There is evidence of an unpleasantly black sense of humour in the selection of epitaphs engraved on some tombstones. The inscription on the grave of Wang Enrong who was executed on 26 June 1918 for murdering a French woman, reads 'Faithful Unto Death', that of Hui Yuhe in the cemetery of Saint-Étienne au Mont who was executed on 12 September 1918 for murdering a fellow Chinese, reads, 'Though Dead He Still Liveth' and Zhang Ruzhi, executed in February 1920, who murdered a French prostitute and her three children, is remembered with the phrase, 'A Good Reputation Endureth Forever'.[40]

Chapter 6

Spies and Suspicions

Taking up his position as editor of the *Peking and Tientsin Times* on 1 December 1914, H.G. Woodhead noted:

> Many of the British residents in Tientsin still seemed to be unaware that there was a war on, and within a few weeks I was receiving protests both from British and neutral subjects regarding articles which they considered might offend German susceptibilities. The view was frankly advanced that the Tientsin Germans were of a different brand from other Germans and that nothing was to be gained by upsetting them. My critics evidently did not read the *Tageblatt*, or another venomous organ published weekly in English by an Italian, *The Tientsin Sunday Journal*. Even in December 1914, the *Peking and Tientsin Times* was giving twice or thrice as much space to German cables distributed by the Deutsche *Uberseedienst* (or 'Half Seas Over Agency' as I used to call it) as to Allied cables ... I saw no reason why a British newspaper should act as a medium for German propaganda ...

Woodhead turned his attention to the *Tientsin Sunday Journal*, writing to the British Legation in Peking on 29 August 1915, enclosing a copy which he said was 'edited within the British Concession from an office adjacent to Gordon Hall by a man named Borioni who holds himself out to be an Italian subject, and printed in the British Concession by the German firm of C. Lee.'[1] Woodhead described it as 'poisonous stuff', 'supported almost entirely by German advertisers'. He wrote, 'the Italian Consul professes to be powerless in this matter' but had apparently advised a group of Englishmen in the Tientsin Club to 'thrash' Borioni.

Woodhead was particularly exercised that this pro-German propaganda was being published in the British Concession and felt that some action could be taken (although Italy was also neutral at this moment in the war). 'The British Consul-General [in Tientsin] sent for me and adopted a very injured attitude over what he felt was an aspersion on his energy. "What could he do?" he asked plaintively. "Get the requisite authority to stop it", I suggested. And in due course he convened an extraordinary meeting of British Concession land-renters to adopt a new bye-law making it illegal to print or publish any periodical in the British area without his written licence.'[2]

The saga continued as the *Tientsin Sunday Journal* moved to the French Concession where it was suppressed after one issue and moved to its spiritual home in the German Concession. When Italy entered the war in 1915, Woodhead 'emphasized the impropriety of an Italian editing a weekly of this kind. After some delay, the Italian authorities deported Signor Borioni', only for his mantle to descend on an American. A reference (by Woodhead) to 'the fact that Borioni had been succeeded by a "misguided Yank"' led to an official protest from the American to the British Consul-General:

> The following week I referred to him as a 'hyphenated egg-exporter' (which was his profession), and the matter was transferred to Peking. Dr Reinsch, the American Minister, called upon and lodged a formal protest [presumably defending an American citizen's right to freedom of speech] with Sir John Jordan, who had been the object of some of the most libellous of the paper's attacks. Some time afterwards the British Minister told me that he had listened patiently to Dr Reinsch's exposition of his grievance and then, pulling a sheet of printed matter out of a drawer, handed it to him and invited him to study it, pointing out that it was all printed in America. It was a collection of German propaganda, including a pamphlet by the late W.J. Bryan,[3] vilifying British rule in India. Nothing more was heard of the American protest, and the egg-exporter shortly afterwards vanished from Tientsin having, it was alleged, secured large payments in advance for locomotives for one of the Government railways – which were never delivered.[4]

Never a defender of any Germans, in Tientsin or elsewhere, the assiduous Woodhead 'derived a peculiar pleasure' from the angry reaction of local Germans to his news sheets or contents bills, pasted up as close as possible to German areas and to the German Legation in Peking.

> One which gave particular offence appeared on the day that the new German Minister, Admiral von Hintze, reached the capital. He had suddenly, in January 1915, landed in Shanghai from a Norwegian tramp [steamer], on which he had crossed the Pacific as a supercargo [a person employed by the owner of the ship to look after the cargo]. At a great reception given by the German community he boasted how he had out-witted the British. Notified of his new appointment while in America, he had crossed the Atlantic as a deckhand employed on a Swedish ship, received the Kaiser's instructions, and re-crossed it as a stoker on a Dutch vessel. In America he assumed the identity of a commercial traveller. He reached Tientsin and Peking to find both places placarded with HINTZE'S 57 VARIETIES.

Woodhead could joke but throughout 1915 and 1916, Hintze met with the Japanese Minister in Peking and the Consul-General in Tianjin, suggesting that Japan might do better by joining Germany, holding out the promise of handing over the German Pacific islands and Jiaozhou. These and other negotiations were not unnoticed by the British and, as one Whitehall official reported mildly, it was not just 'not playing the game, but indicates a certain tendency to a veiled rapprochement between the two countries which is slightly disconcerting'.[5]

Spy fever

With Germans and British citizens living side by side in cities and concessions throughout China, the war brought suspicion and accusations. The thick volume of 'Miscellaneous Correspondence'[6] received by the British Legation in Peking in 1915 contains standard items such as long official reports on 'The Chinese Antimony Position' (antimony was used in shrapnel, therefore of military significance and China controlled half the world's supply), wharf-age dues at Wuhu and the annual costs of 'Constable, Writers and Servants' employed by the Legation, interspersed with reports of sinister enemy activities. A British subject named Rye wrote on 8 November 1915, 'A German spy is living in room 128 at the Waggon Lits [*sic.*], his name is Hellwigh'. There is no record of a response from the Legation. In 1915, the British-owned Grand Hotel des Wagons-Lits was almost entirely staffed by Germans but as China was then officially neutral, Germans were entitled to work and run businesses in China.

The same Mr Rye was assiduous in sniffing out spies and traitors. On 16 November he wrote from the Peking Club, 'Kindly inform Sir John Jordan [the British Minister] that a German subject, C.J. Starck, a well-known smuggler of arms, arrived in Peking with a German officer yesterday morning. He is staying at the German barracks.'

On 13 November, he reported:

> In continuance of my last report re. Germans conducting anti-British propaganda, though in the pay of the Chinese government, I beg to add the name of a German drill instructor by the name of Ziegel. I further beg to point out for the benefit of His Majesty's Consul-General in Shanghai that a Norwegian subject, Jensen, who is the agent at that port for Fritz Materia (the Poldi steel-works) has been commissioned for the task of importing goods and also exporting goods for the Germans. Further, I should ask His Majesty's Consul in Amoy and Swatow to keep an open eye on the Norwegian Consul Haesloop who is a German subject.

Between 5 and 9 August a series of reports were received about a complex and unlikely series of plots involving Germans, Greeks and Jews apparently bent on the destruction of Russian forts in Manchuria and the Chinese Eastern

Railway. The Russian Minister in Peking learnt that 'the Germans have two aeroplanes and a submarine at Manila whither a dangerous German named Din is said to be proceeding ...' The British Consul-General in Shanghai, Everard Fraser, added on 9 August, 'The German's name is Dehn ... Grosse said today that the Petrograd people were offered by some shady people here 40,000 Mausers with ammunition and he had advised to ask for delivery via Nagasaki as the arms did not pass through the Customs ...'[7] It was said that the planes and submarine in Manila were 'all intended for damage to be done to the fortress of Vladivostok: the submarine in particular is to attack and sink transports from Vladivostok to the Dardanelles ... Two Greeks and two Jews have been sent to Manchuria with the purpose of damaging the Chinese Eastern Railway. A box containing explosives and indications of their preparation have been delivered to one of the said Jews, Levine, by the German Legation in Peking.'

One man who caused considerable worry was the Reverend Gilbert Reid. Born in New York in 1857, he attended the Union Theological Seminary, founded by the Presbyterian Church in America but open to all denominations, and set off for Shanghai as a missionary in 1882. In 1894 he founded the International Institute of China in Shanghai and served as editor of the *Peking Post*. On 20 November 1917, Sir John Jordan reported to the Foreign Office in London, enclosing a copy of a letter written to Reid which had been 'allowed to go ahead' through the censor.[8] Jordan described Reid, 'who is American, is well known as one of the most active German propagandists in Shanghai. He is recently said to have been arrested for libelling President Wilson.'

The letter signed Florence Ruah Nance, read:

Dear Dr Reid, I want to thank you for the *Post*. In these days of ultra-censorship it is a joy to find one still unafraid, even eager to lift a voice for the unspeakable Hun! I've wished I could nail my colours on my house-top only it wouldn't represent my whole family. I do wish you'd begin to explain through your columns this 'whyness' of our heap big money difficulties, we folk on a good salary. Lots of folk don't see it's the same old Grasper England who's got us by the throat.

Another enclosure was from C.F. Kupfer of Kuling (Edward Selby Little's mountain resort) who enclosed his annual subscription of $20 and wrote:

You are doing a great work and I feel sure that you will never have it to regret for what you are doing now for the Central Powers. The power of the pen has not lost its influence. The great pity is that so few people do not take time to think [*sic.*] and are not conversant with the history of the Britons. If they were, they would in these days understand the proverb,

'The mills of the gods grind slowly, but they grind exceedingly fine.'
Some day they will see it. I hope you will get the last word.

Shortly afterwards, at the request of the Chinese government, the Reverend Gilbert Reid was deported to Manila, although he was not imprisoned and returned to Shanghai in 1921 where he died in 1927.

Also working 'for the other side', in this case against the Germans, was an enterprising '*soi-disant* German Pole' employed in Tianjin to address the relief parcels prepared there for German prisoners of war in Russia. 'The Russians apparently insisted that each parcel of food or clothing must bear the address in Russian as well as German ... he had been engaged at this task for about a month before it was discovered that he had been addressing all the parcels to friends in Russia. He had to be kept in the Russian Consular gaol until he could be got out of the port to save him from the vengeance of the Germans.'

In an account that revealed the complexity of wartime life in Tianjin with its many different concessions and political groupings, H.G. Woodhead described a failed attempt by 'Austro-Hungarian renegades' to storm the Austrian Consulate and steal important documents which they intended to hand over to the Allies.[9] Dining with 'a prominent British resident and an official of the Municipal Council, the meal was interrupted by the arrival of a messenger from the 'renegades' saying they had to postpone their raid as they could not find enough pistols. The dinner guests could only muster three pistols but Woodhead remembered 'having seen a dozen or so automatic pistols, seized during a recent raid, in the office of the British police station, and remarked what a pity it was that these could not be made available. "Why not," said the official of the Council.

Woodhead then went to the police station with a note for the inspector in charge requesting twelve automatic pistols and 600 rounds of ammunition which he then delivered to Room 67 at the Astor House Hotel (founded in 1863 and flourishing to this day). Later that night he drove to the Austrian Concession to find the streets 'teeming with armed police and marines'. The 'Austrian plotters' told him that someone had betrayed them and they had called the raid off.

> Next afternoon, the police inspector came into my office in a state of obvious excitement and asked me where the pistols were. I said, 'In the hands of the man to whom I gave them last night.' It transpired that an hour earlier, an Austrian marine, carrying a communication from the Austrian to the German Consulate along Taku Road (which passes through the British Concession), had been waylaid by two of the Austrian renegades who accused him of giving them away. Producing pistols, they made him get into a rickshaw, and then, using similar vehicles, one in front of him and one behind, announced that they were going to take him

to their headquarters for an investigation. The trio passed out of the British into the German area, where the marine jumped from his rickshaw and ran down a side street. One of his escort immediately whipped out a pistol and fired. He missed the marine but shot a Chinese interpreter attached to the German police station through the heart.

Woodhead managed to retrieve the pistols (which had not been used in the shooting) from the Astor House Hotel and continued, 'the ringleader told me later that the Tianjin plot had been abandoned, and that they intended, instead, to seize the Austrian Consulate at Shanghai, and also the Austrian-Lloyd steamers interned there. Two of them actually got into the Shanghai Consul's room and demanded his keys, but one of the alleged conspirators then shot his comrade instead of the Consul!

Arms for India
Together with more innocuous poison-pen letters such as that accusing the Belgian woman who ran a hat shop in Tianjin of being a German spy, a complex plot to supply guns to India was received in the British Legation in Peking on 26 September 1915. The possibility of German or Japanese support for rebels in British India was a permanent worry. The report stated:

> Following derived from Kraft on return from Singapore. He seems to play the game. London, India and Bangkok have been informed.[10]
>
> All arms for India will pass through Shanghai and neighbourhood. Kraft mentioned no other place. At present time there are 22,000 Mausers and 8 million cartridges now in Shanghai and neighbourhood awaiting shipment to India by steamer and sailing vessels ...
>
> The scheme for India is that arms shall leave Shanghai on November 1st for India in a vessel believed to be Chinese-owned but flying the Japanese flag with a Norwegian captain, some Japanese mercantile marine officers and Chinese crew and may call at Singapore if coal is running short. This ship is at present plying in ordinary trade in coast ports as a blind and will leave Shanghai on September 15th for Bangkok with an Indian Wm. Dull of whom more later.
>
> Ship will eventually contain 20,000 rifles, 8 million cartridges, 2,500 Browning revolvers with cartridges for each, a quantity of hand grenades and dynamite. On this ship will be one or two Germans or Indians to keep watch on the Captain. Wm. Dull is described as an Indian leader who assisted to throw bombs at Delhi. Is short, very fat, dark, about 25 to 30, small hands and feet, fat fingers, blood-shot eyes, parts his hair on the side ...
>
> Explosives are being made in large quantities in Pootoo Island, Chusan archipelago [Putuoshan, Zhoushandao]. Kraft has had dealing

with reference to a supply of hand grenades with the man who directs the work. This man Kraft knows where the arms are being stored in Shanghai ...

Japanese naval patrols were protecting the Indian sub-continent, but she also sheltered Indian nationalists such as Rash Behari Bose,[11] who was involved in an assassination attempt on Lord Hardinge and a failed mutiny within the India Army. He fled to Japan in 1915 and, despite British attempts at extradition, helped by right-wing Japanese nationalists sympathetic to his cause, managed to stay there until his death in 1945. In an attempt to prevent more Indian nationalists escaping, in 1916 a dozen Japanese merchant ships on the China coast were boarded on the orders of Admiral Grant, nine Indians were removed and shots were fired, none of which helped smooth Anglo-Japanese relations.

German propaganda

Right at the beginning of the war, reporting to the Foreign Office on the progress of the 'joint' British and Japanese action in Qiaozhou, Sir John Jordan included an article from the *Peking Gazette* of 24 August 1914.[12] 'I enclose a calumnious statement which some irresponsible Germans have published. It is only fair to say the better class German opinion disassociates itself from such methods.' Entitled 'The Truth About England', the article began: 'England's policy since the unfortunate Spanish Armada was wrecked on England's coast has been inspired by an insatiable hunger for land and gold.' Describing at length England's perfidy over Indian opium, it continued with the British invasion of the land of the 'peaceful Boers' and informed readers that 'The real instigator of this last war which has set all Europe into flames is England and nobody but England. Russia and France are only British tools.'

There are several references to German attempts to colonise parts of Africa and Morocco, 'seeking an outlet for her teeming millions' whilst England 'found a ready tool in Japan to do her dirty work in Asia and keep Russia, which had already formed designs on India in check.' It ended with the suggestion that Chinese and Japanese 'travel through the different countries of the world and 'look where you find the most civilisation, the most law and order, in the slums of London, to which any policeman could direct you, or the slums of Berlin. Only, let me tell you, in Berlin you might ask 100 policemen in vain to direct you to a slum because there is none there ... England, the most confounded thief of all nations, now playing the role of Champion of the small countries which must not be crushed by a strong power. Haha! What a nation of curs!'

There was much German propaganda published in Shanghai. The 4 December edition of *The War*, published from 38 Nanking Road, proclaimed, 'The longer the war lasts, the more Germany's superiority becomes apparent' and *War Pictures / Kriegs-bilder / Zhan tu* (same date, same address) depicted the impressively bearded Admiral von Tirpitz on its front cover with an extremely provocative and dramatic painting on the back cover of the German warship *Emden* scoring a double hit on the Russian cruiser *Zemtschuk* and a French torpedo boat in Penang harbour.

The activities of the *Emden* in south-east Asian waters infuriated George Morrison who felt that the Japanese, supposed to be protecting Allied shipping in the area, had failed miserably and, at the same time, were possibly protected against attack. He deplored British losses, setting out their financial cost and regarded the fact that Japanese ships appeared to traverse the Indian Ocean with impunity, not threatened by either the *Emden* or German submarines, as evidence of Japanese–German collusion.[13]

Number 33 Nanking Road was a major centre of German publication for *Der Ostasiatischer Lloyd* appeared from the same address, also declaring German invincibility even at moments when this stretched a point. On 27 March 1916, it contained a graphic description of a battle on 29 February when the German auxiliary cruiser *Greif* encountered three British cruisers and a British destroyer. The *Greif* torpedoed a British cruiser of some 15,000 tons but then 'blew herself up', a new definition of invincibility. The three journals, like the *Tientsin Sunday Journal*, were supported by German advertisers: Arnold Karberg and Company (which, in order to continue trading, was to re-invent itself as the British firm Arnhold Brothers) advertised amperes and volt-meters, Naumann, sewing machines, dynamos, Koppel's light rails and cars and Glaeser's, paints and cranes, lathes and drills. Readers were encouraged to read *Wau-wau Satirical Weekly*, published like the others from 33 Nanking Road.[14] From 2 Fuzhou Road, supporters of the Allies hit back, producing booklets including one published in 1917 on the sinking of the *Lusitania* – *Deguo zai haishang de cansha / Germany's murder at sea*, complete with a European-style illustration of distraught mothers weeping over their dead babies.

In Tianjin H.G. Woodhead suspected with 'very good reason' that the German Red Cross, which had its office in the main street of the British Concession, ran a 'Prisoners' Escape Bureau' as a subsidiary enterprise ...[15]

A renegade Austrian marine, who came furtively to my office after dark one night, produced an apparently innocuous postcard addressed to a prisoner of war, and advising the despatch of a parcel. He showed me, however, that it was composed of two thin pieces of card ingeniously pasted together, and that, inserted between them, on a piece of paper, was a map giving the route to be followed and the agents to be visited, when attempting an escape from Khabarovsk. Many prisoners had escaped thence into Manchuria. I handed the specimen over to the Russian authorities who doubtless took steps ...

Some complaints of unpatriotic, if not subversive, action were perhaps due to long-held animosity. In September, Goffe, British Consul in Yunnan, wrote to Sir John Jordan to complain about the activities of the local representative of the British and Foreign Bible Society who he described as 'an impertinent hound – an expression quite inadequate to describe him or my feelings'.[16] Goffe was well known for his intolerance, having nearly lost his post in Macau when he agreed that all Europeans might be invited to tea parties, except the Portuguese (obviously the most numerous and significant Europeans in Macau). He lamely explained that they were frightfully bad at tennis. This time, the accusation was of anti-British sentiments but the missionary (who was presumably of Norwegian origin) wrote to say that he would desist in future but that he did not think 'the occasional hoisting of the Norwegian flag' was proof of disloyalty.

Even within the Allied ranks, there were problems. George Morrison reported in May 1915, concerned that the Japanese were convinced of German invincibility, 'Only ten days ago the Japanese lecturer at the Customs College here, Haraoka by name, told his students that Germany would be victorious in the war, that Russia would shortly be demobilised and that England would be defeated.'[17] And H.G. Woodhead described a failure of British propaganda in Tianjin. British films showing the Battle of the Somme, intended to 'impress with the output of British munitions factories, the perfection of British technical equipment, etc.,' were brought to Tianjin by an impresario under terms that paid the Chinese cinemas as well as remitting one-third of the ticket price to a Service fund, with the result that they were 'screened in the same manner as – but usually at higher prices than – the thrilling adventures of Pearl White.'[18] Woodhead pointed out that the idea was not to impress the 'Allied communities' of Tianjin, but the local people. 'There was, I believe, one display in Tianjin by arrangement with the British authorities, for the benefit of local Chinese officials, after I had pointed out the absurdity of bringing these films all the way out from England only to show them to Allied audiences.'

The *Peking Gazette*, whose German-sponsored article had so enraged Sir John Jordan in 1914, was edited by Eugene Chen in 1915 and his anti-Japanese editorials irritated the British Legation and worried G.E. Morrison. He asked Cai Tinggan, Yuan Shikai's secretary and interpreter on 2 March 1915 if he could 'shut Eugene Chen up' and encourage him to 'restrain himself.'[19] Cai replied:

My Dear Doctor, the world's mischief comes by 'over-doing'. The Germans sinned by 'over-doing'. The Japanese sinned by 'over-doing'.

Eugene Chen is 'over-doing'. I do not know what influence I have with him but I will send Mr Tong of our office to moderate him. I hate to handle a freak myself.

On 4 March, Morrison wrote to Eugene Chen himself: 'You are doing your best to goad the Japanese into reprisals . . . The danger from Japan seems now past but the danger will recur unless the intemperate violence of the *Gazette* can be restrained.'

In May 1917, as discussions over China's possible entry into the war grew heated, Eugene Chen was arrested. The Cabinet Office briefing notes stated:

On 22 May, the Military Governor of Peking left for Shandong, to confer with General Zhang Xun [who was soon to add to the chaos] in regard to supporting the Premier [Duan Qirui] against the President [Li Yuanhong] and Parliament. On the same day, Mr. Eugene Chen, editor of the *Peking Gazette* (whose claim to be a British subject is not recognised by His Majesty's Legation) was arrested by order of the Premier.

Eugene Chen was born in Trinidad in 1878 to Chinese parents, and had studied law in London before being inspired by Sun Yat-sen to move to China, despite knowing little Chinese. He would eventually join the Chinese delegation at the Versailles Peace Conference but he had long been a provocative character.

The next Cabinet Office report continued the story of Eugene Chen's travails in 1917:

'Putnam Weale' [pseudonym of the journalist Bertram Lenox Simpson] of the *Daily Telegraph*,[20] published a leader in the *Peking Gazette* of 24 May, maintaining the right of Mr Eugene Chen to British citizenship and threatening to make an international incident of his imprisonment unless the British Legation secured his release . . . Mr Alston explains that Putnam Weale's real object is political and intended to embarrass the supporters of Premier Duan by securing British intervention on behalf of a journalist whose anti-Japanese bias is notorious. Mr Alston refers incidentally to the relationship known to exist between Mr Chen and the Peking manager of the Deutsch-Asiatische Bank. The Foreign Office . . . desires that nothing should be done to hinder Mr Chen from making good, if he can, his claim to British citizenship, for which purpose his lawyer should be assisted in obtaining access to him. He has been sentenced to four months' imprisonment, a fact which would seem to imply that the arrest was not solely due to his attacks on the Premier, since dismissed . . .

It is clear that the British Legation wanted nothing to do with Eugene Chen and his claim to be a British citizen, and the acting Minister, Alston, was

A MIGHT-HAVE-BEEN CHAIRMAN OF BARCLAYS BANK

Sir Edmund Backhouse was the *dauphin* of a respectable Quaker family, which founded Backhouse's Bank in 1774, a leading bank in the North East,which financed the Stockton and Darlington Railway, the first steam train to carry passengers.

They combined running the bank with good works, such as Alfred Backhouse (*below*) who founded two hospitals in the area. In 1896, they [page 13, plate section] combined with other Quaker bankers

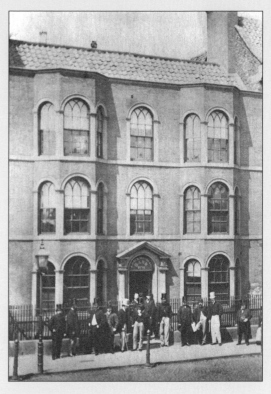

(with whom they were inter-married) to form Barclays Bank.

For the next ninety years, each Barclays chairman was from one of the founding Quaker families, giving the bank a paternalist flavour; had he not gone

bankrupt and had to flee his creditors, Backhouse might have been a candidate to head Barclays Bank. As the borders between different bank types evaporated, Barclays plunged deeply into investment banking at the expense of its traditional business. Quants replaced Quakers as the bank's lodestar.

In addition to deceiving the British government, John Brown and the Bodleian Library, Backhouse pulled the wool over the eyes of the American Bank Note Company. As President Yuan Shikai prepared for the transition to monarchy, he made large bank note orders. Help was needed to consolidate the order in October 1915, so Backhouse stepped in, emphasising his personal ties with Yuan and his top officials and offering to secure an even larger contract for ABNC. The contract that he produced was forged and it emerged that he did not know Yuan or the officials. A few months later, Yuan died and, with it, the requirement for notes with his image on them.

NOTE: Bank history from Barclays Bank Archives. Backhouse history from *The Hermit of Peking*, HR Trevor-Roper, Eland, 1993.

anxious to suggest that not only did he attack Britain's ally, Japan, but his 'relationship' with Heinrich Cordes of the Deutsch-Asiatische Bank suggested sinister German sympathies.

Backhouse's mythical armaments

Also from within Allied ranks, came a scheme thrust upon a very unwilling Jordan in early 1915. It was a proposal that he facilitate sourcing desperately needed munitions for the Allied armies in France and on the Russian front. It was apparently known, or believed, in London, that captured Russian rifles, left over from the Russo-Japanese War in Manchuria (1904–5) were widely available for sale in China. Sir John denied any knowledge of such weapons and pointed out that China was officially neutral and that the export of arms was therefore specifically prohibited by her government. His protests were ignored as the British government worked hard to find ways around such niceties by suggesting that he find 'an intermediary from whom the sale to us would not be open to the same objection'.[21]

With advice from the Chinese Secretary at the British Legation, Sidney Barton (whose wife, according to Morrison, was to enjoy a dalliance with Beilby Alston who at this time was in charge of the China Desk in the Foreign Office in London), Jordan found his intermediary who, he believed, could 'privately purchase 30,000 Mauser and Mannlicher rifles of 1911 and 1912 at £3.10s each, without ammunition'. It was probably Barton who recommended Edmund Backhouse with whom Barton was collaborating on a (never to be finished) Chinese dictionary project in Peking.

Edmund Trelawny Backhouse, a bankrupt embarrassment to his respectable family, had been living, effectively as a remittance man, in Peking since 1899. Apparently a good Chinese speaker, he had helped Morrison with translations of Chinese texts, collaborated with the respectable (and innocent) J.O.P. Bland in a literary hoax about the Boxer Rebellion and affairs of the Inner Court based upon an apparently fictitious diary. He also acquired ancient Chinese books for the Bodleian Library in Oxford (a venture which ended in financial and bibliographical disaster as after some good first batches, Backhouse proceeded to send valueless items against substantial financial advances). In addition he ostensibly acted as agent for the great ship-building firm of John Brown of Glasgow, keen to sell armour-plated ships to the Chinese navy. This latter transaction never came to anything either, but the cover of the ship-building company was invoked by the Foreign Office to help maintain secrecy.

Backhouse entered into the affair with vigour, reporting to Jordan on 30 June that he had located over 150,000 rifles of Austrian and German manufacture in Hankou, Hangzhou, Shenyang, Tianjin and Nanjing where there were also 100 Skoda Maxim guns. By August, the quantities were rising at an astounding rate, '100,000 rifles and also about 350 Krupp machine guns ... and 30,000,000 rounds of ammunition'. After some panics over leaks of information, it seemed as if the mammoth shipment was on its way from Shanghai to Hong Kong. Delays apparently occurred in the Fuzhou area and near Guangzhou but no boats or weapons ever appeared and by the middle of October, it became apparent that:

> the rifles and machine guns so exactly described ... the flotilla of ships and the whole dramatic history of their journey from Hankou to Guangzhou ... which had fetched £2 million from London to Peking ... which had agitated pens in the Foreign Office and the War Office, exercised the Army Council and Lord Kitchener himself, drawn in the personal intervention of the Foreign Minister and the Colonial Secretary, been reported to the Cabinet, the Prime Minister and the King; all this, it now seemed, was an insubstantial pageant, the baseless fabric of a dream, now suddenly dissolved ...

This was a humiliation for Jordan who was recalled on leave for a year. As the Counsellor to the British Legation reported, 'Poor old Sir John has been worrying himself nearly ill over the ... business' and he was replaced by Beilby Alston, serving as chargé d'affaires, who had handled the gun saga from London.

1. In 1792 Britain's King George lll sent Lord Macartney to open up trade with China, but he was politely rebuffed by the Qianlong Emperor, who was used to treating all other countries as subservient. He advised King George 'to display even greater devotion and loyalty in future, so that, by perpetual submission to our Throne, you may secure peace and prosperity for your country thereafter'. He also said, 'We possess all things. I set no value on objects strange or ingenious, and have no use for your country's manufactures.'

2. Amongst Lord Macartney's gifts, dismissed by the Qianlong Emperor, were models of the latest ships and other examples of European technology. Half a century later, even more modern warships, powered by steam, were used against China in the First Opium War. Gunpowder, an undeveloped Chinese invention, was used with devastating effect. The Treaty of Nanjing of 1842 ceded Hong Kong to Britain, opened up five more concession cities and harbours for trading and established the principle of extraterritoriality.

3. After centuries of Chinese contempt for foreigners, it was the turn of the British to show contempt, as China was forced to accept opium in exchange for tea. When China hesitated to sign a second humiliating treaty in 1858, Lord Elgin and an Anglo-French force destroyed Beijing's Imperial Summer Palace. Other nations joined in the carving up of China.

4. Particularly humiliating was Japan's defeat of China in 1894-5, which led to the loss of much Chinese territory and influence. Since 1860, Japan had modernised much more effectively than China. The First World War gave China an opportunity to recover the German enclave in Shandong, but it was awarded to Japan at Versailles. Japan continued its remorseless intrusion into China, culminating in full scale war in 1937.

5. After Japan's crushing defeat of China in 1895, fast-growing Germany wanted a piece of China. Kaiser Wilhelm ll had a dream in which he saw himself as St Michael, leading European nations (all depicted as women) against the 'Yellow Peril', which was going to destroy Western civilization. A substantial colony was acquired in Qingdao, Shandong, soon to be the scene of early drama in the First World War.

6. Aloof America did not seek its own concessions, partly perhaps to avoid the administrative costs; it also enabled Uncle Sam to occupy the high moral ground and not to be seen as a common land grabber. It insisted on an 'Open Door' policy, with equal access to China for all. Great hopes were pinned on American support for China at Versailles, but America and its allies preferred the claims of Japan. China felt betrayed.

7. Concession architecture reflected its European origins. There were shutters on the houses in Shanghai's 'Frenchtown'. In Tianjin, Gordon Hall, with its Scottish baronial look, faced Victoria Park, which was controlled by dozens of byelaws to prevent bicycling, flower picking, dogs and access for Chinese people (except nannies).

8/9. Qingdao (Tsingtau in German) was a model German town, with a fine mansion for the governor. Sun Yat-sen called it 'a true model for China's future'. It was also a major German naval base.

10. The German colony received huge investment from Berlin. It was well ordered, with good schools and other facilities. It attracted many wealthy Chinese to settle there with their families. The Chinese boy salutes the Prussian national anthem.

11. The all powerful Dowager Empress Cixi died in 1908, a day after the Guangxu Emperor had died, with a lot of arsenic in his system. A regency was established for her two-year-old nephew, Puyi. The dynasty had been damaged by the consequenes of the Boxer uprising, leaving it vulnerable to being toppled at any time by a small spark. Revolution was in the air, fanned by Sun Yat-sen, who raised money and hope among overseas Chinese communities.

12. The spark that ended the Qing dynasty was an uprisimg in Wuchang in October 1911, after violent protests over the proposed nationalisation (and transfer to foreigners), on punitive terms, of one of the few indigenously owned railway companies. Other uprisings followed around China, especially the south. The dynasty was in no position to resist. A Republic was proclaimed, Sun Yat-sen was elected the first Provisional President and plans initiated for democratic elections to a bicameral parliament.

13. It was not plain sailing for Sun Yat-sen (*right*) and the Republicans. In Beijing, a wily and tough general, Yuan Shikai (*left*), had been appointed prime minister by the Qing dynasty. Backed by a big army, he was recognised as legitimate by some foreign powers. In return for negotiating the abdication of the child emperor in February 1912, Sun agreed to Yuan being appointed President. Within two years, a likely prime minister was assassinated, Yuan dissolved parliament and Sun Yat-sen was driven into exile. Yuan seemed all powerful.

14. Britain could not help China recover Shandong, because of her naval alliance with Japan, first signed in 1902 and renewed several times. A French cartoon shows France and Russia watching Britain 'again betraying Europe' and plotting to carve up the Chinese cake with Japan. The editorial comment was that the British had been duped by *les malins petits Japonais…* and so it proved, as the alliance went from bad to worse, until Japan blockaded the British concession in Tianjin in 1937 and, in 1941, the countries went to war with each other.

15. At the start of the war in Europe, in August 1914, China declared its neutrality, but was eager to recover the German colony in Shandong. President Yuan Shikai secretly offered 50,000 troops to the British to help achieve this aim – but got no answer.

16. In 1906 the alliance was seen as such a great achievement that the Conservatives boasted of it in their campaign posters. By the end of 1914, with the capture of Qingdao and its aftermath, Britain was growing suspicious of Japanese intentions in China, though still in need of Japanese naval assistance in the Pacific.

17. The British joined forces with the Japanese in capturing the German colony, but were distinctly wary of one another. Britain was represented by the South Wales Borderers, who were shocked at Japanese pillage and rape in the villages.

18. Despite a show of bonhomie between the Japanese and British generals, Mitsuomi and Barnardiston, the British were growing uncomfortable at Japan's aggression.

19. Shortly after the capture of the German colony at the end of 1914, the Japanese government, headed by Okuma Shigenobu, issued an ultimatum to China, known as the Twenty-one Demands. They were designed to make China a vassal state of Japan. America and Britain, caught unawares, were shocked by this sudden and brutal action.

20. A Japanese artist portrayed the conquest of Tsingtao with no reference to the (admittedly small) British participation. It was an early example of an amphibious exercise supported by aircraft and it made a powerful impression.

21. As Japanese and British forces planned their attack on the German enclave at Qingdao, in August 1914, Captain Karl von Müller sailed away in his cruiser, SS *Emden* into the Indian Ocean, where he casued havoc to British interests, destroying or capturing seventeen vessels, disrupting trade, bombing a refinery and humiliating the imperial power in the eyes of its people.

22. The day on which Japan's Twenty-one Demands were presented to President Yuan Shikai, was a 'day of extraordinary shame', in the words of a young student in Changsha, Mao Zedong. The sentiment was echoed all over China; violent riots ensued.

23. President Yuan Shikai was humiliated by the Twenty-One Demands and he made his foreign minister, Cao Rulin, sign them on China's behalf. It did not restrain him getting himself nominated as Emperor and issuing currency with his own image.

24. An (unissued) postage stamp suggests that a constitutional monarchy was considered, but there was no half way house for Yuan. His imperial ambition soon collapsed in contumely and he died in June 1916. His death weakened the centre and triggered the rise of warlordism, which was to dominate China for over a decade.

25. After Yuan Shikai's death, Duan Qirui was prime minister on and off for the rest of the war, though heavily constrained by rivals. China wanted to be present at the peace conference and, in order to earn an invitation to it, sent labourers to France and Russia to release more men to join the armies. This programme got under way in 1917 and almost 340,000 were recruited.

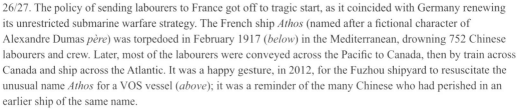

26/27. The policy of sending labourers to France got off to tragic start, as it coincided with Germany renewing its unrestricted submarine warfare strategy. The French ship *Athos* (named after a fictional character of Alexandre Dumas *père*) was torpedoed in February 1917 (*below*) in the Mediterranean, drowning 752 Chinese labourers and crew. Later, most of the labourers were conveyed across the Pacific to Canada, then by train across Canada and ship across the Atlantic. It was a happy gesture, in 2012, for the Fuzhou shipyard to resuscitate the unusual name *Athos* for a VOS vessel (*above*); it was a reminder of the many Chinese who had perished in an earlier ship of the same name.

28/29. The labourers were mostly recruited from the north of China, as they were thought to be tougher and stronger than southerners. Those above are in Weihaiwei, where there was a British 25 year lease, preparing to go to France. The British and French armies thought them hard working and disciplined, if properly handled. They were known as the Chinese Labour Corps, CLC, though Lloyd George preferred 'auxiliaries' in order not to inflame British labour unions who were hostile and objected to them working in UK.

30. Waiting patiently to board the Canadian Pacific's converted passenger liner, *The Empress of Russia* which, with its sister ship, *The Empress of Asia*, conveyed many of the labourers on their voyages to France.

31/32. Conditions on board the Empress liners were desperately crowded. Below deck, over 2,000 Chinese lived on wooden shelves, purpose built in bow and stern, which sometimes collapsed. The CLC workers were crammed in, like 'books in a library'. A lost film poster idealistically portrayed them as Shanghai boulevardiers rather than Shandong peasants.

33/34. The CLC carried out many heavy lifting tasks.

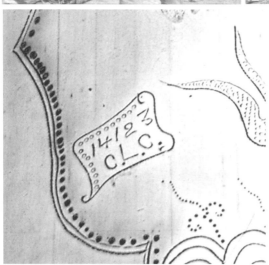

35/36. They had time to produce very varied trench art, including many lovely artefacts out of used shells.

37. More than 1,000 CLC labourers worked in maintaining Britain's secret weapon, the tank. Their vital work here was 'beyond all praise'. A key figure in the CLC structure was the interpreter, of whom there were very few. How would they have coped with translating the parts of a tank, such as sprockets or big ends? But cope they did and the German General Ludendorff was demoralized by the apparently unending stream of tanks made possible by the CLC.

38. To prevent tanks falling into trenches, huge bundles of wood were cut to size, bound into fascines and dropped into trenches to ensure safe transit for the tanks. The CLC proved to be outstanding at this job.

39. One of the CLC's disagreeable jobs was picking up corpses and body parts and digging graves. Chinese labourers look over the hedge at the grave that they dug for the German fighter pilot, Manfred von Richtofen (the 'Red Baron'); he was given a full military funeral by members of the Australian Flying Corps, near Amiens, 22 April 1918.

40. Dr Wellington Koo, 27-year-old Chinese Minister to Washington, receives an honorary degree from his *alma mater*, Columbia University. At the peace conference, he argued forcefully and eloquently in claiming the restoration of Chinese territory. American officials, including the President, were very sympathetic, but his arguments did not prevail.

41. Ishii Kikujirō, Japan's special envoy, strides out confidently in New York, secure in the knowledge that Japan's claims in Shandong were specifically conceded by Britain (and done 'with pleasure') as well as by France, Italy and Russia. They also enjoyed the implicit support of America, so that the Chinese position would be legally weak at the peace conference to be convened at the war's end.

42/43. Lü Zhengxiang, the foreign minister, led the Chinese delegation at Versailles. He was very depressed at the peace conference's development. A particular difficulty was that the Chinese prime minister, Duan Qirui, had signed away Chinese rights in Shandong (in return for Japanese loans) without informing any of the Chinese delegates at the conference, thus cutting the ground away from under their feet. Lü had a Belgian wife and, after her death, joined a monastery in Belgium; it is noteworthy that a member of the Japanese delegation was also a Christian, Count Chinda being a Methodist minister.

44/45. Edmund Backhouse was heir to the baronetcy of his father, Sir Jonathan Backhouse (*left in group above*), partner in a highly reputable Quaker bank which co-founded Barclays Bank. Instead of preparing for a career in finance, he ran up enormous debts at Oxford University and was shipped off to China, where he became a learned and influential sinologist. Because of his supposed relationships in the highest government circles, he was recruited by John Brown, the shipbuilders, and the American Bank Note Company, both seeking Chinese government contracts in the war. Also, the British government sought his help to buy armaments in China. All these relationships and activities proved to be fictitious, if not fraudulent.

46–48. President Wilson (*left*) was an idealist who wanted 'peace without victory', based on the principles of self-determination of all peoples, maintained by a League of Nations. The French leader, Georges Clemenceau (*centre*) – here seen recuperating from an assassination attempt in the middle of the peace conference – wanted France to achieve a total victory, with massive reparations to cripple Germany for all time. Lloyd George (*right*) saw the fallacy of permanently crippling Germany, but did not want the peoples of the British Empire to have self-determination. Wilson's idealism was stymied by the *realpolitik* of the two Europeans.

49. When word came that China had lost out to Japan at Versailles, the whole country erupted in wrath, beginning with riots, led by students, outside the Gate of Heavenly Peace in Peking. This launched the May Fourth Movement, which helped change the course of Chinese history.

50. After the Twenty-one Demands were issued by Japan in 1915, there were boycotts of Japanese goods, and similarly during the May Fourth Movement of 1919, sometimes including the British as well. Notices banning dogs, British and Japanese from restaurants, echoed similar bans imposed on Chinese in the treaty ports and concessions.

51. Chiang Kai-shek, who trained as a soldier in Japan, was a founder member of the KMT, Sun-Yatsen's political party. In war-time Shanghai he developed contacts with the underworld which were to help him in crushing the communists. He emerged from the warlord era as head of a KMT government in 1928, which lasted until the Japanese invasion of 1937. After the defeat of Japan and ensuing civil war, the People's Republic of China was declared in 1949 by Mao Zedong and the KMT took refuge in Taiwan.

52. Chinese labourers got scant recognition, despite the vital work of 340,000 of them in France and Russia. In the Panthéon de la Guerre, a huge panoramic painting of the war, they were painted out to allow for new participants, as the war evolved. Eventually, China was reduced to a tiny corner among the Latin American nations that joined the war on America's coat tails, but played no active part in the war, such as Brazil, Guatemala and Nicaragua.

鞠躬盡瘁

FAITHFUL unto DEATH

53/54. The Chinese dead were buried in their own beautiful graveyard, maintained by the Commonwealth War Graves Commission, at Noyelles-sur-Mer.

DE 1916 A 1918, CENT QUARANTE MILLE TRAVAILLEURS CHINOIS PARTICIPERENT EN FRANCE A L'EFFORT DE GUERRE DES ALLIES ET PERDIRENT PLUSIEURS MILLIERS DES LEURS.
AU LENDEMAIN DE LA VICTOIRE 3000 D'ENTRE EUX S'INSTALLERENT DEFINITIVEMENT DANS CE PAYS ET CREERENT AUTOUR DE LA GARE DE LYON A PARIS LA PREMIERE COMMUNAUTE CHINOISE.
NOVEMBRE 1988

55. In Paris, a plaque recognizes their contribution to the war; 3,000 remained in France, where a good deal of revolutionary activity took place towards changing the course of events in China. Two future leaders, Zhou Enlai and Deng Xiaoping were there.

56. While still at school in 1915, Zhou Enlai spoke out against foreign control of China. In 1919, he participated in the early days of the May Fourth Movement. He went to France in 1920, joining the active Chinese community, many of them left over from service as labourers. He started the Chinese Communist Party in France and returned to join Mao Zedong in the rise of the CCP in China. He was to serve as Mao's faithful, if sorely tried, prime minister between 1949 and 1976, the year when they both died.

57. During the war, Mao Zedong was a student in Changsha, in his home province, Hunan. Later he wrote a poem about the city, which inspired a statue there of him as a young man. He went on, after many tribulations, to found the People's Republic of China in 1949. Unity and dignity were restored to China, but his economic and political experiments were disastrous, causing millions of deaths and stunting the economy for a generation.

58/59. Deng Xiaoping went to France as a 15-year-old student, telling his father that it was '...to learn knowledge and truth from the West in order to save China'. He took various jobs there, while organizing Chinese workers; his militancy and refusal to work made him unemployable for one shoemaker. He returned to become a powerful force in the CCP and changed his name. After Mao's death in 1976, he helped make China an economic power house, while maintaining its status in the world. What would the Qianlong Emperor have thought of China being a top global manufacturer of 'objects strange or ingenious', which he so despised?

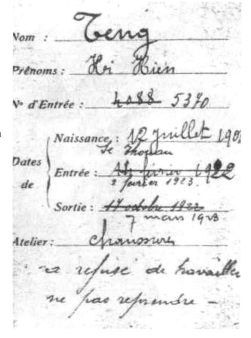

Chapter 7

A crucial year of chaos and decisions: 1917

This was crucial year on all fronts in the First World War. The failure of President Yuan Shikai's imperial restoration of 1915–16 (with himself as the proposed emperor) and his death in June 1916 had left China's government in a more confused state than ever. There was increasing tension between north and south, and turmoil in the provinces.

On 31 January 1917, Germany announced an 'offensive of unrestricted submarine warfare whereby all ships, belligerent or neutral, in the war zone surrounding Great Britain, France and Italy, or on the eastern Mediterranean sea, would be sunk.'[1] Despite considerable popular resistance to entering the European war, this finally pushed America into a stern protest to the German Ambassador and a call to all neutral nations, which included China, to follow suit.[2] In Peking on 9 February, the Chinese Ministry of Foreign Affairs protested against the use of submarines to the German Minister, Admiral von Hintze (who had had to smuggle himself into China to take up his post). The Chinese note protested the threat to 'even legitimate commercial intercourse between neutral states, and between neutral states and belligerent powers' and stated that if nothing changed, 'the Government of the Chinese Republic will be constrained, to its profound regret, to sever the diplomatic relations at present existing between the two countries.'

Admiral von Hintze passed on the German government's somewhat condescending reply (dated 10 March) which expressed 'great surprise' at the threat used by the Government of the Republic of China in its note of protest.[3]

Many other countries have also protested but China, which has been in friendly relations with Germany, is the only state which has added a threat to its protest. The surprise is doubly great because of the fact that as China has no shipping interests in the seas of blockaded zones she will not suffer thereby.

The Government of the Republic of China mentions that loss of life of Chinese citizens has occurred as a result of the present method of war. The Imperial German Government wishes to point out that the Government of the Republic of China has never communicated with the

Imperial Government regarding a single case of this kind, nor has it protested in this connection before. According to reports received by the Imperial Government, such losses as have been actually sustained by Chinese subjects have occurred in the firing line while they were engaged in digging trenches and other war service ... the fact that Germany has on several occasions protested against the employment of Chinese citizens for warlike purposes is evidence that the Imperial Government has given excellent proof of its friendly feelings towards China ...

The note ends with the threat that breaking off diplomatic relations would leave China 'entangled in unthinkable difficulties'. In its response, Germany ignored the fact that in the meantime, on 24 February, 543 Chinese labourers had lost their lives when German submarines sunk the French ship *Athos* on which they were being transported to France. The letter condemned China for sending such labourers to assist the Allies and rebuked the Chinese government for presuming to threaten Germany.[4] China formally broke off relations with Germany on 14 March. America declared war on Germany and Austria-Hungary on 6 April, but it took another five months of frantic negotiation and pressure, both positive and negative, applied by the Allies, as well as bitter internal disputes, before China followed suit and declared war on 14 August 1917.

Germany was not wrong to suggest that China's moves would find her 'entangled in unthinkable difficulties', although these were not created by Germany but by her 'Allies'. They involved a growing series of betrayals, some small, some exceedingly damaging. On 17 February 1917, Liang Qichao, a former leader of the late nineteenth century Reform Movement in China, called upon the British Minister and 'intimated that the Government had decided to sever relations with Germany'.[5] Alston's notes to the British War Cabinet described Liang as 'a noted scholar in close touch with Peking politics but averse to taking office' (although he had, in fact, served as Minister of Justice and would also act as Minister of Finance from July to November 1917). Liang Qichao said that the Chinese Government 'were much exercised in their minds over the financial aspects of the situation. They consider that the preparations to meet that situation involve them in considerable expense and therefore suggest that the Allied governments should consider the suspension of the Boxer Indemnity payments and an increase in Customs tariff.'

Preliminary enquiries made by the Chinese Ambassador to Japan and the Chinese Minister for Foreign Affairs in Peking indicated that the response of the representatives of Japan, France, Russia and Great Britain was that the matter should be delayed as little as possible and that once it had been achieved, they 'would be prepared to invite the Allied Governments to give favourable consideration to China's requests in reference to the indemnity and Customs questions. As regards the question of further financial assistance, which has been mooted, it might be considered if and when China was prepared to take an active part in the war.'

Sun Yat-sen opposes war

The situation was complicated by divisions within China. In early 1917 the journalist, John B. Powell, visited Sun Yat-sen at his home in Shanghai where he was greeted by Sun's bodyguard, Morris 'Two-gun' Cohen, 'who carried a large revolver in his hip pocket, which caused the seat of his trousers to sag grotesquely'.[6] Sun Yat-sen, along with the President Li Yuanhong, opposed the idea of China's participation in the war. 'Dr Sun insisted there was no point in China's declaring war on Germany merely to take sides in a struggle in which China had no direct interest. He declared that China's participation in a war to which the Kuomintang was opposed would precipitate serious domestic dissension. He made the significant statement, "The Chinese people may not be able to distinguish between foreigners of different nationalities and if the simple and honest people are taught to kill Teutons, they might be led to slaughter all white foreigners in the country."'[7]

Sun paid no attention to Shandong and the German-Japanese succession there and did not see, as the Chinese government in the north did, that participation in the war might lead to a resolution of the Shandong problem through the eventual peace settlement.

Sir John Jordan reflected the view of the Chinese government in the north in a despatch of 20 September 1916, although the complications he described also reflected divisions within Japan:

> China desires to come into the War for the main purpose of securing her status as an 'independent state' equal in all things to her Allies. There are also material gains to be derived from her intervention – by the acquisition of German concessions, repudiation of the German share of the indemnity etc . . . Japan opposes her intervention on these very grounds.[7]

On the other hand:

> Japan desires China to come into the war for the main purpose of eventually destroying the status of China as an independent state. By securing for herself the concessions extorted from the Germans and filling with her own nationals the vacancies created by the expulsion of the Germans in the Chinese service, she hopes to have so firmly planted her tentacles throughout China that the country will ultimately fall under her control.

Though America had included China in its appeal to neutral nations to join her in protest, and had herself declared war on Germany, there was a brief hiccup in her attitude. In June 1917, disturbed by the growing north-south split (for Sun Yat-sen was on the point of moving south to Guangzhou to set up a rival military government) and concerned at 'monarchical moves' that might lead to the collapse of China as a functioning republic, America suggested to Britain, France and Japan that they should present a united front and inform China that 'the maintenance by China of one centrally united and responsible government is of first importance both to China herself and to the world . . .'[8] and that 'the entrance of China into the war against Germany is of quite secondary importance as compared with unity and peace of China'.

George Morrison reported that the American Minister was also concerned that 'to declare war on Germany, the assent of Parliament is necessary. Now that there is no Parliament there can be no declaration unless the military act unconstitutionally. They have already been informed by the American Minister that if they do so, they can expect no financial assistance from America, nor presumably from their allies.' The response of the Allies was negative and Japan (which was financially supporting various breakaway military leaders) accused America of interfering in China's internal affairs. Morrison commented, 'Apparently Japan wished it to be thought that only she had the right to interfere in the domestic affairs of China.'[9]

American objections aside, the somewhat disunited Allies embarked upon a protracted series of increasingly negative negotiations over details of indemnity repayments and customs tariffs but such discussions and diplomatic meetings were interrupted by the dramatic events in Peking during the first week in July 1917.

A ten-day Imperial Restoration

In June 1917 General Zhang Xun, widely believed to have German financial support, marched on Peking with 5,000 men.[10] Zhang Xun was a former Qing loyalist who had accompanied the Dowager Empress Cixi on her flight from Peking when the city was occupied by foreign troops after the Boxer Rebellion in 1900 but had subsequently supported Yuan Shikai. Known for his brutality in suppressing the 'second revolution' of 1913, a brief rebellion against Yuan Shikai, Zhang Xun and his soldiers had retained the former Manchu men's hairstyle of a long plait of hair (or queue) so he was known as the 'pig-tailed General'. Zhang Xun's intention was to restore the last emperor, Puyi, to the throne and, meeting little resistance in Peking at first, he declared the accession of the emperor on 1 July 1917 with much flying of the old imperial dragon flags.

The Manchu restoration was described by Sir John Jordan as 'a typical Chinese revolutionary campaign – pure comic opera'.[11] As the Republican forces pulled themselves together, Beilby Alston reported 'Republican guns fired from the neighbourhood of the Shunzhi gate . . . their line of fire just missing the NW wall of the British Legation ... one or two shells at least burst over the Legations.'[12]

George Morrison wrote, with heavy sarcasm, to his wife on 14 July:

> We had an interesting time on Thursday. Firing was terrific. Some 30,000 or 40,000 troops were engaged in a struggle to the death in a confined area. Casualties were 29 killed (14 combatants, 15 non-combatants) and several wounded. You never heard such a terrific banging. In my district several thousands fought and one was slightly wounded.

Whilst Morrison reported that three bombs had been dropped on the imperial palace of the Forbidden City where the new emperor and his family were cowering, according to Alston it was one 'small bomb (dropped from a plane at Nanyuan airport) ... greatest consternation among the imperial family ... this small bomb, which did little material damage beyond killing some goldfish in a pool and wounding a eunuch who was standing by it, was a deciding factor in convincing the imperial family of the hopelessness of their cause.'

It was over by 12 July when the imperial dragon flags 'disappeared from buildings even more quickly than they had appeared' and Zhang Xun's troops, anxious to disappear, cut off their queues: 'pigtails began to fall rapidly outside the Temple of Heaven'.[13]

President Li Yuanhong escaped from his house to the French hospital from where he requested French diplomatic assistance to rescue his family. The young French diplomat Alexis Saint-Léger Léger was 'chosen to go by automobile to pick up the wife, daughters, son and concubines of the President of the Republic.' He waited in the family home, 'in a setting consisting of a Nile-green spittoon, a more-than-life-sized portrait of President Li and an autographed photo of Kaiser Wilhelm surrounded by his marshals ... The furniture was upholstered in rep and the clock was from Bavaria. The Bavarian clock was slow.' He finally filled three limousines with 'the goat-footed Madame Li' and 'numerous concubines dressed in plum-coloured silk' but eventually only 'Madame Li, the three daughters and the dirty child with the silver bracelets stayed ... in my lodgings for three weeks and my draperies still bear the jam smears made by the little hands of a Chinese child.'[14]

General Zhang Xun's troops were rounded up, paid off and sent home by train whilst the general, who had asked for protection in the British Legation 'in case of danger' eventually took refuge in the Dutch Legation. The Dutch Minister, Frans Beelaerts van Blokland, was described as 'very pro-German' and 'unduly benevolent to the Germans' for he had 'seen fit to recall the former German Legation guard from their place of internment outside Peking and had supplied them with arms. Furthermore, M. Beelaerts found accommodation for Zhang Xun inside the German barracks which had been in the charge of the Dutch Legation Guard since the rupture of relations ...'

The Dutch Minister asked if the British would now take charge of Zhang Xun but 'as Zhang Xun had refused the offer made to him to take refuge in His Majesty's Legation prior to and as a means of preventing the outbreak of hostilities, I declined the offer of my Dutch colleague that I should now relieve him of the task of custodian after Zhang's refusal of the very reasonable terms offered him had resulted in actual bloodshed ...'

Beelaerts who later served as Minister for Foreign Affairs and accompanied Queen Wilhelmina to exile in London in 1940–4, was described by a relative as 'very conscientious in looking after German and Austro-Hungarian interests' and a 'real stickler when it came to the observance of neutrality'.[15] His father had been a supporter of Kruger and the Afrikaners during the Boer War, 'which may have coloured Frans's attitude towards the Entente, in particular the English.' Perhaps because of this, German complicity in the Zhang Xun's uprising was hinted at and the French offered him refuge on Réunion.[16] And the Allied Powers successfully pressured the Chinese government to expel Beelaerts.

China declares war

General Zhang Xun's imperial restoration, in which President Li Yuanhong was implicated, led to President Li's resignation and 'retirement' to Tianjin on 17 July. President Li had been cautious about declaring war and joining the Allies. He was succeeded on 1 August by General Feng Guozhang with General Duan Qirui as Premier. Though neither appointment could be ratified by Parliament which was non-existent at the time, this did not stop them from assuming office and declaring war. General Duan Qirui, in particular, was keen to improve China's international standing by joining the war, despite the fact that he was negotiating secret loans to pay his army from Japan, in exchange for offering Japan the right to station troops in Shandong. This secret treaty was to totally undermine the arguments of China's negotiation team at the Versailles Peace Conference.

Warlord divisions

China's declaration of war took place against a growing crisis in the country: Sun Yat-sen formally established his breakaway military government in the southern province of Guangdong on 10 September and fighting between rival warlord generals in south-western China was intensifying. In effect, 'The country was divided into many separate, independent or semi-independent areas, each with a militarist as the supreme power.'[17]

Meyrick Hewlett, British Consul in Kunming, capital of the south-western province of Yunnan, was caught up in the fighting that had begun in 1916 and intensified throughout 1917 as the provincial armies of Sichuan and Guizhou fought the provincial army of Yunnan. The British Consulate stood on a street with a Yunnannese army barricade at one end and a Sichuanese barricade at the other. One evening, 'the Yunnanese allowed the French doctors Mouillac and Poupelain, who had been playing bridge with me, to pass and they got home; not so the French Consul, who was stopped by the Sichuanese and spent the night with me, as did Anderson of the British-American Tobacco Company, to help in case of need.'[18] Next day, Hewlett, as a 'neutral' in this cross-provincial Chinese dispute, was asked to go to the Sichuan headquarters to discuss a cease-fire as 'heavy sniping could be heard unpleasantly clearly':

> I had to climb over the Yunnan barricades, walk across the intervening space and then be pulled over the Sichuan barricades, in one case having to climb a wall by placing a table against it with a stool on the top. All the time sniping went on … Achieving a brief cease-fire, hostilities recommenced with redoubled vigour. Eventually, the city was divided between the Yunnan and Sichuan troops who in turn were divided by the Guizhou troops as being neutral, though their turn came ten weeks later …

After the departure of the Yunnanese troops, the Guizhou army destroyed a sixth of the city including much of the French consulate, leaving the Consul to take refuge with Hewlett. The British consulate was hit but no serious damage was done:

> I buried the ammunition for the Consulate General in a small courtyard to guard against the risk of a major explosion and successfully bandaged up a soldier (of unspecified allegiance) with a nearly severed ear. A few days afterwards I received a message of thanks from his commanding officer who at the same time sent me a man with a shattered arm for treatment. The bone above the elbow was protruding and of course I could do nothing; so telling him that while I was very good at ears I could do nothing with arms, I suggested he should go to the hospital run by the French doctors outside the North gate of the city. I gave him a really stiff brandy …

Economic pressure, minor betrayals

Whilst the periphery was splitting apart, discussions amongst the Allies about financial encouragement to pressure China into declaring war resumed after the excitement of Zhang Xun's imperial venture. In March 1917 China had asked for a postponement of the Boxer Indemnity for ten years without accumulation of interest, the right to increase the Customs tariff to 5 per cent and raise the import tariff.[19] The Allies pointed out that, on the declaration of war, China would immediately benefit by not having to pay the German and Austro-Hungarian share of the Indemnity, but they continued to wrangle amongst themselves offering varying inducements such as the suspension of all payment, with or without interest, just for the duration of the war. There were endless disagreements. 'The Russian minister (without instructions from his government) proposed instead of suspending the Boxer Indemnity (in which Russia has an interest of 29 per cent) the Allies should give China a special loan … the attitude of the Russian and French Ministers, supported by their Italian and Belgian colleagues indicates, in fact, their desire to drive a hard bargain with China and keep her firmly under financial control.'[20]

The Japanese also wanted to introduce changes to import taxes on cotton, not in China's favour but to protect the already enormously successful Japanese cotton industry. The Japanese knew all about fixing tariffs for when Japan achieved tariff autonomy in 1899, it had raised tariffs from less than 5 per cent to 19 per cent by 1911 but no one was prepared to grant China a similar control.[21]

Even after China had declared war, the arguments continued, held up mainly by the inability of the Italian and Russian ministers to get firm instructions from their home governments, and their proposition that 'since China had declared war on Germany without conditions, it was no longer necessary to make such great concessions.' The Italian Minister pleaded national poverty, ('the usual depleted state of the Italian Treasury' wrote Alston) and Prince Kroupensky, 'the present disorganised state of Russian finances'. It was not just Russian finances that were disorganised for the Foreign Minister, who was to be arrested and imprisoned the very next month and replaced by Leon Trotsky, was probably more worried by the state of the war and the coming revolution than arguments about percentages of China's Boxer Indemnity payments.

In September 1917, the British Legation reported (not for the first time) on the 'reservations made by the Italian and Russian Ministers [on the question of postponing Boxer Indemnity payments].[22] In view of the internal conditions in Russia, I presume it would be useless to approach the Russian government to withdraw this reservation so as to cause solidarity and community of action by the Allies and that we cannot expect the Italian government to give way on the point unless we are prepared to induce the Russian government to agree.'

As this memorandum made its way through British government departments, a note was added in red pencil, 'Appeal to the Russians when they have a government and also to the Italians at the same time.' Throughout these months of unsuccessful negotiation, China's financial position was not eased.

Major betrayals

By the time China broke off relations with Germany and Austria-Hungary in March 1917, in anticipation of declaring war on the side of the Allies and with the hope of gaining a place at the peace conference to free herself from

Japanese domination, her future had already been determined by a secret treaty. The British-Japanese Secret Treaty of 21 February 1917 included an agreement that Britain would support Japan's demands at the Peace Conference over the 'German concessions in Shandong and the German Pacific Islands'.

As Lloyd George later explained, 'You must remember that at that time the German submarine campaign had intensified. All our destroyers and torpedo boats were in the Atlantic and we had to make an instant request to Japan to supply destroyers and Japan made the most of the opportunity.'[23]

The subsequent Franco-Japanese Secret Treaty of 6 March 1917, made on the same basis, also promised Japan France's support over the occupation of Shandong, as did the Russo-Japanese Secret Treaty of 5 March 1917. In a Foreign Office minute of 16 February 1917, J.D. Gregory commented:

> In view of the commitment to Japan's post-war claims, we must ... decide whether we are morally justified in giving [China] any sort of encouragement ... in regard to possible advantages to be derived from throwing their lot in with us. Sir John Jordan thinks it would be immoral to do so without telling them about Shandong. On the other hand ... it may be legitimately argued that the case was given away by the Chinese themselves in May 1915 [by submitting to the Twenty-one Demands] and that we are accordingly released from any obligation we have previously incurred in the matter.

Balfour also judged the question of participation at a peace conference as 'hypothetical and inadmissable'. In complete ignorance of the fact that the European Allies had already effectively condemned China to defeat at the Peace Conference, China declared war and prepared to do what she could for her 'Allies'.[24]

Pressure to intern or expel German nationals

Once the Chinese government abandoned neutrality in March, the British, in particular, were determined to press for action against Germans in China. They wanted the Chinese to seize German ships that could be used by the Allies who were desperate for more shipping, to prevent German trade continuing (so that it could be replaced by British trade), and to either intern or expel German nationals.

The seizure of German ships in the harbour at Shanghai was supervised by W.F. Tyler of the Chinese Maritime Customs who had tried to volunteer for active naval service at the beginning of the war, but was told by Sir John Jordan that the Admiralty considered that he was serving his country better where he was. He was amused by this response because 'at the time I was acting as Neutrality Advisor to the Chinese Admiral, and the power most to be guarded against in that respect was Great Britain. It was a position that was anomalous and very delicate.'[25] The Inspector-General of Customs, Sir Francis Aglen, had asked him on 8 August 1914 to undertake the task of advising 'from behind the screen'. He asked the British Consul-General in Shanghai, Sir Everard Fraser, who told him that Sir John Jordan had 'cordially concurred' with his appointment (and later told Tyler, 'You are suffering like many others for the cause') but Fraser said nothing 'about the delicacy of the job – about what our mutual relationship might be. There were British, French and German gunboats on the Yangtse which had to be interned. At the river ports, the British Consuls and the Commandants of the vessels played the game; they acquiesced in disarmament as a necessary feature of the situation. The Germans were troublesome and, owing to Admiral Li's weakness, were not adequately dealt with.'

In February 1917, when America had broken off relations with the Central Powers, Tyler started planning for 'the probable course of events: a breach of relations followed eventually – absurd as it might seem – by China declaring war against the Central Powers.' On the basis of events elsewhere in the world, he assumed that German steamer captains 'would have instructions to sink their vessels and cause as much inconvenience as they could in an enemy port' and it was essential to be prepared to seize the vessels before this could happen. He was accused by 'influential Englishmen' of being alarmist and he found himself without much support.

However, 'on 14 March at 5 o'clock in the morning, an officer brought me a message from the Admiral that diplomatic relations would be broken off that day at noon.' Tyler decided, entirely on his own initiative (and contrary to his responsibility for China's neutrality in acting in advance of diplomatic events), that seizure of the ships should be carried out 'some hours before the diplomatic breach'.

> There was a factor of psychology ... I felt certain that the German captains had instructions to sink their vessels; equally I felt certain that those men – mild in their isolation and comparatively unaffected by the German crowd hypnosis – would not be keen about the doing of it. They would take steps to sink their ships at noon because they had to; but if we seized some hours earlier there would be a good excuse for non-fulfilment of these orders.

Tyler's preparations were detailed. Instructions to boarding officers stipulated that officers would only carry revolvers whilst the men would 'be armed with rifles and bayonets and with 100 rounds of ammunition. In order to prevent the vessel being scuppered, they were to proceed to the engine-room to check the Kingston valve.' A note, anticipating diplomatic events, was prepared to be handed to each ship's captain: 'I have been instructed to take charge of your vessel on the discontinuance of diplomatic relations between China and Germany. I do not take possession of your vessel but merely police charge.' It detailed the procedure for inventory and receipts and left the question of internment to others, 'Except in the matter of leaving your ship in my charge you are under no restraint whatever.'

Tyler quoted a leading article from the *North China News* which described the 'prompt, swift and effective' action by the Chinese navy, carried out with exemplary 'discipline and courtliness'. It was discovered that three out of the six German vessels seized had, indeed, been prepared for destruction.

> Taken completely by surprise, the officers of the *Sikiang* were seen to throw their bombs overboard when the Chinese naval guard boarded. This vessel had her gangways hauled up and the boarding was effected by boarding ladders. On the *Dieka Rickmers*, the Captain, having been warned by the officer of the guard of the advisableness of giving information if he had any explosives on board, decided after an interval of consideration to act on that warning, and he showed the officer four bombs in one of the engine cylinders.

The bombs were, apparently, not intended to be exploded in the cylinder, it was a place of storage.

After the crew had been taken off the *Albenga*, 'one bomb was found inside a boiler and another in the double bottom.' All the bombs found were of identical design and construction:

> They were rectangular tins containing about three pounds of dynamite fitted with a detonator and a length of Bickford fuse – a slow match that would burn for several minutes after ignition. Such a bomb would, we understand, blow a very considerable hole through a ship's bottom, or completely wreck a boiler or engine.
>
>   The fact that these bombs were of the same pattern indicates that there was a concerted and organized official scheme to sink the vessels, which was only forestalled by the promptness of the Chinese naval action.

Tyler looked at the bombs himself and was interested to discover one which contained no dynamite but was filled with signal lights, 'whose only effect would be to make a smell. That captain was determined not to sink his ship; but there were his officers to consider, and later there might be the need to explain why his bomb had not exploded; and those burnt-out signal lights would evidence that the dynamite had been defective.'

The British Government favoured the deportation of all German and Austro-Hungarian nationals, the first proposal being that they be sent to India, but this was dropped in favour of internment in Australia (although Australia subsequently got cold feet for fear of German reprisals). They proposed that the Chinese government bear the costs of deportation but in early October, the British Government was even considering bearing the costs of transportation and maintenance of some 4,000 persons itself, for in November, Sir John Jordan reported that 'the Chinese authorities have neither the courage, nor the funds, nor the necessary administrative machinery to effect a general internment. It is essential in Allied interests to get enemy residents out of China as soon as possible.'[26]

The Chinese government promulgated regulations concerning enemy subjects which did not go far enough to please the British, whose disapproval was tinged with ridicule.

> Mr Alston apparently favoured internment against deportation but points out a purely fictitious difficulty i.e. lack of tonnage when in reality there were 35,000 tons of enemy shipping in Shanghai. The Chinese, having issued a proclamation to the effect that enemy subjects would not be interned but could continue to carry on business if they liked or could leave the country, then proceed to issue elaborate regulations regarding internment camps. In fact they appear to have enjoyed an orgy of regulation-making – the regulations being as usual self-contradictory or meaningless.[27]

As this report circulated through British government departments, further notes were added, 'The Chinese government's attitude towards enemy persons generally shows how necessary it is for us to secure their deportation en bloc. Chinese surveillance of internment camps would be a farce.' One of the regulations issued proposed the confiscation of maps and explosives but stipulated that fowling pieces, aeroplanes, knapsacks and saddles should simply be 'kept by local officials for the duration'. The regulation that prohibited enemy subjects from 'travelling and undertaking picnics' called forth much British hilarity although since picnicking in the temples in the Western hills or at the summer palaces and imperial tombs was the preferred weekend activity of foreigners in Peking, it could be construed as a logical, even mildly punitive, prohibition.

Sir John Jordan wrote with some sympathy of China's efforts to comply with Allied demands for deportation of enemy subjects:

> The Chinese have committed themselves to the task and are quite willing to carry it out, but not until the Allies make good the promises they gave when China entered the War. These related chiefly to the suspension of the indemnity and the revision of the tariff. In neither case have the Allies as a body kept faith with China.[28]

Noting the months of 'fruitless discussion' on financial concessions and the abandonment of the Australian deportation plan for which China was not responsible, he stated that 'the Chinese Government in spite of internal weakness has so far loyally carried out their obligations.' In the event, repatriation of Germans (some 2,000) was terminated in 1919 after the war ended, with the betrayal of China's hopes at the Versailles Peace Conference.

By contrast with China's efforts, several commentators noted the failure of Japan to restrict German mercantile activities in Japan, despite the state of war that existed between the two countries. George Morrison reported after a visit to Japan in 1916:

> As regards Germany, the Japanese attitude is one of neutrality. The Germans in Japan carry on their business as usual. German business houses are still active. German banks are still open. There is no restriction – or rather only a very modified restriction upon the movement of Germans throughout Japan. Two explanations are given of this attitude. The military party in Japan, indoctrinated with German militarism, have never up to quite recently admitted the possibility of Germany's defeat in this war. British merchants will tell you that the benevolent treatment of Germans is due to the fear of further revelations regarding the navy scandals in which Germans and the great firm of Mitsui have been implicated. Still another explanation is given – which seems to be widely credited – that a bargain has been struck between the Germans and the Japanese which permits freedom of German activity in Japan in return for immunity of Japanese shipping from German submarines. Up to the present only one Japanese steamer of any importance has been sunk by a German submarine.[29]

A year later, he returned to the theme of immunity:

> Japan being held to have done naught in any way commensurate with her duty to her Allies, no ship of hers having been called to exchange a hostile shot with any German ship. And her mercantile fleet having enjoyed an immunity from submarine attack which is at least remarkable, not to say suspicious.

Chinese troops and ships for Europe

Although internment or deportation were issues thrust upon the Chinese by the Allies, China herself made offers to supply naval ships and troops to fight with the Allies. In a 'Very Confidential' message from Peking on 4 September 1917, the British Naval Attaché at Peking reported that two cruisers and three destroyers . . . for patrol purposes in Far Eastern waters' had been offered by a member of China's National Defence Committee.[30] Though there was some doubt that 'the practical utility of this offer, if made, may not be great, it would in my opinion be politic to give it due consideration as it would undoubtedly create an excellent effect here [in Peking] besides assisting to draw together factions in the Navy.' Although the British Admiralty 'stated that it would accept the offer if and when it is made officially', a note in the file dated 27 September 1917 stated, 'Unfortunately, the Chinese government seem to have very little hold over the Navy, the greater part of which has gone over to the Southern Party [Sun Yat-sen's Kuomintang]'.

The offer of Chinese troops to join Allied forces in Europe was complicated by French and American initiatives and very different British views on where such troops should be deployed. Sir John Jordan sent a telegraph to the Foreign Office on October 16 1917:

> The Premier informed me on 13 October that the Chinese government proposes to send from 30,000 to 40,000 [men] for co-operation with the French. He added that America was willing to provide funds to enable the Chinese government to send and equip this force. The US Minister confirms this information. I gather the French propose to ask Allied Shipping Commission to supply transports.[31]

The proposal was robustly opposed:

> The French are embarking on a policy of wasting Allied tonnage for which they will receive no military return whatever ... No one, with the exception of our military attaché in Peking has ever suggested that even the best Chinese troops would stand shellfire on the Western Front for five minutes ... The French are becoming too fertile of ideas ... in view of the fact that they are more or less dependent on us for tonnage, they are moving rather fast.

A pencilled note on the file reads, 'Personally I think the scheme idiotic.'

The British, with tonnage, some of which was required to ship the hundreds of Chinese labourers to the Western Front, and with their many other imperial fronts in mind, sent messages backwards and forwards through the War Office, Foreign Office and India Office about the possibilities of graciously taking up the offer and deploying Chinese troops elsewhere:

> The fighting value of Chinese troops is doubtful and the difficulty of transporting them to Mesopotamia or East Africa apparently insurmountable ... the effect upon the native mind of our employing Chinese would presumably be most prejudicial to our prestige ... finally there is the danger that, were we to accept the offer [of Chinese troops], Japan would insist on training and finding officers for the Chinese forces and would thus take the first step towards gaining control over the whole Chinese army ...[32]

The response of the Under-Secretary of State for Foreign Affairs, Lord Robert Cecil was: 'Chinese troops would certainly not be acceptable to the

Government of India for service in Mesopotamia' and he repeated this statement less than a week later, appending it to a despatch that the War Office was 'considering the despatch of a Chinese military force to Egypt' after yet another proposal that small bodies of troops might be 'employed in the firing line on the Gaza front and not for police or patrol duties in the Delta ... they should be under their own officers to give the Japanese no opportunity to provide officers.'[33]

In the end, despite repeated offers of naval and military assistance, no Chinese troops were deployed by the Allies anywhere. However, some 5,000 skilled Chinese mechanics and labourers were sent to support British troops in Basra and 227 died there. They were not part of the Chinese Labour Corps whose contingents continued to make their valued contribution in France and suffer injury and death. And, despite the Chinese government's seizure of German shipping in Chinese ports, leasing almost all to the Allies, and despite the offers of troops and ships, at the Versailles Peace Conference, both Britain and Japan (which had not sent a single soldier) accused China of having chosen not to contribute to the Allied cause during the war.

Chapter 8

After the war, the disappointment

Armistice

When the Armistice was declared on 11 November 1918, there was rejoicing throughout China. The American Minister, Paul Reinsch, wrote, 'Amidst troubles, Peking rejoices'.[1] He described an official reception for the Associated Powers. 'As each Minister arrived, the national air of his country was played by the Marine Band. When the Russian Minister came in, the band, without special instructions, played the old Russian Imperial hymn. Prince Koudacheff was moved, for this anthem was now outlawed in his country, he came to me in tears.' They moved to the Forbidden City which was 'massed with troops ... The President bowed to all the flags and made his address, aeroplanes appeared, dropping innumerable Chinese flags and messages of felicitation, printed in gold on red ... rockets were sent skywards, exploding. They released paper figures of animals as well as soldiers and weapons ... which floated for a long time in the air ...'

Prince Koudacheff had reason for gloom since the new Russian Bolshevik government had signed an armistice with the Germans on 15 December 1917, withdrawing from the war, and British and Japanese troops moved into Siberia. Sir John Jordan wrote at the time:

> The position of the Russian Legation and of Russia generally in China is pathetic ... Prince Koudacheff has been an excellent colleague and I feel keenly for him. The other day he received instruction to hand over charge to the next senior member of the Legation who sympathised with their political views. The offer was made successively to every member of the staff, from the Counsellor down to the latest student interpreter. All declined the honour and disassociated themselves ... the only exception being the student interpreter, who confessed to socialist leanings but was not prepared to accept the offer.[2]

China's hopes were now focused on the Peace Conference, held at Versailles from January to May 1919 which – it was expected – would be conducted on the basis of President Wilson's idealistic Fourteen Points. Both Chinese diplomats and members of the Chinese Labour Corps put their faith in President Wilson, with whom Wellington Koo travelled from America to arrive in Brest in the evening of 13 March, where they were greeted by a group of Chinese Labour Corps workers.[3] Though an ally, at the Peace Conference,

China was not accorded the same status as 'the big four', America, France, Italy (which withdrew temporarily, in April 1919, furious over not been allocated Fiume) and Great Britain, or even Japan which had the same number of official delegates (five) as the 'big four' and was occasionally allowed in to make it the 'big five' but was treated 'as something of a joke'.[4]

Shortly before the Versailles Conference began, George Morrison railed against Japan's acceptance at the top table, recalling the time in 1915 when Japan refused to permit China to join the Allied cause.[5]

> On 23 November 1915, when British, French and Russian ambassadors in Tokyo approached the Japanese government with a request that Japan would join them in bringing China into the Alliance ... Ishii, on behalf of the Japanese government peremptorily refused his consent ... at a critical time when the entry of China into the war would have been of material assistance to the Allies ... the Japanese government refused to permit that assistance ... This surely can never be forgotten.

Such activities clearly had been forgotten or ignored, for Lloyd George told his colleagues at Versailles he had never heard of the Twenty-one Demands, and the sympathies of his Foreign Minister, Arthur Balfour, were entirely with Japan. Balfour declared that China did not have the right to be handed something 'she could never have recovered for herself'.

In a letter to Lord Curzon, written on 20 September 1919, he expanded his view (having either never known or merely forgotten Yuan Shikai's offer of Chinese soldiers in the summer of 1914, nor Yuan Shikai's plea to both the UK and the USA for help in taking over Shandong). He described himself as:

> moved by contempt for the Chinese over the way they left Japan to fight Germany for Shantung, and then were not content to get Shantung back without fighting for it, but tried to maintain that it was theirs as the legitimate spoils of a war in which they had not lost a man or spent a shilling.[6]

Unaware of such views, China prepared for Versailles.

Two delegations to Versailles
In Shanghai a conference attempting to make peace between the Peking government and the government that Sun Yat-sen had established in the south in 1917, was failing rapidly, with the result that there were two Chinese delegations sent to Versailles, one from the north and one from the south. The official, northern, delegation was led by the Foreign Minister, Lü Zhengxiang [Lou Tsen-tsiang] (at whose eighteen-course dinner party in 1913, Sir John Jordan had removed his jacket and his decorations) and included advisors, such as G.E. Morrison and senior diplomats, Wei Chenzu,

THE FOURTEEN POINTS

1. Open diplomacy; no secret treaties
2. Freedom of the seas
3. Free trade
4. Arms reduction
5. Colonial claims settled
6. Independent development of Russia
7. Belgium evacuated and restored
8. Recovery of France's lost territory
9. New Italian borders
10. New Balkan borders
11. Autonomy for the peoples of Austria-Hungary
12. A new Turkey, with autonomy for non-Turkish peoples
13. Polish independence
14. An association of nations to guarantee independence of all states.

[Text & comment: http://www.ourdocuments.gov/doc.php?flash=true&doc=62]

On 8 January 1918, President Wilson proposed to the US Congress his Fourteen Points as a basis of peace after the war. Apart from its high moral tone, the speech carried great weight around the world, because the belligerents were exhausted, bankrupt, starving and stalemated. The Entente Powers and (after their defeat) the Central Powers depended on America for food. They were massive debts between the Allies and to America, which (hopefully) might defer or waive their debts and provide new money.

American foreign policy was normally not interventionist. In 1801 President Thomas Jefferson spoke of 'peace, commerce and honest friendship with all nations, entangling alliances with none'. President Wilson was re-elected in 1916 largely because he had kept America out of the Great War. It was against the grain of history for America to take sides in a war between European nations and then to take a decisive lead in framing the peace. No Iowa hog farmer would want to take up arms over the Polish corridor or the invasion of Manchuria.

America had to be woken from its isolationist slumber; the brutal manner of Germany's attacks on American shipping in early 1917 served that purpose. America then devoted huge enthusiasm and organisational skills to the war. But once peace was made, was there a risk that America would revert to its traditional isolationism and repudiate Wilson's Fourteen Points?

Minister in Brussels, He Weide, Minister to France and Alfred Sze (1877–1958) Minister to the Court of St James, although its most impressive member was Wellington Koo, an American-educated lawyer and diplomat, whose legal finesse and eloquence impressed all who heard it as he argued China's case for the return of ex-German concessions in Shantung, now held by the Japanese.

Appointed Chinese Ambassador to the United States in 1915, Wellington Koo had had an informal conversation with America's President Wilson just before leaving for Paris and had been invited to travel on the same boat as the American delegation, which he regarded as a promising sign. Wellington Koo and many others in China had been encouraged by President Wilson's Fourteen Points, a vision of how peace might be achieved and international relations be conducted in the future, enunciated on 18 January 1918.[7] In point five, for example, Wilson had advocated 'free, open-minded and absolutely impartial adjustment of all colonial claims, based upon the principle that in determining all such questions of sovereignty the interests of the population concerned must have equal weight', a message that offered hope to the Chinese.

The American minister, Dr Reinsch, had organised the translation of many of President Wilson's speeches into Chinese and a volume was published in Shanghai in 1918 so they were quite widely known and much was expected of them. Although China was nobody's colony, foreign occupation of Shandong and the Treaty Ports and leased territories like Weihaiwei, all governed by extraterritoriality, felt to many like colonial occupation and invasion of sovereignty.

In France, Wellington Koo charmed the French Prime Minister Georges Clemenceau who was unimpressed by the Japanese delegation, complaining of their ugliness. Wellington Koo, he declared was, 'like a young Chinese cat, Parisian of speech and dress, absorbed in the pleasure of patting and pawing the mouse, even if it was reserved for the Japanese. His irresistible flow of eloquence used to irritate Baron Matsui [Japanese Ambassador to France], a massive chunk of Japanese mentality . . .'[8]

Sun Yat-sen's rival military government in southern China proposed a joint delegation of northern and southern representatives (three to two) but this was refused and, in the end, only one southerner, C.T. Wang (Wang Zhenting, 1882–1961), was added to the list with the other official delegates. That there were any southern representatives was a surprise since Sun Yat-sen had written in 1917 against China's plan to declare war, arguing for strict neutrality and stating that since Germany had done less harm to China than the Allied countries, it would be better to declare war on the latter. He had also argued that entering the war might cause trouble within China which would allow Japan to take further advantage. However, after the complete

FROM NUMBER ONE GOOD MAN TO PARIAH

President Wilson arrived in Paris to a tumultuous welcome in December 1918. One Chinese called him 'the number one good man in the world'. Mao Zedong, then a student in Changsha, thought that America might be a good model for the future. Despite public acclaim, the allied leaders were sceptical. Contrasting them with the Ten Commandments, Clemenceau dismissed them by saying '*Le bon dieu n'avait que dix*', while Lloyd George mocked the 'sacred text'.

Britain did not want the natives of its empire to have a say in their future. Italy demanded territory occupied by Croats, Tyroleans and Slovenes. France wanted to squeeze vast compensation out of Germany. Japan did not want to restore Shandong to China. Germans soon learnt that Wilson's idealistic peace plans did not apply to them.

« Débarrassez-moi de ce chiffon de papier. »

Welcome to Wilson Outglows Pomp of Napoleonic Days

Even Clemenceau, Who Thought He Knew Paris, Is Amazed and Declares Fervid Greeting Is the Greatest Ever Accorded in History of the World

President Clemenceau is portrayed in *l'Humanité* as telling one of his minions to ditch the Fourteen Points, *ce chiffon de papier*, or not worth the paper they were written on. At the end of the day, Wilson's idealism was wrecked not only by the self-interest of the victorious nations, but also by the US Senate which rejected American membership of the League of Nations. China's disillusionment with Wilson was total when he abandoned the principle of self-determination of peoples and allowed Shandong to remain under Japanese control. One slogan summed up Chinese disillusionment with Wilson and his Fourteen Points FOURTEEN=ZERO!

NOTE: *Atlanta Constitution* cartoon 15 December, 1918. *New York Tribune* headline, 18 December 1918; Clemenceau cartoon, *l'Humanité* 17 June 1919.

break with the Peking government and the formal establishment of the military government in the south in September 1917, Sun's government changed direction and declared war on Germany.[9]

Sun Yat-sen's representative, C.T. Wang, was the son of a Chinese Methodist Minister, 'a prize graduate of both a prominent mission school in China and a leading university in America [Yale], an active director of the YMCA and the leading Chinese Christian in China at that time.'[10] Though C.T. Wang had been appointed to lobby America for southern representation, Sun Yat-sen's government suddenly refused to sanction his participation and appointed its Vice Minister of Foreign Affairs, Wu Chaoshu, as the southern representative in Paris. Wu never managed to get to the conference where C.T. Wang participated, working with Wellington Koo.[11]

Even the journey to Versailles was fraught with difficulty, apparently caused by continuing Japanese provocation, according to one account. Lü Zhengxiang's Belgian wife had a narrow escape during the train trip through Korea:

> At an early morning stop of the train in Korea, Mrs Lu, an early riser, was walking up and down the station platform for a little exercise. Two Japanese soldiers crowded Mrs Lu off the platform; she fell almost three feet to the ground below. Though a rather large woman she was fortunately not seriously hurt, but she screamed so loudly that she awakened her husband. He rushed out in his pyjamas and rescued Mrs Lu, but when they returned to their stateroom, they found all Dr Lu's government papers relating to the Versailles Treaty had been stolen. Only the Japanese government was interested in these papers.[12]

Arriving at the Hotel Lutétia in Paris, Lü Zhengxiang and his party found that the southern delegation was also staying there. This enhanced the atmosphere of mistrust and mutual suspicion, despite the fact that both sides held the same ambitions. There were the mysteriously mislaid papers, accusations against Lü of bribes taken from Japan and (against Wellington Koo) of improper liaisons. Recently widowed, Koo was accused of consorting with a Japanese woman. In fact he was courting Huang Huilan, the Overseas Chinese daughter of the Indonesian sugar king, to whom he became engaged in November 1920.[13]

Secret Treaties

Lü Zhengxiang, who was dogged by reports that he had taken bribes from the Japanese, became increasingly depressed throughout the conference, frightening his wife by disappearing for days (just as Chinese politicians did in China to avoid difficult moments). Both he and Wellington Koo were unaware of the secret treaties that Russia, Britain, France and Italy had made with Japan in early 1917, promising to support Japan in its claims to Shandong, in exchange for desperately needed armaments and ships. However, the delegation from Sun Yat-sen's government in the south which, despairing of support from Europe or America, was in contact with the Socialist International in Paris and increasingly drawn to Bolshevik Russia, received copies of the treaties (with Russia at least) from a Russian journalist in Paris.

Eugene Chen, an Overseas Chinese born in Trinidad, who had trained as a lawyer in London and embarrassed the British Legation in Peking when editing the outspoken, anti-Japanese *Peking Gazette*, was a member of the Sun Yat-sen delegation. To his surprise:

> pulling out papers from the large envelope, he started to read the copies of the secret treaties made by the Western powers and Japan regarding, 'the rape of China' or the 'Shantung question' ... These secret documents had fallen into Bolshevik hands after the Communist revolution in 1917, when they had gotten hold of the Czarist files and archives. Eager to make trouble at Versailles, the Russians were more than glad to give Eugene the evidence of the betrayal of China.[14]

In fact, the Russians seem to have been distributing damaging copies of secret treaties in which the Czarist government participated with the Allies quite widely to the delegates to the Versailles Peace Conference. They revealed details of the Anglo-French carve-up of the old Ottoman Empire in the Sykes-Picot agreement of 1916 to the Arabs, causing a similar uproar.[15]

It is not clear how much even Woodrow Wilson knew about the secret treaties signed by Lloyd George and Clemenceau. His biographer suggests that when Wilson arrived in Paris for the conference, 'this [discussion with the Japanese delegation and mention of the secret Anglo-Japanese agreement of 1917] was practically the first Wilson had heard of this secret treaty.'[16] His Secretary of State, Robert Lansing, told the Senate Foreign Relations Committee in August 1919 that he had no knowledge of the secret treaties before the Peace Conference. When the British Foreign Secretary Balfour went, unwillingly, to America in April 1917 to brief President Wilson who had just declared war on Germany, it does not seem that he took the texts of the secret agreements with him. As one Foreign Office official wrote, 'the trouble is that there is absolutely no record here of what documents were taken by Balfour or what were subsequently sent to him ... it is therefore simply a question of memory, in which, as you know, Balfour is not particularly strong.'[17]

That President Wilson may not have known about his European Allies' secret treaties was bad enough, but the most damaging secret treaty of all was the Sino-Japanese Treaty of September 1918, in which the Chinese government acceded to Japan's occupation of Jiaozhou and arrangements for the management of the Ji'nan–Qingdao railway, in return for a 25 million yen loan. Japan's chief negotiator at the Conference, Foreign Minister Baron Makino alluded to this 'agreement' at a meeting in the Quai d'Orsay on 28 January 1919. It is clear from the transcript of the meeting, which was attended by thirty-four people, including President Wilson, Clemenceau, Lloyd George, Orlando and their advisors and the Japanese and Chinese delegations, that the 'agreement' was quite unknown to all but the Japanese, and Wellington Koo was shocked to discover its existence.[18] Whilst he would argue that earlier 'treaties' had been forced upon neutral China by Japan, this one was more difficult to explain away.

Although the end result had already been determined in 1917 by the Allies' secret treaties, the handover of German concessions in Shandong to Japan was not made without argument. From December 1918 Paris filled with the representatives of twenty-seven nations, with advisors, lawyers, journalists and economists, and the delegates to the conference working on fifty commissions investigating different aspects of the war and the content of the peace treaty.

Away from the larger sessions, from 24 March 1919, the 'Big Four', Clemenceau, Lloyd George, Woodrow Wilson and Prime Minister Orlando of Italy, met almost daily, in comfort and in secret, usually in President Wilson's residence in the Hôtel Murat, occasionally in Clemenceau's gloomy office or Lloyd George's apartment, for 145 sessions of private discussion intended to sort out the world's problems by themselves, including the relationship between China and Japan over Shandong.

Harold Nicolson, a junior member of the British delegation deplored not only the secrecy of these meetings but the fact that the 'Big Four' devoted so much time to details of borders and populations, largely because there had been no discussion between the Allies of what sort of peace treaty they were trying to achieve. The French Ambassador to Washington had presented a programme of procedure to President Wilson in November 1918 but this had been ignored by Wilson who did not like the tone of the message. Nicolson noted that the effect of ignoring the programme was 'deplorable in the extreme'. He also revealed how often the Big Four were ignorant of the background of the matters they were deciding, with Lloyd George declaring that he had never heard of Teschen (or the Twenty-One Demands) and President Wilson hampered by 'the slowness' of his 'mental processes …'[19]

Present at some of these meetings, Nicolson recorded 'the tired and contemptuous eyebrows of Clemenceau, the black button boots of Woodrow Wilson, the rotund and jovial gestures of Lloyd George's hands, the infinite languor of Mr Balfour slowly uncrossing his knees …'[20]

The difficulties the Big Four faced were demonstrated by the departure of Prime Minister Orlando in late April, furiously disappointed by the refusal of his colleagues to acknowledge Italy's claim to Fiume and Dalmatia. Italy had joined the Allies and declared war on Germany and Austria-Hungary in May 1915, after signing the secret Treaty of London (April 1915) by which Britain, France and Russia promised Italy a large part of Slovenia and the northern Dalmatian coast. Thus Orlando came to Paris assuming that the terms of the treaty would be followed, but President Wilson, having already compromised his Fourteen Points over Tyrol and the Polish Corridor, explained to him that the Treaty of London had to be set aside.[21] His explanation was that, since Austria-Hungary no longer existed, the terms of the Treaty of London no longer applied and did not have to be followed. In the light of the arguments over Shandong, this ready abandonment of a secret pre-war treaty is significant.

Wilson also had to face considerable pressure from American public opinion. There was hostility to Japanese immigration, expressed most strongly in California, a problem also faced by Lloyd George since both Canada and Australia were firmly against Japanese (and Chinese) immigration, so the treatment of Japan, as a major ally at the Peace Conference, was a delicate matter.

Chapter 9

Anatomy of a Betrayal: the interpreter's account

Clemenceau's official military interpreter, Paul Mantoux, recorded the exchanges between the Big Four, including those concerning China and Japan, and they reveal the development of the arguments from a mood of initial complacency, through intense pressure on the Japanese delegation (which had almost no effect at all and may have entrenched the Japanese position) and considerable hypocrisy over adherence to, or abandonment of, international treaties, whether signed under duress or in secret.

On **29 March 1919**, Wilson, Clemenceau, Lloyd George and Orlando met, primarily to discuss Hungary. President Wilson, aware of the Japanese delegation's anger at being excluded from these private sessions began:

> **Wilson**: I have something to say about our meetings. We ought to explain to the Japanese why we are meeting without them. I worry about upsetting them.
> **Clemenceau**: The truth is that we meet to look at a small number of specific questions in which, in fact, Japan has no interest.
> **Wilson**: True, but should we not tell them, in order to avoid difficulties?
> **Clemenceau**: I agree, although I think there are questions that are better discussed between ourselves. It would be easy to let them know the nature of these questions and we could add that we will invite them here as soon as possible.
> **Lloyd George**: When we discuss the future of the German colonies, their presence will be necessary.
> **Clemenceau**: When can we get back to Klotz's project on reparations?
> **Lloyd George**: I'm ready.
> **Wilson**: So am I.

At this stage, Wilson was anxious not to upset the Japanese, but all seemed to agree that the basic question that might concern them was the future of German colonies as a whole, including the Pacific Islands that were of interest to the US (because of their relative proximity to the Philippines, and to Australia and New Zealand for the same reason) and the subject was not yet posed as 'the Shandong question'.

*   *   *

Despite their apparent concern for the Japanese delegation, on **15 April**, Wilson, Clemenceau, Orlando and the British Foreign Secretary, Arthur Balfour, discussed Luxembourg, Lemburg and territorial questions such as the Danish frontier, Heligoland, the Belgian frontier, Danzig and Marienwerder, before Balfour raised the question of submarine cables in the hands of the Japanese:

Balfour: Japan has a demand: they want to keep the three lines they have taken over. One of those cable lines belongs to a private company and the Japanese are prepared to purchase it.

Wilson: I have an observation to make. All these submarine cables, as well as the other important lines across the Pacific, pass through a small island called Yap [one of the Caroline islands, previously in German hands and captured by the Japanese]. I want this island to be internationalised because if it belonged to the Japanese, they could, at whim, cut communications between the different parts of the Pacific, especially between the US and the Philippines.

Balfour: And there is still the question of Jiaozhou.

Wilson: For China, it is not only for economic reasons that they want to get rid of all foreign concession in Shandong. It is because the area evokes the most sacred and historic memories [as the birthplace of Confucius] that she is particularly keen to remove foreign influence. On the other hand, what the Japanese want above all is not Jiaozhou, which they have offered to hand back to China, but a concession in Shandong. My sympathy is with China, and we should not forget that in the future, the greatest danger to the world could well arise in the Pacific region.

Balfour: When Japan entered the war, China being neutral, Japan demanded to hold on to what they could take from Germany. We consented. Since then, there has been a treaty between Japan and China. We have asked for it but have heard nothing so far. They say that they [the Japanese] have agreed to return to China that which they have taken from the Germans. But they also say that given the sacrifices they made in order to take Jiaozhou, it should be ceded to them, so that they can return it to China later. It is a matter of national pride.

Wilson: We must first of all see the Sino-Japanese treaty. The Japanese are very tricky in negotiations. I know from experience that they are very ingenious in the interpretation of treaty terms ... [He is presumably referring to the sinister verbal contradictions of the Lansing–Ishii agreement.]

Clemenceau [changing the subject]: We still have to hear this week from the powers directly concerned in the treaty with Germany: Belgium, Poland and Bohemia. We must give each one a morning.

*   *   *

On **18 April**, Orlando, Wilson, Clemenceau and Lloyd George met to discuss the borders of western Poland.

Wilson: I found out this morning about the two treaties between China and Japan on the subject of Jiaozhou. The first envisaged that after ceding Jiaozhou to Japan for the Peace Treaty, it would be returned to China on condition that Jiaozhou Bay be opened to Japanese trade, and a Japanese concession be established on a site chosen by the Japanese government. Subsequently, China and Japan signed another treaty relating to the railway between Jiaozhou and Ji'nan by which China retained the power of civil administration of the territory around the railway but shared policing and railway administration with Japan, as was done before with Germany.

Lloyd George: For the moment, we are only concerned with what we need to include in our treaty with Germany. I do not see why Jiaozhou should be treated differently from all the other German overseas possessions which we have decided should be handed over by the Germans to the Five Great Powers to deal with as they see fit.

Wilson: That is also Lansing's opinion [the US Secretary of State] and I think it is the best solution. It would be useful to have a serious conversation with the Japanese on the subject. It is not in their interest to make an enemy of China; the future of the two countries is closely linked. We should advise the Japanese to be generous with the Chinese and promise them, if they follow our advice, to encourage their peaceful relations with the Chinese Republic. It would help us maintain our authority if we, too, publicly renounced our spheres of influence in China. I do not think that these zones are of any great benefit, but we are concerned with the maintenance of peace in the Far East. I fear great danger to the world if we do not take care.

Lloyd George: We could look into the question, on condition that the principle of the 'open door' is maintained in China ...

Wilson: In my opinion, once the fever of Bolshevism dies down, Europe will be spared another great war for a long time, but I fear it is not the same for the Far East. I'd compare the seeds of conflict which are developing there to sparks, hidden under a thick blanket of leaves, which spread invisibly over the months, until they suddenly burst forth in one of those great forest fires that we sometimes see in America. This is what we must try to avoid.

Lloyd George: We will tell the Japanese that the formula for Jiaozhou will be the same for all other German overseas possessions.

Wilson: If the Japanese are on our side, they must follow the same methods as we do.

Lloyd George: As far as spheres of influence are concerned, if China is open to the commerce of all nations, I think the British public will accept our renunciation of a privilege that is purely nominal.

Lloyd George's proposal for Jiaozhou was adopted. Wilson and Lloyd George seem to have felt that they had settled the matter between themselves and, with Japan, theoretically, on their side, there the matter might have rested, but for the obdurate refusal of the Japanese to accept the idea that Jiaozhou should be treated like all other German overseas possessions. Japan was insistent that her rights in Shandong should form part of the treaty, not be left for later discussion.

*   *   *

On that basis, on **22 April**, Wilson, Clemenceau, Lloyd George and Orlando (who was to leave Paris a couple of days later in tears over the treachery over the Treaty of London) summoned the Japanese delegates, Foreign Minister Baron Makino and Viscount Chinda, the Japanese Ambassador in London.

Clemenceau to President Wilson: This morning I re-read our treaty with Japan. It ties us to them, just as it does Great Britain. I thought I should let you know.

Baron Makino (reading out a long statement): On 15 August 1914, Japan sent an ultimatum to Germany, calling on her to hand over the leased territory of Jiaozhou. As Germany did not respond within the fixed period, a military action ensued, carried out with Great Britain. Jiaozhou was taken in November 1914.

In January 1915, a first negotiation [he refers to the contentious Twenty-one Demands in this emollient fashion] began between Japan and China over Jiaozhou and the possession of Germany in Shandong province in order to assure that it would be impossible for Germany to regain her position in China after the war and become, once again, a danger to the Far East. The Convention of 25 May 1915 was the result of this negotiation. By this, Japan declared herself prepared to hand back Jiaozhou to China at the end of the war, on condition that the bay remained open to international trade, that a Japanese concession be established on the bay, and that a retrospective agreement sort out the possessions and privileges of the Germans in China.

At the beginning of 1917, Japan, in agreement with the Allies, did everything she could to persuade China to abandon neutrality. In March 1917, the Republic of China broke off diplomatic relations with Germany and declared war in August. In September 1918 ... there was a new exchange of notes between China and Japan dealing with matters left undecided in the previous Convention. Japan promised to dismantle the civil administration she had set up along the Qingdao railway. It was agreed that the Chinese would police the line, with Japanese instructors and supervisors. The administration of the line and the construction of new railway lines would be shared between Japan and China. At the same time, the Chinese took out a loan of 25 million yen.

Japan is prepared to return Jiaozhou with conditions that seem perfectly just if you consider what she did to take the territory from the Germans. The Treaty of 1918 simply completes that of 1915. To take any other route would be to run counter to agreements made by both parties.

The Chinese delegation claims that her declaration of war with Germany *ipso facto* annuls the German lease on Jiaozhou ... We feel you will do right by Japan, taking into account the efforts she has made during the war, and do so by not offending her national honour.

Wilson: And the underwater cables mentioned in the text, did they belong to Germany?

Makino: Yes, they were the property of the German government.

Wilson: I have tried to explain to you the results of the conversations I had yesterday with Clemenceau and Lloyd George. You know my views and I'd like my colleagues to explain theirs.

Lloyd George: We are in the same position with Japan as we are with Italy. We have made agreements to which we must hold [an extraordinary statement as they were about to abandon the Treaty of London]. As for Jiaozhou, we are bound by the Convention of 1917, signed by our Ambassador in Tokyo. The question that remains is whether the final fate of the territory of Jiaozhou should be mentioned in the treaty we sign with Germany. In the Anglo-Japanese Treaty of 1917, Great Britain agreed to support the claims of Japan in Jiaozhou and Shandong. The Japanese made similar promises over the territories south of the equator [the Marianas and Carolinas]. I do not think it necessary in the treaty with Germany to set out how territories seized by the Japanese will be reassigned, any more than those which will be returned to the Dominions [Australia and New Zealand]. It should be enough to say that Germany loses those territories. What becomes of them is our business. We will ask for a mandate from the League of Nations for Australia and New Zealand, and I'm sure Japan will support us in this.

Makino: Certainly, for the islands south of the equator.

Lloyd George: This has nothing to do with Germany, it is for us to decide. I'm prepared to support Japan in what she has requested. But if she insists that her rights be mentioned in the treaty with Germany, Australia and South Africa will insist on the same treatment. We would have to sort out the mandates and how the system would function, and we do not have time to do this before our negotiations with Germany.

Chinda: Do you plan to do the same with Jiaozhou and the South Pacific? The system of mandates applies to populations incapable of self-government, which does not apply to Jiaozhou. If you wish to delay the solution and only ask Germany to sign a clause renouncing her claims, then it is simply a question of time. But we have an order from our government that if the territories and rights that we claim are not put into our hands so that we can fulfil our obligations to China, then we should not sign the treaty with Germany.

Makino: Our treaty with China must be carried out. Its terms are known in China and if it is ignored, this will be a serious matter for Japan.

Chinda: It is a simple matter. There is a Convention between China and Japan. There is no need for a long discussion and we are not convinced that a delay will help at all.

As Japanese tempers were clearly rising, President Wilson started asking for details of the proposed management of the railway and of the mines in the Jiaozhou area, before Lloyd George, who had to represent the views of the British Empire pointed out that his difficulty was that 'Mr Hughes [Prime Minister of Australia] will certainly say, "You have put Jiaozhou in the treaty, why have you not included the cession of New Guinea to Australia?"' [Baron Katō elsewhere referred to Hughes as 'a peasant'.]

Wilson: Once again, I am the only one who is a truly independent judge of the matter. Clemenceau and Lloyd George are tied by their agreements. Personally, I am not convinced that England and Japan, in signing their treaty, had a clear right to dispose of the Pacific Islands.

Lloyd George: They were German islands, the property of the enemy.

Wilson: Peace in the Far East depends upon good relations between China and Japan. That is what concerns me. I see that there are pre-determined agreements which leave us with our hands tied. But if Japan does not demonstrate to the entire world her desire to help China achieve the same independence and the same freedom to develop as other nations, if Japan does not show that she wants, not to impose, but to help her with her capital and technological superiority, then suspicion and hostility will be created in China. It must be acknowledged that the relationship between Japan and China is not one of mutual respect, but this must be created for the future of peace in the Far East. What I fear is that if Japan sticks firmly to the terms of these treaties, she will appear to be thinking only of her own rights and not of her duties ... I should like to see the treaty make provision for the Five Powers to act as trustees in the matter of the ending of rights previously held in China by Germany. The

Five Powers could then look into how the treaties between Japan and China on the one side and those between Japan, France and Great Britain, should be carried out, and how they could be modified as necessary, not through external pressure but with the consent of the interested parties themselves ...

I have another proposal, which is that we agree that all powers who have rights of extraterritoriality, of stationing troops etc., in China, agree to renounce them at the same time, so that China would be on the same footing as all the other great nations with no other sovereign nations having designs on her territory. As you know, there are plenty of inflammatory elements in China, and we must be careful not to light a fire that no one can put out. For no nation on earth can control a nation of 400,000,000 souls. You also know China's feelings about Shandong, associated with her oldest and most sacred traditions. I fear that careless action could provoke a movement in China based upon the most profound sentiments of the soul.

I must add that I respect international agreements, even if I might have preferred that they had not been signed, and I do not propose to ignore them.

Baron Makino assured the company of Japan's desire to 'do everything that will aid the prosperity of our neighbours'.

Wilson: I have a better idea of where we stand now. Do you want to meet the Chinese here? Or would you prefer to explain your position directly to them? As they are members of the Conference, we cannot reach any final conclusion without their presence, and their consent.

Makino: It is appropriate to hear them. However, we do not wish to have any discussion with them. When there are preconceived ideas, it takes time to dismiss them. I greatly regret the misunderstanding that exists, but we will not be able to dispel it that way.

Lloyd George: Do you mean Japan would prefer to speak to China without us, or meet them here?

Makino: What I want to say is that we will not discuss it with them.

Wilson: In that case we must see the Chinese right away.

Lloyd George: Should we not take advantage of this moment to tell the Japanese plenipotentiaries what we have been doing these last few days? We have sorted out problems which do not concern Japan, such as the question of Danzig and the Sarre. The only question which concerns Japan is that of reparations ... The problem of the Kiel Canal which might interest you, is not completely sorted.

Makino: When are you inviting the Chinese delegation? We do not wish to appear before you as supplicants.

Wilson: The Chinese are rather afraid of you, and I think it would be best if we hear them on their own so that they can explain themselves freely.

Chinda: That is desirable. What we do not want is a direct discussion with them.

Wilson: We will inform them of the statements you have made this morning.

Makino: We insist upon the manner of the handover of Jiaozhou to China. It must be handed back directly by Japan. Our government insists on this.

The same afternoon, Lü Zhengchang and Wellington Koo were summoned (without the Japanese delegation) to meet Clemenceau, Lloyd George and Woodrow Wilson. Prime Minister Orlando was not present.

Wellington Koo argues against treaties signed under duress
Lü Zhengchang and Wellington Koo, Chinese delegates, are introduced.

Wilson: You know our interest in the Jiaozhou affair. We saw the Japanese this morning. The problem is complicated by prior agreements. It appears that at the moment China entered into the War there existed an exchange of notes between China and Japan dated 25 May 1915. Japan promised, after the cession of the territory of Jiaozhou by the Germans, that the territory would be returned to China: the Chinese government took note of this declaration. Another exchange of notes took place in 1918 in which Japan set out conditions which China accepted. In the meantime, France and Great Britain had signed treaties with Japan in which they agreed to support Japan's claims at the Peace Conference with reference to German concessions in China and the German islands of the Northern Pacific for which Japan would support British claims about the Southern Pacific.

Lloyd George: You must remember that at that moment, the submarine campaign had intensified. All our torpedo boats and anti-torpedo boats were in the Atlantic. We had to make an immediate request to Japan to send us destroyers and Japan took the best advantage she could. We were in a very difficult situation.

Wilson: You see how embarrassing this is. Lloyd George has explained the circumstances in which Britain signed the treaty with Japan; M. Clemenceau says that his treaty with Japan was even more formal.

When you explained your position at the Quai d'Orsay [in front of the Council of Ten] your argument was that your declaration of war with Germany annulled your treaties with that country. That is true but it did not annul your treaties with Japan, in particular the convention that you signed after the declaration of war.

My proposal is that territories and rights in dispute should be handed to the trusteeship of the five Great Powers. They will try to find an amicable modification of the treaties. At the same time, they will themselves make a proclamation of a general renunciation of spheres of influence in China, of extraterritoriality and all the privileges until now accorded to foreign powers on Chinese soil so that China stands on an equal footing with the other powers.

Japan is against the first part of this proposal. We are in a difficult position because of the treaties tying England and France.

When I asked the Japanese what was the exact significance of the preconditions they impose on the retrocession of Jiaozhou, they said that it was because of the three mines that belong to the Ji'nan–Qingdao railway company. These mines, as well as the railway itself, will be run jointly by China and Japan. The Japanese say that they are prepared to remove their civil administration from the area traversed by the railway, leaving troops stationed only at the terminal stations. Even these troops would be withdrawn if a general agreement to renounce all foreign privileges in China was agreed by all the powers. The Japanese say that their only desire is to co-operate with China. You must tell us what you make of their proposition.

Wellington Koo: The treaties we signed with the Japanese were the result of a form of ultimatum.

Lloyd George: What was this ultimatum?

Wellington Koo: In January 1915, after the seizure of Qingdao, the port was open for commerce. The Chinese government demanded the removal of Japanese troops who occupied the interior of the province up to 200 or 250 miles from the sea. On the pretext of regarding this as an inimical act, Japan presented Twenty-one Demands to China. The first of these was that Japan would henceforth supply political advisors to the Chinese government.

We resisted as best we could. Tired of delays, on 7 May 1915, Japan launched an ultimatum, demanding a response within 24 hours, failing which, she would take such measures as she judged necessary. This ultimatum left China in a state of consternation. Europe was preoccupied with the war and could do nothing.

Lloyd George: Did you not appeal to the United States?

Wilson: Yes, we protested against Japan's attempt to deny China's sovereignty. The Japanese tried to keep it secret but we knew about it.

Wellington Koo: Secrecy was imposed on us with severe threats … The treaty we signed was the result of the ultimatum. Thus it is very different from a treaty that is freely agreed. Japanese troops remained in Shandong province and their presence there gave rise to incidents and disorder. There have been endless complaints, and China has made several demands for the removal of these troops. Japan has ignored these demands. On the contrary, she has set up a Japanese administration all along the railway, for more than 250 miles with Japanese courts and Japanese police following Japanese laws and regulations. There is serious agitation in Shandong province. The Chinese government fears that it will end in violence. It would welcome an amicable solution.

Lloyd George: Did the Germans have police all along the railway?

Wellington Koo: No, the line was protected by Chinese troops.

Lloyd George: So, by your treaty, the Japanese obtained more than the Germans. If you had to choose between your treaty with the Japanese and the simple transfer of German rights and privileges to Japan, which would you prefer?

Wellington Koo: Japan is so close to us and is so strongly established in Manchuria where it has troops and controls the railway to Peking, that the presence of Japan in Shandong has created a much more serious situation than with the Germans. Peking would be caught in a pincer movement [between Manchuria and Shandong].

Lloyd George: But, and this is a question for England and France, too, if you had to choose between the transfer to Japan of the rights enjoyed by the Germans or the execution of your Sino-Japanese treaty, which would you choose?

Wellington Koo: If we had signed the treaty willingly, there might have been a choice.

Lloyd George: I repeat the question. We are not bound by the Sino-Japanese treaty. Do you want to consult your colleague on this?

Wellington Koo: I have consulted him. In the Sino-Japanese treaty, restitution by Japan is purely nominal. If you compare the two treaties, I think that, all things considered, the German treaty is more limited. I must stress the dangerous situation that could potentially arise should Japan be granted only the same rights as those enjoyed by the Germans. We only ask for that which will maintain peace in the Far East. The painful experiences of the last three years in Shandong have made this clear to us. I want you to understand the exigencies of the situation.

Wilson: This morning I tried to speak as if I was representing the interests of China. I stressed the importance of the resolution of this problem to peace in the Far East and the world. It is essential to all of us that China should be treated on an equal basis, with an 'open door' to commerce with all nations, in their interests and her own. We find ourselves in an extremely delicate situation. The United States protested at the time against the Twenty-one Demands Japan wanted to impose on you.

Lloyd George: I remember that Sir Edward Grey [British Foreign Minister at the time] did so too.

Wilson: We are trying to get ourselves, as best as possible, out of a difficult situation. The United States is not tied by any previous agreements. Since this war began through the protest of the western nations against the violation of a treaty, we must, above all, respect treaties, although I deplore the conditions which led you to sign your treaty with Japan in 1915.

Lloyd George: It was a different situation in September 1918 when the second Sino-Japanese treaty was signed, because by then, victory was on our side.

Wellington Koo: The treaty of 1918 simply completed that of 1915.

Wilson reads the treaty of 1918.

Lloyd George: Our treaty with the Japanese only envisaged the transfer of the rights of the Germans to the Japanese. I would like to see the two [treaties] examined and compared by experts who could tell us which is more favourable to China. We will also give the Chinese delegation time to make an examination. This is our only possible course since we are tied by our treaty with Japan. If the transfer, pure and simple, of German rights to Japan is the least unfavourable course for China, this is all that we are bound to offer Japan. We do not have to offer Japan the benefit of the terms of a treaty signed under duress and behind our backs.

Wilson: I remember the nature of the ultimatum. Through the Twenty-one Demands, Japan wanted to provide political advisors to the Chinese government, to play a part in the policing of all the major cities. She demanded a monopoly – a half share – of all arms and munitions sales and a dominant position in the exploitation of all the mines of central China. The Chinese were forced to accept some of these terms.

Lloyd George: Are they still in place?

Wellington Koo: Yes, which is why we are asking for the support of the Conference.

Wilson: Japan, as well as China, and all of us will be a member of the League of Nations. All members of the League of Nations guarantee the territorial integrity and national independence of the others. That way, China will have the protection she has never had before, and we, on our side, will have the right to intervene in the Far East, which we have never had before. When we protested in 1915, according to international law, Japan could say to us, 'This has nothing to do with you'. But the founding Act of the League of Nations states that anything that threatens the peace of the world is the business of all the participants and the intervention of any of them cannot be considered an unfriendly act. This system will have its effect on the Far East.

I am prepared to warmly recommend the proposal of a general renunciation of the special rights of foreign powers in China. I recall that Japan was prepared to accept the proposal. The consequences would include the disappearance of the Japanese police, of Japanese courts etc., and we would have a means of action. This is a hope for the future and the best we can do at present.

The current difficulty is that, whatever the origin of the Sino-Japanese treaty, whatever our reservations about an agreement obtained by threat, the same doubts do not apply to the Anglo-Japanese and Franco-Japanese treaties. Even if your treaty was annulled, these would still exist. And they permit Japan to take what once belonged to Germany. This is what leads us to ask whether you prefer to accept your treaty or the Anglo-Japanese and Anglo-French treaties?

Lloyd George: I'd like to see this question examined by three experts: French, American and English.

[This proposition is accepted]

Wellington Koo: I have two things to say. In the first place, China is at a crossroads. Much of the nation wants to co-operate with the western powers, and that is also the desire of the current government. But if we do not obtain justice at the Conference, that will throw us into the arms of Japan. There is a group in China that is for 'Asia for Asiatics'; if we fail in our mission, I'm afraid that the reaction will be strong.

Secondly, the agreements made by France and England, under the pressure of circumstances, at a critical moment, are they still applicable today? Circumstances changed from the moment that China became your ally. Moreover, the principles upon which peace should be based are incompatible with Japan's ambitions.

In thanking you, I do not wish to dwell too much on the serious consequences that might follow. It is important to know whether we can create a half-century of peace in the Far East or are we going to create a situation which could lead to war within a decade?

Wilson: These are serious considerations. But the Great Powers' respect for treaties that they have signed is not a denial of justice. The principles that we uphold here cannot have the effect of destroying valid treaties; they cannot be invoked to nullify previously agreed obligations. I do not accept that respect for treaties can be considered unjust.

In the past, China was treated unjustly and that is what we want to change in the future. But the only solution to these current difficulties is for China to join the League of Nations. It is not the individual protests of states but world opinion that should work. The world is full of sympathy for the great Chinese people and knows that its future depends upon the fate and opinions of these 400,000,000 people. But we must not confuse justice and the repudiation of treaties, however unfortunate.

Wellington Koo: The position you have taken is solely based upon the circumstances of the war.

Lloyd George: We cannot go down this route. These were agreements that we entered upon seriously, when it was a question of saving the world, including China, from German domination. Nothing would have stopped Germany, had she won, from taking over China. Remember that the phrase 'iron glove' was first used about China.

At a serious moment, when the life of our people was in danger, we appealed to Japan. Not only did we get the support of the Japanese fleet at a critical moment, but, without Japan, we could not have taken Jiaozhou. It is not possible for us to say to the Japanese, 'we were happy to meet you during the war, but now, goodbye'.

Our sympathy for China is unquestionable. We understand your difficulties in Shandong province and we are prepared to do for you everything that our treaties allow. We will be happy to welcome China into the League of Nations and offer her all the protection that the League will be able to offer. I am sure that China has in front of her a future as glorious as her past but we cannot regard treaties as pieces of paper that can be torn up once the need has passed.

Wilson: I accept that these are unfortunate treaties. But they were signed to protect the world and China from German domination.

Wellington Koo: They are only justifiable in the European context.

Lloyd George: If Germany had won here, she would have been mistress of the world. America was not prepared to resist her: the world was at her feet.

Wilson: Germany was not content with the Hamburg–Baghdad project. She knew of, and had the intention of exploiting the famous wealth of the Far East. The Kaiser had declared himself the enemy of your race and we all remember his speech on the 'Yellow Peril'. He would not have tried to govern France and England, he needed to conquer them and carry off everything that suited him. One of the results of the war was that we saved, most notably, the Far East.

All we can say to you is that you should look carefully at the alternative we offer you.

The Chinese delegates retire.

*   *   *

Wilson: I am conscious of the apparent contradiction between my attitude to this question and that of Italy. The difference is that Austria-Hungary has disappeared. If she still existed, I would not oppose the enactment of the Treaty of London. And the Yugoslavs and Italy like us will join the League of Nations.

As far as Japan is concerned, we must do what is necessary to get her to join the League of Nations. If she stays outside, she will do as she wishes in the Far East. You heard them this morning saying that they would not sign the treaty if we did not respect our contractual obligations to them.

Lloyd George: The way in which they terrorised the Chinese into signing their treaty is one of the most unscrupulous in history, especially when it concerned a gentle and defenceless people.

Wilson: Yes, but I'm most worried that we should not create a chasm between East and West.

Lloyd George: That is the strongest argument and the Chinese are not sufficiently aware that, without us, they would today be at the mercy of the Germans.

Clemenceau: Shall we go back to the question of Spalato [Split]? ...

It is clear that, whilst Lloyd George and Wilson were about to betray Italy by reneging on the Treaty of London, they had decided to stand firm upon the secret treaties with Japan. Wellington Koo's arguments about forced treaties and treaties signed due to the exigencies of war being invalid were to be ignored. Wilson and Lloyd George were keen to get the Chinese to accept the 'better' of two treaties. Unfortunately, the Japanese delegation were not only impatient but had a threat up their sleeve. If Clemenceau can be characterised by an obsession with German reparation, Lloyd George was having to juggle the strong feelings of the Dominions, while President Wilson was concerned, above all, with his projected League of Nations, and the need to get Japan to join.

On **28 April**, Lloyd George reported that, in discussions with Balfour, the Japanese had remained adamant over their demands and refused to accept occupation of Shandong under the conditions previously established by the Germans. President Wilson expressed his concern about American public opinion, 'nothing will inflame American public opinion more than the idea of an injustice in China in Japan's favour. The news I have from America makes it clear that public opinion is strongly behind me over the line I have taken on the Italian question and that I am expected to take the same attitude over the Japanese question.'

Japan trumps President Wilson

The same day, **Balfour** reported that Baron Makino had told him, '"Despite the great interest we have in the foundation of the League of Nations, we cannot join without protesting against the refusal to adopt the principal of racial equality. We cannot accept both the refusal of this principle and the rejection of our claims in Jiaozhou. We ask that you let us know where we are on that latter question before the session on Monday." I told him that the explanations made by the Japanese delegation were acceptable to the heads of state. But the Japanese want to be seen this afternoon.'

Lloyd George: If not, what will they do?

Balfour: I think they will make a protest against the refusal to accept the principle of racial equality. But if they don't get satisfaction over Shandong, they might go further.

Wilson: Might they go as far as to withdraw from the League of Nations?

Balfour: Not if they expect a satisfactory solution of the Shandong problem.

Wilson: I cannot go back to America saying that I have abandoned China. If the Japanese give back Jiaozhou and content themselves with economic rights without military advantage, it would seem that they treat the Chinese better than the Germans did.

There was a final discussion on **29 April** in which Wilson and Lloyd George attempted to restrict the Japanese military and police presence in Shandong by explaining how railways were policed in Britain and America. The Japanese refused to consider any such arrangements and Viscount Chinda raised a final question about prisoners of war, asking for reparation for the 4,000 German prisoners the Japanese had taken in Shandong, demanding reimbursement (which was refused by Lloyd George). The Japanese delegation released a final statement of intention on 30 April:

The policy of Japan is to hand back the Shandong peninsula in full sovereignty of China, retaining only the economic privileges granted to Germany and the right to establish a settlement under the usual conditions at Qingdao.

The owners of the railway will use special police only to ensure security for traffic. They will be used for no other purpose.

The police force will be composed of Chinese and such Japanese instructor[s] as the directors of the railway may select and will be appointed by the Chinese government.

Although after days of wrangling about railways in Shandong and their policing and control, the Japanese appeared to have moderated their demands over policing, they had achieved their prime object which was the acknowledgement that Jiaozhou would be handed directly to Japan for eventual, date unspecified, return to China, without having to go through an 'indirect' handover involving Germany. The details of railway control were left aside and the Japanese knew that, as in Manchuria, they could virtually do as they pleased, without having to resort to the threat not to join the League of Nations.

The Japanese announcement of 30 April was transmitted to China and as it became widely known over the next few days, it provoked massive demonstrations, first in Peking on 4 May and then many other cities. In the 'Summary of the Conditions of Peace' issued on 10 May 1919, the direct transfer of rights and privileges from Germany to Shandong was set out:

> Germany cedes to Japan all rights, titles and privileges, notably as to Jiaozhou, and the railroads, mines and cables acquired by her treaty with China of 6 March 1898, and by other agreements as to Shandong. All German rights to the railroad from Qingdao to Ji'nan, including all facilities and mining rights and rights of exploitation, pass equally to Japan, and the cables from Qingdao to Shanghai and Qifu, the cables free of all charges. All German state property, movable and immovable, in Jiaozhou, is acquired by Japan free of all charges.

Meanwhile, the Chinese delegation continued to try and ameliorate the situation and sent notes to President Wilson.

* * *

14 May, conversation between President Wilson, Clemenceau, Lloyd George and President Orlando [who had returned to the peace conference]

> **Wilson**: I have received two notes from China. The first demands the abrogation of the treaties between China and Japan, the second demands the withdrawal of all foreign troops from Chinese territory and that the foreign post offices and consular rights etc., be withdrawn. Mr Lansing proposes to reply that these problems will be put before the League of Nations as soon as it is constituted.

Clemenceau and Lloyd George agree.

* * *

On **25 June**, as reported in a conversation between Wilson, Clemenceau, Lloyd George, Baron Sonnino [Italian Foreign Minister], Baron Makino, China proposed to sign the Peace Treaty 'with reservations'.

> **Clemenceau**: I have received a letter from the Chinese delegation saying that they can only sign the treaty with reservations. I propose to reply that if they have reservations, they cannot be admitted to the signing ceremony.

Wilson: I thought that sovereign nations had the right [to reservations] when signing.
Clemenceau: We haven't allowed it to Romania or Serbia.
Wilson: Mr Lansing says that this is normal international procedure.
Lloyd George: They either sign or they don't sign. What does a signature mean if the signatory says at the same time that he rejects the clause that is of special interest to him?
Baron Makino: We need to know exactly what the contents and implications of these reservations are. If they were accepted we would be compelled to make corresponding reservations.
Wilson: It is a protest against our solution to the Shandong question.
Baron Makino: If it is only a protest, I have nothing to add. But it might mean something more.
Wilson: The question would have to be put to the Chinese delegation. It is based upon instructions from their government.
Lloyd George: If this reservation means that the Chinese do not accept the articles of the treaty that concern them, what does a signature mean?
President Wilson: We can ask M. Pichon to ask the Chinese delegation on our behalf. (Agreed).

*   *   *

On **26 June**, conversation between President Wilson, Clemenceau and Lloyd George.

> **Clemenceau**: Wellington Koo has told me that the Chinese delegation will protest, which is necessary for Chinese public opinion, but it is in the hope of a final revision of the treaty clauses relating to Shandong. Should this protest letter be written before or after the signature of the treaty? I would prefer it to be written afterwards.
> **Lloyd George**: Certainly.
> **Clemenceau**: Otherwise it might encourage Romania to do the same.

*   *   *

The wartime achievements of Japan were praised in the *New York Times* of 1 August 1919:

> Japan destroyed at one stroke the German power in the Far East by the reduction of the fortress of Qingdao; hunted out the enemy warships roving the adjoining seas; patrolled the South Sea, the Indian and Pacific Oceans during the whole period of the war; conveyed the troops of Australia and New Zealand to the battlefields of Europe and Asia, co-operating on the Mediterranean with the allied fleets in their operations against the enemy submarines; prevented the infiltration of German

SHANDONG, THE LAST STRAW

"Going to Talk to the Boss"
(Chicago News, 1919.)

President Wilson's idealistic proposals for a 'peace without victory', his Fourteen Points and his League of Nations were widely admired. America had made a huge military and economic contribution to victory over the Central Powers. During the war, America's gold reserves rose by almost $300 million, matching a comparable fall in those of the other belligerents – with a notable exception; Japan not only added nearly $150 million to its reserves, but also achieved its strategic objectives in increasing its financial grip on China, while being allowed to retain the German enclave in Shandong.

At the start of the Versailles Peace Conference, Wilson seemed the most powerful man on earth, but his authority was drained away by nations pursuing their own interests. Britain, France and Japan eviscerated much of his precious Fourteen Points. *Realpolitik* trumped idealism, with China one of the largest losers.

More humiliating than his setback abroad was his setback at home. The president overlooked how his powers were circumscribed by Congress. Opposition to the League got under way while he was still at the conference. Particularly objectionable was Article X, requiring all states to go to each others' aid in the event of aggression – a direct erosion of the US Senate's power to declare war. On his return from Versailles, he embarked on an 8,000 mile tour to get support from the American people, but suffered a serious stroke, though described as a nervous breakdown in the press.

The New York Times.

"All the News That's Fit to Print."		THE WEATHER

VOL. LXVIII...NO. 22,534.   ...   NEW YORK, SATURDAY, SEPTEMBER, 27, 1919. TWENTY-FOUR PAGES.   TWO CENTS

PRESIDENT SUFFERS NERVOUS BREAKDOWN, TOUR CANCELED; SPEEDING BACK TO WASHINGTON FOR A NEEDED REST;

Wilson's Secretary of State, Robert Lansing, was critical of the Shandong decision, which 'had done more than anything else to strengthen opposition to the Treaty'. The decision was, in his view, 'the last straw'. Wilson feared that, unless Japan got its way, it would boycott the League. Lansing disagreed and felt that 'even though Shandong had not been delivered', Japan would have joined the League, but he felt that his duty to follow the decision of the president.

Wilson was unable to compromise with his opponents, so that the US Senate, led by Senators Borah, Lodge and Johnson, rejected the peace treaty and thereby membership of the League of Nations. The cartoonist depicts the three senators refuring to give the lady (peace) a seat on the subway.

NOTE: Headline *New York Times* 27 September 1919. Lansing: *Wilson and China* by Bruce Elleman, Routledge, 2002.

influence and the spread of Bolshevism into East Siberia; subscribed to the allied loans to the full extent of her financial capacity; provided the [Allied] powers with munitions and war materials, and stood ever ready to respond to the call of her allies in case of necessity.[1]

George Morrison, advisor to the Chinese delegation but confined to bed with the kidney disease that was soon to kill him, fulminated against this view that Japan had been any help to the Allies. He was convinced that Germany and Japan, though officially enemies, were in collusion. Why had the *Emden* not attacked any Japanese ships in the Indian Ocean? Why had no Japanese ships attacked the *Emden*? Why, indeed, had the Japanese suffered no German attacks at all on her ships in the Indian Ocean?[2]

And Clemenceau, who had sat in on all the Council meetings with the stubborn and insistent Japanese delegates, commented, 'Who can say that in the war she played a part that can be compared, for instance, to that of France? Japan defended its interests in the Far East, but when she was requested to intervene in Europe, everyone knows what the answer of Japan was.'[3]

In his *Memoirs of the Peace Conference*, published in 1935, Lloyd George declared that China's contribution had been 'insignificant'.[4] This was in the context of an argument about war reparations which equated 'contribution' above all with population.

> The small powers had made their contribution and some of them had endured sacrifices and sufferings greater than even those to which the Great Powers had been subjected; and they were entitled to a voice in the peace settlement. We had to decide the numbers which should be given to each of the Allied countries who were not in the rank of the Great Powers, and whether the numbers should be fixed on the basis of population or of the contribution made to the struggle by each. China had a population of 400 millions, and the assistance she rendered was insignificant, compared to the efforts and sacrifices of Serbia, Belgium, Roumania, or Canada and the other British Dominions.

It is perhaps significant that Lloyd George made no reference to Japan in this context.

* * *

The Chinese delegation to Versailles had been doubly betrayed. The secret treaties with Japan between Britain, Russia, Italy and France, signed in 1917 meant that, throughout the rest of the war, the Allies were bound to agree to Japan's conditions. The delegation could not have known about these treaties but, more devastating and more humiliating, the existence of the second secret treaty with Japan, signed by the Chinese government in 1918, was quite

CHINA AND THE LEAGUE OF NATIONS

THE GAP IN THE BRIDGE.

The last of President Wilson's Fourteen Points was as follows *A general association of nations must be formed under specific covenants for the purpose of affording mutual guarantees of political independence and territorial integrity to great and small states alike.*

Wilson is rightly given credit for being the main architect of the League of Nations. Drawing on the report of Britain's Phillimore Commission and Wilson's own ideas, the president's trusty advisor, Colonel House, prepared detailed plans. After extensive consultations with many others, the Covenant of the League of Nations was agreed and came into force in January 1920; there were 42 founder nations, but not the United States, whose absence was a serious weakness.

China was a founder member, as was Japan, and took its resposibilities seriously. In 1921, when a dispute arose between Germany and Poland over Silesia, China provided one of four representatives on the commission to resolve it. In disputes between peaceful nations, such Finland and Sweden over the Åland Islands, the League could play a useful role. But it was doubtful if the 'territorial integrity and political independence of China would be safeguardeded' by the League, as President Wilson reassuringly claimed. When there was naked aggression, as Italy's attack on Abyssinia, the League proved to be powerless. The Italian dictator, Benito Mussolini, with his usual braggadocio, remarked 'the League is very well when sparrows shout, but no good at all when eagles fall out'.

The League totally failed to deal with Japanese aggression against China. On 18 September 1931, the Japanese created a small explosion on a railway line in Manchuria, casting the blame on Chinese saboteurs. Negligible damage was done, but it gave Japan a chance rapidly to take over the whole of Manchuria and set up a puppet state Manchukuo, under the last Chinese Emperor, Puyi, before the League could act.

A commission, under Lord Lytton, visited the area and made an investigation, even examing the damaged rail – no doubt by then denuded of incriminating evidence. His report in October 1932; was not much more than a rap over the knuckles, but sufficient for Japan to walk out of the League.

If the League was powerless against aggressor nations, it did a lot of good and established several bodies which have survived to this day, such as the World Health Organisation and International Court of Justice. In 1946 the League was dissolved and replaced by the United Nations, which was better structured to enforce its decisions than the League.

unknown to the delegation, which may also have been unaware of the contents of the 1915 treaty. They saw copies for the first time in 1919 when 'Mr Lloyd George was of the opinion that any arrangements made during the war should be placed before the meeting ... M. Clemenceau agreed to produce them and asked if the Japanese delegates would do likewise? Baron Makino said he had no objection to doing so ...'[5]

It is no wonder that Lü Zhengxiang became seriously depressed, and it required considerable mental agility from Wellington Koo to continue to argue for China's rights.

After the disappointment of Versailles, Wellington Koo continued a distinguished career as China's first representative at the League of Nations, serving as Foreign Minister and Minister of Finance and as Chinese Ambassador to France and Britain before becoming a judge at the International Court of Justice in the Hague. Lü Zhengxiang succeeded him as Chinese representative at the League of Nations but after the death of his wife in 1927, he became a Benedictine monk in Bruges.

Although it might have seemed that the Allies were in agreement over China, the negotiations were complicated by problems between Japan and America over the question of 'racial equality'. Woodrow Wilson's major preoccupation was to establish a 'League of Nations' which he saw as a natural sequence to the Versailles Peace Conference, a means to avoid future wars. When Italy walked out of the Conference and appeared unlikely to sign up to the League of Nations, it became increasingly important to Wilson that Japan should stay in. Mindful of widespread prejudice which was enshrined in law in the United States and elsewhere, Japan wanted a proposal about racial equality inserted into the covenant of the League of Nations. 'Racial equality' was not included in the League's covenant as it was opposed by many, particularly in America with its many anti-Asian exclusion laws (such as the Chinese Exclusion Act of 1882 and the Californian Aliens Act of 1913 designed to prevent Japanese from acquiring land) and Britain with its imperial dominions. The Australian Prime Minister Billy Hughes upheld the 'White Australia' policy and said that 95 out of 100 Australians opposed any idea of equality. However, having gained most of what they wanted, the Japanese delegation did not follow up its threat not to join Woodrow Wilson's League of Nations.

Eugene Chen was perhaps, in a small way, partly responsible for one of Wilson's greatest disappointments, the fact that the United States itself did not join the League, for Chen supplied copies of the secret treaties, not only to Sun Yat-sen (further increasing his disillusion with Europe and America), but also to 'Republican senator, William E. Borah, chairman of the committee of foreign affairs, who at that time was leading a campaign against ... Wilson's project, the League of Nations', providing extra ammunition for

Borah's campaign, which led to the United States senate refusing to join the League.[6] Although Borah did not take over the chairmanship of the Foreign Relations Committee until 1924, it is generally agreed that his impassioned speech against America joining the League of Nations carried the Senate with him.

Both Chinese delegations refuse to sign
Despite near impossible political differences between the two Chinese delegations to the Versailles conference, they were united in their opposition to Japan's occupation of Shandong. Both delegations refused to sign Articles 156 to 158 by which 'Germany renounces, in favour of Japan, all her rights and privileges, particularly those concerning the territory of Jiaozhou' and all the railways, submarine cables, properties, archives and title-deeds relevant to the territory.

China gained nothing from Versailles, not even the equal treatment as a sovereign state that had become increasingly important. As news of Japan's effective victory in Articles 156–8 spread after Japan's announcement of 30 April, Chinese students in Paris surrounded the Hotel Lutétia, effectively preventing the delegations from leaving for Versailles, had they intended to do so. And when the news of the failure to address Japan's occupation of Jiaozhou reached China, it provoked massive angry demonstrations.

Painted out of the War
From the moment of France's victory on the Marne in September 1917, two well-known academic artists, Pierre Carrier-Belleuse (1851–1933) and Auguste-François Gorguet (1863–1927) began work on an enormous, collaborative and celebratory painting, the Panthéon de la Guerre, 402 feet by 45 feet, incorporating 5,000 portraits in classical architectural settings. The Panthéon was completed in October 1918 and exhibited in a specially constructed building in Paris where it could be seen in the round. At the beginning, it included portraits of five allied nations, but by 1918, it included twenty-three (although four were represented only by their flags).[7]

France occupied the prime space, and Belgium and Britain each had their own space, whilst others shared: Italy and Portugal, Rumania and Russia, Serbia and Montenegro, and Japan shared a space with Greece. America was added later, occupying the third section but crowded in with other, mainly Latin American allies: Brazil, Costa Rica, Cuba, Guatemala, Nicaragua and, squeezed in inappropriately, China and Siam. At one point, a group of members of the Chinese Labour Corps were included but, when America entered the war, they were painted over. The painting eventually ended up in the National World War I Museum in Kansas City, cut down to fit its new home and re-painted to reflect America's role in the war.

Chapter 10

China's reaction

4 May 1919

When the news of the failure to address Japan's occupation reached China quickly by the new technology of telegraph and newspaper reports, it provoked the massive demonstrations of 4 May 1919, first started by students at Peking University. They had been buoyed up by hope that President Wilson might remain true to his 'Fourteen Points' of 1918 and ensure that China benefitted from 'free, open-minded and absolutely impartial adjustment of all colonial claims'. Disappointment was intense. Some 3,000 students gathered in the centre of Peking at the Qianmen Gate on the southern side of what is now Tiananmen Square.[1] They carried banners reading 'Oppose the Big Powers', 'China for the Chinese', 'Give Back Qingdao' (the last written in blood) and called for a boycott of Japanese goods.

The police attempted to drive them away by force but the demonstrators went on to the Legation Quarter where they hoped to deliver a petition on behalf of 11,500 Peking students to President Wilson asking that he follow his own 'Fourteen Points'. Refused access to the Legation Quarter, they moved on to the residence of Zhang Zongxiang, who had been Chinese ambassador to Japan since the time that the Twenty-one Demands were signed. Breaking up an old iron bedstead, the students beat him with the bed-legs until he was covered in bruises that 'looked like fish-scales all over his body' and left him for dead (though he eventually recovered).

They then rushed on to the house of the Minister of Communications, Cao Rulin (who had been ordered by Yuan Shikai to sign the Twenty-one Demands). 'Cao's ornaments, his antiques . . . all of them were just smashed to pieces, and the many perfume bottles in his wife and daughters' rooms were all broken into shards on the floor. The smell of perfume filled the air . . .'[2] As the house was set on fire, Cao fled over the back wall. Thirty-two protestors were arrested only to be released on 9 June as demonstrations, strikes and boycotts of Japanese goods sprang up all over China. There were clashes between Chinese students and the police in Tokyo and in China, strikes in Shanghai, Wuhan, Tianjin, Ji'nan, Xiamen and other cities which continued throughout the year. Rickshaw pullers in Shanghai refused to carry Japanese passengers, Japanese shopfronts were smashed and newspapers refused to take any advertisements for Japanese goods.

In Tianjin, Zhou Enlai, the future premier of China, recently returned from Japan where he had been learning about Marxism through Japanese books on the subject, joined fellow students in publishing a Tianjin Students' Union *Bulletin* advocating reform and democracy and dedicated to publicising 'new thought'.[3] The *Bulletin* was condemned by the local police and suppressed. Zhou Enlai joined a massive demonstration on the Shandong question in Peking on 1 October and returned to Tianjin for a protest rally attended by 40,000 people on 10 October.

On 20 December, he was arrested at a meeting of 30,000 students and others protesting over the Fuzhou incident in November when Japanese Consulate guards had shot and killed a number of Chinese students engaged in boycott activities there. After six months in prison, he began planning a study trip to Europe through the Chinese-French Educational Commission, set up by Cai Yuanpei (1868–1940). Originally intending to study at the University of Edinburgh, Zhou Enlai was put off by the language requirements and the cost, and settled on Paris instead, where he studied French and worked in the Renault factory at Billancourt, probably only for a couple of weeks before he acquired funding from Yan Xiu, founder of Nankai Middle School, and the Comintern.

Another future leader, Deng Xiaoping, worked in the Hutchinson rubber factory at Montargis before starting a bean-curd shop in Paris at the suggestion of Zhou Enlai.[4] The future of Communism in China might have been very different had Zhou Enlai been one of the handful of Chinese students in Edinburgh. In France, where there were many radical students on work-study programmes, he joined his left-leaning fellow students in a Communist cell in 1921.

The boycotts, strikes and demonstrations resulting from the decisions made at Versailles came to be known as the May Fourth Movement. Not truly a movement, it was more of a spirit or inspiration. Intellectuals in particular, were inspired with a new nationalism, a desire to transform, improve and strengthen China, as epitomised by the aims of Zhou Enlai's student *Bulletin*. It gave impetus to growing trends such as the move to abandon old-style literary language in favour of the vernacular which could be understood by a wider range of readers who were served by a massive increase in publishing of newspapers and journals that had begun in the early years of the Republic. One of the most influential was the left-wing journal *Xin Qingnian/New Youth* founded in Shanghai in 1915 by Chen Duxiu (1879–1942). Chen became Dean of Peking University in 1917, was a co-founder of the Chinese Communist Party in 1921 (with Li Dazhao) and promoted socialism and Marxism in *New Youth* from 1919.

Li Dazhao (1888–1927) was appointed Librarian of Peking University and employed the young Mao Zedong in the reading room there in 1918, where he attended lectures on socialism and, with Li Dazhao's encouragement read Marxist works, before returning to his home province and starting his own radical journal in Changsha. Both Li Dazhao and Chen Duxiu were employed by the President of the University, Cai Yuanpei who had gone to France to study in 1905 and done so much work there to attract and set up a support network for Chinese students (which continued into the 1920s) and provide teaching material which was supplied to the Chinese Labour Corps workers, before returning to China in 1916 to take up his appointment at Peking University in 1917.

These formidable intellectuals were at the forefront of the May Fourth Movement, and the first great demonstration was led by Peking University students. Beyond the immediate political reactions to the Versailles Treaty, the movement to transform and radicalise China was led through publications in the vernacular language, such as *New Youth* where Chen Duxiu wrote, 'Down with the ornate, obsequious literature of the aristocrats – up with the plain expressive literature of the people!' Lu Xun (1881–1936), one of the greatest Chinese writers of the twentieth century (described as 'the saint of modern China' by Mao Zedong) was an early contributor to *New Youth*, declaring, 'I write fiction to "serve life" and furthermore to reform life.'[5]

Despite the growing split between rival 'governments' in north and south China, and despite the rise of militarism in the provinces, the May Fourth Movement was crucial in inspiring China's intellectuals and thinkers to find practical ways of modernising China, and in creating a positive new nationalism. It was a form of self-strengthening, born out of despair. And there was much to despair of. In 1917–8, the regional military commanders were active in the south-west with fighting between the armies of Yunnan, Guizhou and Sichuan and Premier Duan Qirui, who should have been preoccupied with affairs of state and China's participation in the war, but was fighting against rebellious military factions in Hunan province. Then the Hubei province militarists declared independence from the central government and 'By the end of January 1918, Yezhou (Hunan) was recovered by the allied Hubei-–Guangxi forces, and the rebellious Hubei militarists were fighting northern troops in western Hubei to a standstill.'[6]

The warlords Wu Peifu (1874–1939) and Zhang Zuolin (1875–1928) based in the Beijing area and in Manchuria respectively, fought each other in major wars twice. Wu Peifu, who had been effectively in charge in Peking in 1922, was driven back to Zhengzhou in Hunan province and Zhang Zuolin, who captured Peking in 1926, was driven back to Manchuria by Chiang Kai-shek's Nationalist forces where his train was blown up by Japanese soldiers in 1928. Feng Yuxiang (1882–1948) famous as 'the Christian general' rumoured to baptise his troops with a hose-pipe, had, like Wu Peifu, risen through Yuan Shikai's New Army, and seized Peking in 1925, inviting Sun Yat-sen (who died there in 1925) to come and form a government. The power struggles between the warlords caused devastation to local populations and considerable instability, with twenty-six people holding the office of prime minister between 1916 and 1928.[7]

The Northern expedition of Chiang Kai-shek's army, which fought unsuccessfully against the Japanese in Ji'nan (the capital of Shandong province) as it moved northwards, reached Peking in 1928. This did not mean the end of local warlord battles by any means despite the technical unification of China when, in that same year (and just before he was blown up by the Japanese) Zhang Zuoliang pledged the allegiance of Manchuria. It was also true that by 1928 foreign occupation of China appeared to be declining with Japan's withdrawal from Shandong in 1922, rather forced upon her by the Washington Naval Conference of 1921–2, and the Chen-O'Malley agreement of 1927, that returned the British concessions in Hankou and Jiujiang, although it was not until 1943 that all the other British concessions were formally handed back to China.

Through the 1920s, as warlord battles continue to rage and Chiang Kai-shek's army moved northwards from the Kuomintang's base in Guangzhou, two other threats arose. Though Japan ostensibly withdrew from Jiaozhou in 1922, her imperial designs on China were by no means over. Turning her attention from Shandong to concentrate on Manchuria, she invaded the province in September 1931, put the ex-emperor Puyi on the throne of 'Manchukuo' in 1934 and launched a full-scale invasion of China in 1937, taking Peking in July and Shanghai in November.

* * *

The First World War had provided Japan's first opportunity to invade and exploit China, an opportunity that was carried through with determined savagery to the end of the Second World War. Before Pearl Harbor, Britain and Japan remained allies, signing yet another agreement, the Anglo-Japanese Tianjin Agreement on 19 June 1940. The UK promised to co-operate in all ways to suppress 'all activities prejudicial to ... the security of the Japanese forces'. Japan had taken Tianjin in August 1937 and when three suspected Chinese saboteurs had taken refuge in the British Concession, Japan instituted a blockade until the agreement was signed. Worse, on July 18, it was announced in the House of Commons that there would be a three-month closure of the British-controlled Burma Road to arms, ammunition, lorries, petrol and railway supplies to China, at the request (or demand) of the invading Japanese. In response to queries, it was stated that HMG was 'mindful of ... obligations to the National Government of China'[8] (for whom the Burma Road was a lifeline in the war of resistance against Japan), and desirous to 'see China's status and integrity preserved ...'

In the invasion of China, Japan's brutality was thorough and widespread, one of the most shocking being the orgy of massacres and rapes in Nanjing that lasted for three weeks from mid-December 1937.[9] Still a subject that arouses intense feeling in China, exacerbated by Japan's tendency to pass over the subject in school history books, the number of dead is still impossible to verify exactly with estimates ranging from 40,000 to 300,000. Missionaries and businessmen trapped in Nanjing reported 1,000 rapes (often fatal) per night. One of the witnesses of the horrors was the local director of Siemens, John Rabe, who left a diary listing these numbers, but the Japanese themselves left evidence. Hideous photographs of their victims, stuck through with bamboo poles, grotesquely murdered, were taken by Japanese soldiers and sent to a pharmacy in Shanghai to be printed. Another, still-remembered, outrage was the 'Three-alls' ('kill all, burn all, loot all') policy used by the Japanese Army to destroy villages and crops throughout the northern provinces of China from the winter of 1941.

As Japan's invasion of Manchuria took hold, Chiang Kai-shek, Chairman of the Nationalist Government of China 1928–1931, Chairman of the National Military Council 1931–1946, announced on 7 April 1933 that Chinese Communist bandits were a greater threat than the Japanese. With hindsight, it can be seen that he chose the wrong enemy for by directing his (Chinese) troops against (Chinese) Communist troops and failing to resist effectively the Japanese invasion, many feel that he doomed his Nationalist Army to failure. The brutality of the Japanese provoked resistance and the effective guerrilla warfare against the Japanese fought by Mao Zedong and the People's Liberation Army inspired many.

A factor in the growth in interest in Bolshevism and Marxism in China was the widespread disappointment and disillusion with America as President Wilson's 'Fourteen points' were not enacted in China. Sun Yat-sen's delegates to the Versailles Peace Conference were in touch with the Bolshevik representatives there and, in the spring of 1920, a Soviet delegation headed by Grigori Voitinsky arrived in China and made contact with Li Dazhao and Chen Duxiu of Peking University. By the summer of 1921, there were six Communist cells in China and, in July 1921, the Chinese Communist Party (CCP) was founded in Shanghai with Mao Zedong as one of the delegates. Under Soviet orders, with Lenin issuing the directive, the CCP joined forces with Sun Yat-sen's Kuomintang to form a united front against warlords and the government in the north.

The Soviet Russian view was that, according to Marxist texts, a Communist revolution could only be achieved by the urban proletariat and that it was essential to inspire the workers in China's cities to rise up. Several Chinese Communists, including Mao Zedong, who came from peasant backgrounds, felt that peasants could be equally inspired and, since China was essentially a nation of peasants, with only a tiny urban population, it was more profitable to work in the countryside. This approach was intensified when Chiang Kai-shek's army, arriving in Shanghai on its 'Northern Expedition' on 12 April 1927, turned upon the Communist-organised workers who had 'liberated' the city as part of the 'united front' and massacred more than 100, injuring many more.

Mao and others abandoned Chinese cities and concentrated their efforts on mobilising the peasantry. In October 1927 they set up the Jiangxi Soviet in the Jinggang Mountains on the border area between Jiangxi, Hunan and Hubei provinces. There, they worked with the peasants until October 1933 when Chiang Kai-shek launched a fifth 'encirclement campaign' to drive them out and they set off on the Long March of over a year, travelling 9,000 kilometres, to the north-western province of Shanxi. There, in the mountain town of Yanan, they continued to work with the local peasants, organising land distribution and communal work, setting up clinics and schools, but, most significantly, organising guerrilla warfare against the hated Japanese. Chiang Kai-shek had wasted an enormous amount of effort in driving the Communists out of the Jinggang Mountains and his preference for destroying Communists rather than Japanese was a major factor in the growing opposition of Chinese intellectuals, whose patriotism had been fired by Versailles and by hatred of the Japanese.

When the Second World War ended, and with it the Japanese invasion, Chiang Kai-shek's Kuomintang, turned its fire on the Communists in a civil war that ended in October 1949, when Mao Zedong proclaimed the foundation of the People's Republic of China. Scholars still argue about how the Communists, with virtually no external support, whilst Chiang Kai-shek was supported by both America and the Soviet Union, managed to sweep to control of the country. It is not widely known that Stalin, convinced that only a Kuomintang-led 'united front' could defeat the Japanese, signed a non-aggression pact with Chiang Kai-shek in 1937, sent Soviet military advisors to Chiang's army and, offering credit of some $100,000,000 in 1938–9, supplied 600 aircraft, 1,000 guns and howitzers and 8,000 machine guns, whilst in Mao Zedong's Communist base in Yanan, there was only a Soviet advisor.[10]

Despite the lack of military support, the Chinese Communist armies defeated Chiang's well-supplied troops, whose morale was low, due to corruption and a lack of care. Military achievements aside, most experts agree, that one of the significant aspects of Mao's victory was that it was inspirational, that Chinese students and intellectuals, in particular, saw the Communists as the successful vanguard of the new spirit of nationalism which had grown out of the disappointment at Versailles.

National humiliation at the hands of foreigners has been a fairly constant theme in twentieth and twenty-first century Chinese nationalism. Opium and the mid-nineteenth century Opium Wars mark the moment when modern history begins in Chinese history books, and the subsequent hundred years saw the 'carve-up' of China into areas of special interest to different foreign powers, all keen to make money out of China. Although some of the foreign inhabitants of China were charitable and idealistic, and assisted China's development through the introduction of modern medicine and female education, in particular, the sense of invasion, occupation and external control still rankles, and still remains part of how China views the outside world.

This attitude is clear in public statements made by Fu Ying, Vice Minister of Foreign Affairs of the People's Republic of China, who served as China's Ambassador to Australia 2004–2007 and Ambassador to the UK 2007–2010 (UK–China relations having been raised to ambassadorial level in 1972). In an interview with the *Financial Times*, she said:

> China has such a long history of its own, the only continuous culture for 5,000 years. But it also has had about 200 years of a very sad history, with foreign occupations. That hurt China. That is why the Chinese remember the suffering more than the victories. China has a sharp sense of crisis.[11]

In the 2015 Fullerton Lecture in Singapore, she expanded on the theme of suffering, with what might be an indirect reference to President Wilson's Fourteen Points:

> Chinese people are not at all indifferent to what happens in the world and the experience from the colonial era left a deep imprint on the Chinese outlook on international relations and order, with an emphasis on inclusiveness and fairness.
>
> In the nineteenth century, western gunboat diplomacy forced open China's door and turned China's view of the world upside down. Ever since, China started to integrate into the western-dominated modern world, not without pains, hardship and setbacks.[12]

Compared with the humiliation of the Opium Wars, the disappointment of the First World War and Versailles is of a slightly different nature. It came at a time when news travelled faster, when young Chinese were beginning to venture abroad in search of a modern education, and when they read in the new journals and newspapers about events outside China. The fact that China had aided the Allies by sending labourers, by seizing German ships and offering troops, that China had participated in the war, and had hoped to be respected as an ally, and that President Wilson appeared to offer hope for liberation from colonial exploitation, made the disappointment of Versailles more acute.

Yet though the subsequent decades were incredibly difficult, culminating in the Sino-Japanese War and the ensuing civil war, the enthusiasm for transformation that grew with the May Fourth movement in a reaction to Versailles, eventually led to the moment in October 1949 when Mao Zedong proclaimed, 'The Chinese people have stood up'.

Chronology of Recent Chinese History

The Chinese have a longer view of their history than Westerners do of theirs, matching its long continuity, so the Ming dynasty was seen as a recent golden age by some Chinese. President Nixon once supposedly asked Zhou Enlai what he thought had been the impact of the French Revolution on western civilization. Zhou Enlai considered the question for a few moments. Finally, he turned to Nixon and replied, 'The impact of the French Revolution on western civilization – too early to tell.' It is a good story, often misquoted and perhaps untrue, yet illustrative of the Chinese view of history.

China's extent varied considerably over the centuries. The Ming dynasty ruled over a heartland of mainly Han Chinese peoples. Their successors, the Qing dynasty, incorporated Manchuria, its homeland, as well as Mongolia, Tibet and Xinjiang. Much control was lost through foreign incursions and unequal treaties during the nineteenth and early twentieth centuries.

Manchu (Qing) dynasty, 1644–1912

1644 – Manchus descend on Beijing from the north-east and end the Ming dynasty, looked back on by some as a golden age. The Manchu queue was forced on the Han Chinese, on pain of death, but the Qing maintained the traditional administrative system. During the reign of the Kangxi, Yongzheng and Qianlong emperors (1662–1796) the economy and arts flourished. The empire extended into Tibet, Central Asia, Mongolia, Taiwan and Siberia; several tributary states recognised the Qing ascendancy. Foreign trade was largely confined to Guangzhou. Chinese who went abroad were 'deserters of the Celestial Empire' and liable to execution. China became the largest empire in the world, xenophobic, aloof, technically self-sufficient.

1792–3 – Britain's King George III sent Lord Macartney to open up trade with China, but he was politely rebuffed. Further attempts by Britain, Russia and Netherlands were made over the next fifty years to open up trade, with scant success.

1796–1804 – Famine, corruption, anti-Manchu resentment and Ming nostalgia sparked the White Lotus rebellion.

1839–1842 – Lin Zexu, imperial commissioner, destroys opium stocks at Guangzhou. First Opium War. Treaty of Nanjing cedes Hong Kong to

Britain, provides for five open trading cities (Treaty Ports) and established extraterritoriality. Also, $21 million compensation was demanded from China.

From 1851 – Imperial weakness, national humiliation and natural disasters trigger Taiping, Miao, Nian, Dongan and other rebellions all over China. Tens of millions of casualties and displacements. Recruitment of Chinese labourers accelerates worldwide.

1856 – Second Opium War. Treaty of Tientsin (1858) opened up eleven more ports for trade. The Chinese refused to comply, leading to an Anglo-French invasion and the looting and destruction of the Imperial Summer Palaces outside Beijing (1860). Britain and France set up their own concessions in the Treaty Ports, while America participated in shared concessions in Shanghai and Tientsin (Tianjin). Russia gained much territory in the Amur region and around Lake Balkhash (now in Kazakhstan).

1861–1895 – After two disastrous wars and much foreign intrusion, the Self-Strengthening Movement started to improve technical, administrative, linguistic, military and diplomatic capacity. New enterprises and institutions created. Representatives sent overseas and legations opened. Progress was regularly held up by conservative opposition.

1884–1885 – Tonkin War enabled France to acquire Northern Vietnam.

1893 – Ban on foreign travel lifted.

1894–1895 – China defeated by Japan in Korea, seen by China as a tributary state. Japan gained Taiwan and effective control of Korea. More countries get concessions in China. Big expansion of foreign controlled railways.

1896 – Russia wins right to extend Trans-Siberian Railway through Manchuria.

1898 – Germany leases territory in Shandong, including Qingdao, creates mining and railway companies. Hundred Days' Reform proposed by Kang Youwei to the Guangxu Emperor, who issued edicts to modernize the country. He was thwarted by the conservatives and put under house arrest by the Empress Dowager Cixi.

1899 – US Secretary of State John Hay proclaims 'Open Door' policy for China; its territorial integrity to be maintained, all nations to be free to trade there and missionary activity permitted.

1898–1900 – A disastrous drought in Shandong triggered a protest by peasants against the alien Qing dynasty – the Boxer Uprising. It was soon diverted into a general protest against foreigners, especially their missionaries and railways. It spread across Northern China, with the slogan 'Support the Qing, destroy the foreigners'. Foreign legations in Beijing were besieged. An international force came to the rescue, which engaged in much pillaging of Beijing. Savage revenge was meted out on the Boxers. China had to pay the $450 million Boxer Indemnity.

1902 – By now, eight European countries and Japan held territory in China; America had shared concessions. Anglo-Japanese Alliance agreed; extended 1905 and 1911.

1904–1905 – Japan inflicted severe defeat on Russia in a war over Manchuria and Korea.

1908 – Guangxu Emperor died of a big dose of arsenic or medicine or both, followed by Empress Dowager Cixi on the next day. Regency established for Puyi, just short of three years of age.

1910 – Japan annexed Korea, having been increasing its grip there since 1895.

1911 – Rebellion in Wuchang, followed by others all over China. Proclamation of Republic and Sun Yat-sen's election as its Provisional President. Mongolia declares independence.

The Republic and the Great War, 1912–1919

1912

February: Yuan Shikai, having been appointed prime minister the previous year, negotiated the child emperor Puyi's abdication and elected Second Provisional President. Yuan Shikai had the powerful Beiyang Army behind him, based in Beijing, while Sun Yat-sen was the leader of diverse elements scattered around China and among Chinese communities abroad. Yuan assured Sun that 'never shall we allow the monarchical system to reappear in China'.

August: Guomingdang Party (KMT) formed by Song Jiaoren, an associate of Sun Yat-sen. Song organised elections to a new bicameral parliament and campaigned for need to curtail presidential powers, being abused by Yuan Shikai.

December: elections left KMT in a dominant position and Song Jiaoren as a likely prime minister.

1913

March: Song assassinated, evidently on orders of Yuan Shikai, though not proven.

April: Yuan negotiated £25 million Reorganisation Loan from international banks, excluding US banks, mainly to finance his Beiyang Army; it was considered unconstitutional. China very weak financially and economically. Since 1820 China's GDP per capita was down by 8 per cent, while the GDP of Japan, Europe and America increased by 200, 300 and 400 per cent.

May: Yuan concedes China's reduced status in Mongolia to Russia.

July: to curb Yuan's abuse of power, KMT launched a 'second revolution' in seven southern provinces. By year's end, KMT is crushed, its members expelled from parliament and Yuan confirmed as President, with international recognition.

1914

January: Yuan dissolves parliament.

May: a new constitution cements Yuan's power; he argues that democracy has not worked. He replaced civilian with military governors in the provinces – seeds of the subsequent warlord era.

August: start of the Great War in Europe. China declared neutrality, but aims to recover German colony in Shandong. President Yuan offers 50,000 troops to UK to that end, but received no answer. Instead, bound by treaties, UK and Japan co-operated in a campaign to recover it.

November: Anglo-Japanese victory; both nations gave assurances of its unconditional restoration to China – not done until 1922.

December: Yuan revives the rituals of worshiping Heaven, as traditionally done by emperors, suggesting his own imperial aspirations.

1915

January: without consulting its British allies, Japan presents its Twenty-one Demands to President Yuan; they would make China a Japanese vassal. Chinese officials prepare to lobby for a place at a future peace conference. Though as yet non-belligerent, China hoped to earn a place by providing labourers rather than combatants.

March: public outrage in China and surprise abroad at the Twenty-one Demands.

May: Yuan accepts a slightly watered down version of the Demands, but his reputation is dented.

June: Possible use of Chinese labour explored by France.

July: Chinese offer of 300,000 labourers (with 100,000 rifles) deemed 'hardly practicable' by the British.

November: Yuan arranges to be proposed as Emperor at a special representative assembly. This provoked widespread revulsion, even among his allies.

December: the governor of Yunnan started a rebellion against Yuan, soon followed by other provinces.

1916

January: French mission reaches China to arrange recruitment of labour, via a private company, in order not to compromise Chinese neutrality.

March: funding for Yuan's accession ceremony cut. Yuan abandons his imperial title.

June: Yuan died of uremia, compounded by demoralization and disgrace. Internal politics confused in China, with the rise of warlordism and a north–south split. Duan Qirui, one of three potential successors indicated by Yuan on his deathbed, became prime minister for most of rest of Great War. An authoritarian and militarist, he faced constant opposition, mainly from the south.

August: Japanese-Chinese clash at Zhengjiadun, Manchuria, provides chance for Japan to place advisors in Chinese armed forces. First Chinese labourers reach France.

November: Huge military losses induce a new British policy on Chinese labour, supported by the recently appointed War Minister, Lloyd George. Recruitment starts.

1917

February: Germany announces unrestricted submarine warfare. America, China and others protest. Some 543 Chinese labourers and 209 sailors bound for France on SS *Athos* drowned in the Mediterranean; later, most labourers were shipped across the Pacific to Canada, then by train and then by sea across the Atlantic. Britain secretly agrees 'with pleasure' to support Japan's claims in Shandong, contrary to assurances of November 1914.

March: China severed relations with Germany. Much debate within factions and regions about advisability of declaring war on Germany; Sun Yat-sen thought it 'utterly absurd'.

April: America declared war on Germany. Great optimism in China that America will be supportive at the peace conference. Chinese labourers with British forces in France numbered 35,000; eventual total was about 100,000 (British) and 40,000 (French). In addition, 200,000 supplied to Russia.

June: Britain appeals to Japan for shipping and naval assistance, in accordance with the Anglo–Japanese Alliance and secret agreements.

July: Warlord Zhang Xun engineers restoration of Puyi to the throne, but it lasted only twelve days.

August: After much delay and debate, China declares war on Germany and Austria-Hungary. Military government set up in Guangzhou by Sun Yat-sen, accentuating China's north-south split; factions of Yuan's army remained strong in the North.

October: Bolshevik Revolution in Russia creates new excuse for Japan to intervene in Manchuria.

November: Lansing-Ishii Agreement between America and Japan confirms Open Door policy, but appears to condone Japanese encroachment in China.

1918

January: President Wilson, without telling his allies or sounding out his political opponents in America, announces Fourteen Points as a framework for peace. Public welcome and private scepticism in Europe. Enthusiasm in China at the concept of self-determination, seen as a chance to expel foreign enclaves and extra-territoriality.

September: Influenced by Japan's numerous loans to China, Duan Qirui, prime minister, secretly agrees that Japan can retain its Shandong interests – this was to place a big obstacle to China's claims to recover its territory at the peace conference.

November: Armistice ends Great War. Celebrations all over China. President Wilson's Fourteen Points accepted as basis for peace, including self-determination and the League of Nations; doubts as to practicability not broadcast, especially as America now holds vast financial superiority over all other belligerents.

1919

January: Versailles Peace Conference starts with seventy delegates from twenty-seven countries.

April: Italy, one of the Big Four, walks out because it was not granted Fiume and Dalmatia. Japan demands its rights in Shandong, which had already been secretly conceded to Japan by the Allies and agreed to by the Chinese government the previous September. The Chinese delegation argued that, under President Wilson's policy, secret agreements and those extracted by force should not be valid. However, Wilson overlooked his policy of self-determination on this occasion, but obtained a promise from Japan that it would be restored to China in due course. If both Italy and Japan had walked out of the conference, the chances would be dim for Wilson's coveted League of Nations. China, therefore, refused to sign the Treaty of Versailles.

May: the outcome of the peace conference was received with consternation in China. It gave rise to the May Fourth Movement, which was to change the course of Chinese history.

July: Soviet government, not yet fully in charge of Russia, disowns Tsarist unequal treaties; this unilateral and unique expression of equality and friendship was to have much influence in China.

October: Repatriation of most of the Chinese labourers.

November: US Senate rejects the Treaty of Versailles and League of Nations.

The later Republic, 1920–1949

1920 – Formation of League of Nations, with China as a founder member, but without US participation. Two future leaders of China go to France – Zhou Enlai organizes workers and Deng Xiaoping works in various industrial jobs. About 3,000 Chinese labourers and students remained in France after the war. Some engaged in political activities, aimed at change in China.

1921 – Chinese Communist Party (CCP) founded by Mao Zedong and others. Mongolia, independent, falls into Soviet sphere.

1922 – China recovers sovereignty of former German concession in Shandong, at the nine nation Washington Naval Conference.

1923 – On Moscow's suggestion, KMT and CCP form alliance 'First United Front', whereby CCP members join KMT as individuals.

1924 – Whampoa Military Academy founded by KMT with Soviet help, to train revolutionary army; initial participation of CCP.

1925 – Death of Sun Yat-sen. Leadership of KMT passes to Chiang Kai-shek.

1926 – Northern Expedition, led by Chiang Kai-shek, with the aim of unifying China, taming the warlords and at the same time turning on the CCP.

1927 – KMT-CCP alliance ruptured. CCP members purged and murdered. Start of civil war in China.

1928 – KMT Nationalist government, under Chiang Kai-shek, achieves international recognition, having reduced (but not wholly eliminated) warlordism; capital moved from Beijing to Nanjing. KMT demands renegotiation of foreign presence in China.

1931 – Japan occupies Manchuria. Mao and colleagues form Jiangxi Soviet, fighting off several KMT attacks. Eventually they had to abandon their base and embark on the Long March (1934–1935) to new base in Shaanxi.

1932 – Japanese puppet state, Manchukuo, created; the last Qing emperor, Puyi, made head of state and, two years later, emperor.

1937 – Second Sino-Japanese War; Rape of Nanjing results in up to 300,000 deaths, widespread pillage and rape. In the face of Japanese aggression, KMT and CCP resume alliance, but deep distrust lurks below the surface.

1939 – Second World War starts in Europe.

1941 – Japanese attack US Navy at Pearl Harbor; USA declares war on Japan.

1945 – Manchukuo invaded by Soviet Union. Atomic bombs force Japan surrender. After end of war against Japan, civil war resumed between Nationalists (led by Chiang Kai-shek) and Communists (led by Mao Zedong).

1949 – After Communist victory, Mao Zedong announces formation of the People's Republic of China. Chiang Kai-shek sets up KMT regime in Taiwan.

Appendix 2

Key Personalities in the War

Abbreviations: **KMT** – Kuomintang (pinyin Guomindang), nationalist political party, formed in 1912; Sun Yat-sen was its initial chairman; after his death in 1925 Chiang Kai-shek became its leader. **CCP** – Chinese Communist Party, formed in 1921; Mao Zedong was one of its fifty-three founders.

Alston, Sir Beilby (1868–1929). British diplomat who served in a variety of posts. Counsellor at British Legation, Beijing 1911–1917 and *chargé d'affaires* in Sir John Jordan's absence. He then served in Vladivostok and Tokyo, before returning to Beijing as Minister Plenipotentiary in 1920–1922. Later he served in Argentina and Paraguay, before being appointed Ambassador to Brazil in 1925; suffering from ill health, he died *en poste* in 1929.

Balfour, Arthur J. (1848–1934) former British Prime Minister, became Foreign Secretary in Lloyd George's coalition government of December 1916. He gave his name to the 1917 Balfour Declaration, which provided a home for the Jews in Palestine, leading to the state of Israel. He thought that China did not deserve to recover her territory, as they would have been unable to recover it on their own; for the Chinese, he had 'feelings of contempt'. Under him, the Foreign Office acceded 'with pleasure' to Japan's claim to retain Shandong.

Backhouse, Sir Edmund, Baronet (1873–1944). Scion of a distinguished Quaker banking family, orientalist, linguist and author. Fleeing his creditors, he settled in Beijing, where he lived, on and off, for over forty years, mostly masquerading as a Chinese scholar. His two books about the Manchu court created the presumption that he had excellent high level contacts, so he was able to act as a British spy in the war and agent for international companies dealing in armaments and bank notes. His transactions proved to be mainly mythical, if not fraudulent. Towards the end of his life, he wrote *Décadence Mandchoue*, also possibly mythical, which purports to provide a unique and shocking glimpse into the hidden world of China's imperial palace with its rampant corruption, grand conspiracies and uninhibited sexuality. It had to wait until 2011 to be published.

Barnardiston, Major General Nathaniel (1858–1919). Commanded British forces at siege of Qingdao, which had a relatively minor role, contributing

1,500 troops as against 23,000 Japanese. The British involvement was criticised by the Chinese, with no off-setting benefit to Britain.

Beelaerts van Blokland, Frans (1872–1956). Dutch diplomat. Minister in Beijing. Representing a neutral power, he looked after the interests of Germany and Austria-Hungary in China so conscientiously that Britain and France asked the Chinese government to have him removed. Later he became Minister of Foreign Affairs, chief advisor to Queen Wilhelmina during her exile in London (1940–1944) and Vice President of the Privy Council.

Cao Rulin (1877–1966). Educated in Japan and, before the war, was part of the pro-Japanese movement in China. As Vice Minister for Foreign Affairs, dealt with Japan's Twenty-one Demands of January 1915. Succeeded in mitigating their harshness somewhat; Yuan Shikai shrewdly delegated the signing (and the ensuing opprobrium) onto him. During the May Fourth riots of 1919, his house was burnt down by an angry mob, but he escaped. Later, became a director of several mining companies.

Chen, Eugene (Youren) (1878–1944). Lawyer, born in Trinidad, where he became a successful solicitor; his father had fled to the West Indies after participating in a rebellion against Qing dynasty. Chen's first language was English and he started life as a British subject. He joined Sun Yat-sen as an advisor to the new Republic in 1912. Later he became a journalist and newspaper founder. After attending the Versailles Peace Conference, he was influential as a diplomat, one of his main themes being recovery of Chinese rights from foreign powers. His career was buffeted by the fluid state of politics; on several occasions, he found himself in and out of office, prison and exile. He returned to Shanghai in 1942. The Japanese hoped that he would join their puppet government, which he declined to do, calling them a 'pack of liars'.

Chiang Kai-shek (1887–1975). Nationalist leader. Military training in Japan. Joined Kuomintang (KMT), Sun Yat-sen's political party. Sun established Whampoa Military Academy to create an army for unifying China; Chiang appointed its head. Soviet Union provided help, insisting on CCP participation in KMT. Succeeded Sun on his death in 1925 as KMT leader. In 1926 Chiang headed Northern Expedition, aiming to unify China. In 1927 Chiang began eliminating CCP but, after savage civil and global wars, he was defeated by Mao Zedong and retired to Taiwan in 1949, taking many of the nation's treasures and most of its financial reserves with him.

Chinda, Count Sutemi (1857–1929). Japanese diplomat. Obtained a BA degree from DePauw University, a liberal arts college in Greencastle, Indiana, with strong roots in the Methodist movement. Chinda served as Ambassador to USA 1912–1916 and United Kingdom 1916–1920. No doubt influenced by his time at DePauw, Chinda became a Methodist minister; it is noteworthy that one of his opposite numbers at the Versailles Peace Con-ference, also served the Christian church. Lü Zhengxiang, China's foreign minister, was a Roman Catholic, who became a monk after the war.

Churchill, Winston S. (1874–1965). British politician. As First Lord of the Admiralty, he was held responsible for the failed Dardanelles Campaign in 1915. He left office to serve in the army, remaining a backbench MP. As such, on 24 July 1916, he argued – somewhat apologetically – for the use of Chinese labourers to permit the release of able-bodied men to serve in the front line. A minister in the twenties, out of office in the thirties, he was Prime Minister from 1940–45 and 1951–55.

Clemenceau, Georges (1841–1929). Radical French politician. Early career in medicine and journalism. Prime Minister 1906–1909 and 1917–1920. Sympathetic to both Japan and China, collector of oriental art and opponent of racism and colonialism. Main objective at Versailles Peace Conference was to demolish German power once and for all. Acquiesced in Japanese retention of Shandong.

Conty, Alexandre-Robert (1864–1947). French diplomat, minister to China 1912–1917. He was one of the first to advise China that it should aim to obtain representation at the peace conference which would follow the war. He antagonised the Chinese by his haughty behaviour and consistent efforts to get China to support the Entente Allies; it did not help that France insisted on expanding its concessions in Shanghai (successfully) and Tianjin (un-successfully). He was declared *persona non grata* and returned to Paris in September 1917, shortly after China declared war on Germany. Later, he served as ambassador to Brazil.

Cordes, Heinrich (1866–1927). German diplomat turned banker in China. Studied languages and law, gaining honours in Chinese, at the University of Berlin. Spent several years as Chinese Secretary to the German Legation in Peking; described as the 'power behind the throne' there, having to an extent 'gone native'. Being married to a Chinese wife and having several children with her made him unusual in the expatriate community and more embedded in China than his German contemporaries. After the Boxer Rebellion joined Deutsch-Asiatische Bank in 1901 as deputy manager in Tianjin, being pro-moted to manager in Beijing in 1905. He offered a loan in 1916 to President Yuan Shikai, hoping to wean him off the idea of joining the Entente Allies, but in the following year (after Yuan's death) China declared war on Germany.

Deng Xiaoping (1904–1997). Wealthy Sichuan farmer background. In 1920 went to France to study, telling his father the reason 'to learn knowledge and truth from the West in order to save China', but he had to take jobs in various industries. In 1927 returned via Moscow, to become a powerful force in the CCP. In and out of favour with Mao. After Mao's death in 1976, he moved China in a new direction, making it an economic power house, while maintaining the status in the world that Mao had created. What would the Qianlong Emperor have thought of China being a top global manufacturer of 'objects strange or ingenious', which he so despised?

Duan Qirui (1865–1936). Soldier and politician. Under patronage of Yuan Shikai, he was an effective military commander in the Beiyang Army. Broke with Yuan over his declaration as emperor, but was one of three nominated as a possible successor in his will. Served as Prime Minister intermittently during the war. In return for Japanese loans to fund his army, he agreed to Japan having rights in Shandong; it weakened China's case at the Versailles Peace Conference.

Matsui Keishirō, Baron (1868–1946). After graduating in law at university, Matsui joined the diplomatic service. After serving in Washington, Seoul and London, he was assigned to Beijing in 1902, remaining there for a long tour of duty until 1913. During the Great War, he was Japanese ambassador to France and a Japanese delegate to the Versailles Peace Conference, where Japan worsted the Chinese by being allowed to retain the German enclave in Shandong, on whose recovery the Chinese had set their hearts.

Ishii Kikujirō (1866–1945). Japanese diplomat and politician, Minister of Foreign Affairs, 1915. Special envoy and later ambassador to the USA, with which he felt it was important to maintain good relations, if Japan was to prosper. In November 1917 signed the Lansing-Ishii Agreement with Robert Lansing, US Secretary of State, under which both parties agreed to maintain the 'Open Door' policy. Later became President of the Council and Assembly of the League of Nations. Opposed Japan's Tripartite Pact with Germany and Italy in 1940, which was likely to be seen as anti-American.

Jordan, Sir John (1852–1925). Of Irish origin like many British officials who served in China. Spent some thirty years in China altogether. British Minister in Beijing throughout the war. Close relationship with Yuan Shikai. Continued to be a much sought-after advisor on Chinese matters after his retirement as minister.

Wellington Koo (Gu Weijun) (1888–1985). After university in Shanghai, he earned an MA and PhD in liberal arts, law and diplomacy at Columbia University. President Yuan Shikai's English secretary in 1912; minister to the USA in 1915. As one of China's representatives at the peace conference in 1919, he made a powerful case for the return to China of all concessions and the end of extra-territoriality, but his arguments did not prevail. For brief periods, in 1924 and 1926, he was President and Premier of China; otherwise, he spent his career overseas, serving as Ambassador to France, UK and USA and Vice President of the International Court of Justice, The Hague.

Lansing, Robert (1864–1928). American lawyer. Counselor to the State Department in 1914. Secretary of State, in succession to William Jennings Bryan, in 1915. In November 1917 signed the Lansing-Ishii Agreement with Ishii Kikujirō, on behalf of Japan, under which both parties agreed to maintain the 'Open Door' policy in Japan. At the same time, America agreed to recognise Japan's 'special interests' in China – contradicting the 'Open Door' policy and permitting Japan to continue its occupation of Shandong. Lansing later felt regrets at this ambiguity.

Alexis Saint-Léger Léger (1887–1975), also known by a pseudonym, Saint-John Perse, combined, like his older contemporary Paul Claudel, successful careers in French diplomacy and literature. He served as secretary to the French embassy in Beijing. Post war, after impressing the many times prime minister, Aristide Briand, he rose to be Secretary General of the Quai d'Orsay. His poetry earned him the Nobel Prize in 1960.

Li Hongzhang (1823–1901). Soldier, politician and modernizer. After the Second Opium War, he was one of the architects of the Self-Strengthening Movement but progress was hampered by conservative forces surrounding the dynasty and provincial rebellions. Visits to UK, USA and other foreign countries – contrary to the national ethos of the day – strengthened diplomatic ties, but critics alleged he was consorting with the enemy and taking bribes.

Li Yuanhong (1864–1928). Chinese general and politician. Commanded the rebel army in 1911; Sun Yat-sen's vice president in 1912. When Yuan Shikai wrested the presidency from Sun Yat-sen in that year, Li retained the vice presidency, without any effective powers, for the following four years until Yuan Shikai's death in June 1916. One of three nominated as a possible successor in President Yuan's will, he succeeded him as president for one year. Later served again as president twice, once for a year and once for five days – such was the erratic and unstable nature of politics in China in that era.

Liang Qichao (1873–1929) was possibly the most influential journalist of his time in China. A brilliant student, he helped organize the Hundred Days Reform in 1898 with Kang Youwei; they were encouraged by the Guanxu Emperor, who wanted to make big changes in China after the humiliating defeat by Japan in 1894–5, but the plans were thwarted by the Empress Dowager Cixi. Liang had to flee to Japan and travelled the world promoting reform in China. After the revolution in 1911, he returned to China; he was a strong supporter of China joining the Entente and declaring war on Germany. After the war he continued to write prolifically and teach at universities.

Liang Shiyi (1869–1933) was described as the 'Brains of China' and likened to Machiavelli. His diverse career in transportation, finance and politics spanned the end of the Qing dynasty, the years of Yuan Shikai's supremacy and, despite periods of exile, the post-war period. He saw the merits of joining the war against Germany and promoted the sending of Chinese workers to France – armed or unarmed – as a means of earning a place at the peace conference. His later career was blighted by his association with Yuan Shikai's attempt to get himself made Emperor. A master of public relations, he thought that China was not ready for democracy and set out an extensive justification of Yuan's imperial plan in the *New York Times* of 4 June 1916.

Lloyd George, David (1863–1945). British politician, Chancellor of the Exchequer 1908–1915. From May 1915 he gradually took a leading political role in directing the war. Prime Minister December 1916 to October 1922. Much impressed by the Chinese Labour Corps and supported its recruitment; in order not to upset British trade unionists, he wished to call the labourers 'auxiliaries', but this name was not adopted. Did not support China's aspiration to recover Shandong at the peace conference, owing to secret treaties signed with Japan.

Lü Zhengxiang (1871–1949) born a Protestant, converted to Catholicism. He married a Belgian wife. Believed in the compatability of Christianity and Confucianism. International education in Shangahi enabled him to master French. Diplomat and interpreter; attended peace conferences at The Hague Conferences in1899 and 1907. Premier of China twice and Foreign Minister four times. Led the Chinese delegation at the Versailles Peace Conference, very disappointed by the result. After his wife's death in 1927, became a monk in Belgium, authored several books and made an honorary bishop.

Manchu emperors (Qing dynasty). The Guangxu Emperor (1871–1908), after an attempted campaign to modernize China in 1898, had been sidelined from power by the Empress Dowager Cixi (1835–1908); they died on successive days. In 1908, two-year-old Puyi (1906–1967) became emperor, under a regency – a scenario ripe for the revolution which ended the Qing dynasty. Restored as emperor by Zhang Xun for eleven days in July 1917, complicating negotiations over China's entry into the war. Japanese puppet ruler of Manchuria 1932–1945. Imprisoned in 1949 for ten years. Lived out his later life quietly as a gardener and literary editor in Beijing.

Mao Zedong (1893–1976) of middle status farmer background. Student in the war, mostly in Changsha, Hunan. As a young man he believed that there was much to learn from America and Europe, to conquer China's backwardness. Disillusioned by Versailles. In 1921 he was one of fifty-three founders of the Chinese Communist Party. After years of infighting, civil war and global war, he emerged as national leader and declared the formation of the People's

Republic of China in October 1949. He restored China's unity and status. His autocratic tendencies and policies hampered economic progress. Today he is officially judged as 70 per cent good and 30 per cent bad.

Mitsuomi, General Kamio (1856–1927). Commanded Japanese forces at siege of Qingdao, the German colony in Shandong, at the start of the war. The town was taken with a force of 23,000 Japanese supported by 1,500 British troops. Later, Kamio became governor of Qingdao.

Morrison, George E. (1862–1920). Australian adventurer, traveller and writer. Correspondent of *The Times*, known as 'Morrison of Peking'; sometimes relied on Sir Edmund Backhouse for stories and translation. Openly supported the republican movement. Advisor to President Yuan Shikai in 1912, after the establishment of Republic. In 1917, his library of China books sold to form basis of Oriental Library in Tokyo; he felt – no doubt correctly – that Beijing would be an unsafe home for them after his death.

Makino Nobuaki, Baron (1861–1949). Japanese statesman. After a brief career in diplomacy, serving in Britain and Austria-Hungary, spent most of his career in politics, initially at the provincial level and then nationally. He occupied a variety of ministerial posts for nearly thirty years and, in retirement, continued to be influential behind the scenes as a liberal, thus incurring the enmity of the militarists who attempted to assassinate him in 1936. At the Versailles Peace Conference, he argued for a racial equality clause to be included in the League of Nations, but withdrew it as part of the bargaining with the allied leaders in order to secure the greater prize of Shandong.

Orlando, Vittorio (1860–1952). Italian Prime Minister after the disastrous battle of Caporetto in 1917. As one of the 'Big Four', he walked out of the peace conference in April 1919, when President Wilson vetoed Italy's claims to Fiume and Dalmatia, on the promise of which Italy had joined the Entente Allies in 1915. One result was that Wilson found it more difficult to deny Japan's claims to Shandong, as a Japanese walk-out (on top of the Italian one) would have killed his League of Nations plan stone dead – which anyway was later to be rejected by the US Senate.

Plüschow, Günther (1886–1931). German aviator, explorer, war hero and author. Caught in the Japanese siege of Qingdao in August 1914, he managed to escape with the governor's final despatches. His plane crashed in a rice paddy and he set out for Germany on foot. After many adventures, he ended up at Gibraltar, where he was arrested by the British and was taken to England for internment in Castle Donington, Leicestershire. He managed to escape and return to Germany – the only German combatant to escape from Britain in both World Wars. Later he explored Patagonia by air and was killed when his plane crashed near Lago Argentino. He wrote several books; three films were made or inspired by him.

Reinsch, Dr Paul S. (1869–1923). American lawyer and academic. Served throughout the war as Minister to China. In 1917 encouraged China to join the war against Germany and offered financial support. Gave the impression that the German colony in Shandong would be returned to China after the war. Reprimanded by Secretary of State Robert Lansing for being too forthcoming to the Chinese, not knowing of Lansing's green light to Japanese aspirations in Shandong.

Shigenobu, Ōkuma (1838–1922). Unusually for a Japanese politician of his time, studied Chinese literature and English language. Advocate of Western culture and science. Promoted conversion of Japan from feudal to parliamentary system. At various times, Foreign Minister and Finance Minister. As Prime Minister, for second time, responsible for Twenty-one Demands in January 1915. Their aim, to subjugate China, provoked widespread protests in China and consternation in USA and UK.

Song Jiaoren (1882–1913). With Sun Yat-sen, founded KMT. In 1912 election, KMT won over 40 per cent of the seats in both House of Representatives and the Senate. During the election campaign, he had vehemently argued for limiting presidential powers. He was obviously in line to be prime minister, but was assassinated in 1913. All the main conspirators disappeared or were themselves assassinated. Few doubted that President Yuan Shikai was behind the crime. After Song's death, a second revolution was put down and the KMT banned by Yuan, who ruled supreme until his death in June 1916.

Straight, Willard (1880–1918). American banker, diplomat, publisher and reporter. Represented the J.P. Morgan bank in China. Very influential on oriental matters in government circles, he was arranging the arrival of the American delegation to the Versailles Peace Conference, when he died of the global influenza epidemic. Might the Chinese have got a different deal if he had survived? His son, Whitney Straight, settled in England, served as a pilot in the Battle of Britain and became managing director of British Overseas Airways Corporation after the Second World War.

Sun Yat-sen (1866–1925). 'Father of the Nation'. Qualified as a doctor in Hong Kong in 1892. Abandoned medicine for revolution in China and engaged in plotting and fund raising in Europe, Asia and North America. Stimulated several unsuccessful revolts against the Qing dynasty, until the Wuchang rebellion of 1911 (of which he had no prior knowledge, being in Colorado) led to establishment of Republic. Sun relinquished the proffered presidency to Yuan Shikai, who subverted elections won by Sun's associates.

After Yuan's death, Sun's political party, KMT, at Soviet instigation, co-operated with the Communists, but turned on them after Sun's death.

Takaaki, Katō (1860–1926). Studied law at Tokyo Imperial University, where he graduated at the top of his class. Joined the Mitsubishi group which sent him to London. In 1887 joined the diplomatic corps and was appointed ambassador to Britain in 1894, at an unusually young age. In 1900 appointed foreign minister, a position he held subsequently for three further spells. As ambassador to London and foreign minister, was a principal architect of the Anglo-Japanese Alliance (1902, with later amendments), which was to be major factor in the politics of China during the Great War. He was ambassador to Britain a second time, 1908–1912; prime minister 1924–26. He died in office from pneumonia.

Tang Shaoyi (1862–1938). The first prime minister of the Republic of China, for only three months in 1912; he resigned because of President Yuan Shikai's unconstitutional conduct. After the war, served in Sun Yat-sen's military government in Guangzhou, but again resigned on constitutional grounds. After retiring from politics in 1937, he entertained the possibility of heading a puppet government after the Japanese invasion in that year. As a consequence he was assassinated on KMT's orders.

Truptil, Georges (born *c*.1870). French colonial soldier and adventurer. As a young lieutenant, participated in an expedition to study the course of the River Mekong. Appointed lieutenant colonel in December 1915, he was put in charge of recruiting Chinese labourers for industrial and military support activities in France. In order to preserve the impression that China was not violating its neutrality, the task was entrusted to a specially formed private company, Huimin, which included Liang Shiyi, a close associate of President Yuan Shikai.

Varè, Daniele (1880–1956). Italian diplomat and author. He wrote three novels, the most well known of which, *The Maker of Heavenly Trousers*, was set in Beijing during his time there as a diplomat (two periods 1912–1920 and 1927–1931). Later he served as Italian ambassador to Denmark, but was ousted by Mussolini, among other Italian diplomats. It availed him nought that, in Beijing, he had been the boss of Galeazzo Ciano and turned a blind eye to his naughty night life. Ciano was then a young diplomat, soon to wed Mussolini's daughter, Edda, and be appointed foreign minister.

von Hintze, Paul (1864–1941). German sailor, diplomat and politician. Son of a cigar maker from the assiduous middle classes of Prussia. In 1898, as a young naval officer, he found himself in confrontation with Admiral Dewey, when America was seeking control of the Philippines, where Germany had a potential interest. Naval attaché in St Petersburg in 1903, where he greatly impressed the Kaiser, leading to his appointment as ambassador to Mexico, soon after the revolution of 1910. He served as Minister to China, 1914–1915. After a spell as ambassador to Norway, he became foreign minister of Germany but was ousted after three months, being of a liberal inclination and keen to promote an armistice.

von Maltzan, Baron Ago (1877–1927). German diplomat. Minister in Beijing at outbreak of the war; he had unofficial discussions with President Yuan Shikai, with a view to the voluntary return of Shandong to China, but was pre-empted by Japan's military seizure of the colony, with British help. Later German ambassador to the USA. Killed in an air crash in 1927. His papers about China were looted or destroyed by Soviet troops in 1945.

von Spee, Vice Admiral Maximilian (1861–1914). Commander of Germany's East Asia Squadron in Qingdao. In August 1914, before Japan's attack, sailed his two armoured cruisers, *Gneisenau* and *Scharnhorst*, plus supporting vessels, out of Chinese waters. Harried British ships across the Pacific and Indian Oceans. Imposed severe losses on British Navy at Battle of Coronel, off the coast of Chile. In December 1914 von Spee's attempt to raid the Falkland Islands ended in disaster; most of his best ships and 2,200 German lives lost, including his own. A new battleship, *Admiral Graf Spee*, named after him in 1934, was also lost in the South Atlantic, scuttled at Battle of River Plate in December 1939.

Wallenberg, Gustaf (1863–1937). Swedish diplomat. Minister in Beijing. Later ambassador to Japan. Scion of one of Sweden's most notable families, which has provided leaders in business, politics, philanthropy and the arts. Grandfather of Raoul Wallenberg, who organised an audacious and courageous campaign to save Jews in Hungary in 1944–1945.

Wilson, T. Woodrow (1856–1924). President of Princeton University and Governor of New Jersey, before election to the US presidency in 1912. China took heart at America's entry into the war in 1917; Wilson's idealism, the Fourteen Points and League of Nations had great appeal. Expecting the return of Qingdao, China was bitterly disappointed by Wilson's failure to insist on his policy of self-determination and the revocation of secret treaties or treaties signed under duress – notwithstanding that he insisted on it in the case of Italy. Protestors in China contemptuously dismissed the Fourteen Points as 'Fourteen = Zero'. In the end, the Treaty of Versailles was not ratified by the Senate, Wilson's health having so deteriorated that his ability to negotiate with the Senate was fatally impaired.

Woodhead, Henry G.W. (1883–1959). Influential British journalist, active in China from 1902 over several decades. Editor of the English language newspaper *Peking & Tientsin Times*. He expressed a traditional British point of view in strong and graphic language. His approach is summed up in the title of his 1929 book *Extraterritoriality in China: The Case Against Abolition* which Chiang Kai-shek's KMT government had called for in the previous year.

Xu Shichang (1855–1939), one of three nominated as a possible successor in President Yuan's will, was president of China for almost four years, but his rule was weakened by increasing warlordism. Cracked down on the May Fourth Movement in 1919. Under his presidency, China refused to sign the Treaty of Versailles and sent troops to participate in the Russian Civil War. Failed to retain control of Mongolia, which again declared independence in 1921, falling from the Chinese into the Soviet sphere of influence.

Yuan Shikai (1859–1916). Chinese soldier and politician, sponsored by the modernizer Li Hongzhang. Active in Korea 1885–1894, but left before being tarnished with China's defeat by Japan. Controlled the Beiyang Army, enabling him to negotiate the end of the Qing dynasty and his own presidency of the Republic of China in 1912. Then he cracked down on Sun Yat-sen's party and the elected parliament, consolidating all power in his hands. At the start of the war, sought to recover Shandong, by military or diplomatic means. When he got himself declared emperor, he lost all support and soon died. After his death, the country became more disunited for a decade, with warlords fighting each other for control.

Zhang Xun (1854–1923). 'The Pig-Tail General', loyal to the Qing dynasty and, after its demise, to Yuan Shikai. Defeated the second revolution of 1913, which had been launched to arrest Yuan's seizure of absolute power. Continued to wear the queue or pig-tail (and require his troops to do so) as symbol of loyalty to the Qing dynasty. In July 1917 attempted to restore Puyi as emperor; the attempt ended in farcical failure after eleven days and Zhang thereafter retired from public life.

Zhou Enlai (1898–1976). Chinese politician, from a scholar/official background. Educated at modern schools in China. Higher education in Japan, but disillusioned by Japanese militarism. In 1919 participant in May Fourth Movement. Went to France in 1920. Active in Chinese community, many of whom had originally come to France as labourers. Organized the Chinese Communist Party in France. In 1924, came back and rose with the CCP in China. He was to serve as Mao's faithful, if sorely tried, premier between 1949 and 1976, the year in which they both died.

Notes

Chapter 1: Japan sees an opportunity

1. Gunther Plüschow, *My escape from Donington Hall: preceded by an account of the siege of Kiao-chow in 1915* [*sic.*], London, John Lane, 1923, p. 23.
2. John von Antwerp Murray in Russell H. Fifield, *World War One and the Far East: the diplomacy of the Shantung question*, New York, 1952, p. 5.
3. Weihaiwei on the northern coast of Shandong province, was the summer anchorage for the British Navy's China squadron, leased in 1898.
4. Fifield, pp. 5–11.
5. Plüschow, p. 29.
6. John Dixon, *A Clash of Empires: the South Wales Borderers at Tsingtao*, 1914, Wrexham, 2008, p. 97.
7. Lo Huimin, *The Correspondence of G.E. Morrison*, vol. 2, Cambridge University Press, 1978, p. 556.
8. Dixon, p. 56.
9. Dixon, p. 53.
10. Plüschow, p. 68.
11. Sir John Jordan, Jordan Papers, National Archive, FO 350/12.
12. Dixon, p. 114.
13. Despatches of Brigadier General N.W. Barnardiston, Supplement to *The London Gazette*, 30 May 1916.
14. Dixon, pp. 124, 147–8.
15. Dixon, p. 126.
16. Lo Huimin, p. 665.
17. Ian Nish, *Alliance in Decline: a study of Anglo-Japanese relations 1908–1923*, London, Bloomsbury, 2012, pp. 138–9.
18. Dixon, p. 230.
19. *On the Emden, Prince Joseph von Hohenzollern, Emden: my experiences in SMS Emden*, London, 1928, and L. Sandhaus, *The Great War at Sea*, Cambridge University Press, 2014.
20. Lo Huimin, p. 661

Chapter 2: New China, the 'infant republic'

1. Lord Macartney, *An Embassy to China: being the journal kept by Lord Macartney during his embassy to the Emperor Chi'ien-lung*, 1793–4, London, Folio Society, 2004, p. 165.
2. Frances Wood, *No Dogs and Not Many Chinese: Treaty Port life in China 1843–1943*, London, John Murray, 2000, pp. 9–17.
3. National Archives, FO 228/1801–2.
4. Lo Huimin, p. 645.
5. O.M. Green, *The Foreigner in China*, London, Hutchinson [1924], p. 156.
6. Lo Huimin, p. 692.
7. Herbert Croly, *Willard Straight*, New York, Macmillan, 1925, p. 384–5
8. Croly, pp. 422–7.

9. W.F. Tyler, *Pulling Strings in China*, London, Constable, 1929, pp. 233–7.
10. Salt Gabelle: the French term 'gabelle' originally meant 'tax' but was applied particularly to an unpopular tax on salt levied from the thirteenth century and, by extension, to the tax on salt in China levied by the Imperial Chinese Customs which was run by foreigners.
11. Jordan Papers, FO 350/12.
12. Goldsworthy Lowes Dickinson, *Appearances: being notes of travel …*, London [n.d.], pp. 67–8.
13. Daniele Varè, *Laughing Diplomat*, London, John Murray, 1938, pp. 91–2.
14. Tyler, p. 226.
15. Sir John Jordan, 'Some Chinese I have known', *The Nineteenth Century and After*, DXXVI, London, 1920, p. 957 and Jerome Chen, *Yuan Shikai*, London, Allen and Unwin, 1961, p. 202.
16. Paul Samuel Reinsch, *An American Diplomat in China* [1922, reprint ed.], p. 3.
17. Jordan Papers, FO 350/13, 6 January, 1916.
18. St. John Perse [St. Léger-Léger's penname] *Letters*, Princeton University Press, 1978, p. 313.
19. Reginald Fleming Johnston, *Twilight in the Forbidden City* [1934], Hong Kong, Oxford University Press, 1985, p. 101.
20. Edward Selby Little, see Bob Molloy, *Colossus Unsung*, New Zealand, Xlibris, 2011, pp. 96–8.
21. Nish 2012, pp. 81–2, 109.
22. H.C. Thompson, *The Case for China*, London, Allen and Unwin, 1935, p. 132
23. Tyler, p. 226.
24. Lo Huimin, pp. 678, 737.
25. William J. Oudendyk, *Ways and Byways in Diplomacy*, London, 1939, pp. 35, 139.
26. Varè, p. 96
27. Brooke Astor, *Patchwork Child: early memories*, New York [1962] 1993, pp. 59, 81, 124. Maurice Cazenave was French chargé d'affaires in the early 1900s and subsequently became a financial agent.
28. Oudendyk, p. 36.
29. Stursberg, p. 87
30. Astor, pp. 63–4.
31. Varè, p. 121.
32. Oudendyk, p. 34
33. Robert Bickers, *Getting Stuck In For Shanghai*, Beijing, Penguin, 2014, p. 11

Chapter 3: Japan: not playing straight

1. Croly, pp. 238–51, Sir Eric Teichman, *Affairs of China*, London, Methuen, 1938, p. 22.
2. Dominic Lieven, *Towards the Flame: empire, war and the end of Tsarist Russia*, London, Allen Lane, 2015, p. 195.
3. Sir John Pratt, *War and Politics in China*, London, Jonathan Cape, 1943, pp. 149–50.
4. Croly, pp. 235, 258.
5. www.firstworldwar.com/source/anglojapanesealliance1902htm [accessed 30 April 2015].
6. Robert Lansing, *War Memoirs of Robert Lansing, Secretary of State*, London, Rich and Cowan, 1935, p. 281.
7. Pratt, p. 150.
8. Croly, p. 431.
9. Nish, p. 105.
10. Jordan Papers, FO 350/12. Katō Tomosaburo was an admiral, subsequently Naval Minister and Prime Minister of Japan.

11. *The Problem of Japan* 'by an ex-Counsellor of Legation in the Far East' [Sidney Osborne], Amsterdam, Van Langenhuysen, 1918, p. 83.
12. Nish, p. 150.
13. Paul French, *Carl Crow – a tough old China hand*, Hong Kong University Press, 2006, p. 64.
14. It was returned to China in 1922 after pressure at the Washington Conference of 1921 on naval disarmament, but less than a decade later, Japan invaded Manchuria.
15. 19 March 1915, Jordan Papers, FO 350/14.
16. *The Problem of Japan*, pp. 252–7, French, p. 66.
17. Nish, p. 162.
18. 19 March 1915, Jordan Papers, FO 350/13.
19. National Archives, Cabinet Papers CAB 24/146, 12 June 1917.
20. Lo Huimin, p. 374.
21. The British attempt to force China to sign the Simla Agreement and a subsequent disagreement over Tibetan membership of the Chinese parliament and their credentials was going on in September 1916.
22. National Archives, FO 371/2658, 18 September 1916.
23. National Archives, Cabinet Papers CAB 24, 146.
24. Lo Huimin, p. 647.
25. Lansing, pp. 302–3.
26. Pao-chin Chu, *V.K. Wellington Koo*, Hong Kong University Press, 1981, pp. 19, 24.
27. Chan Lau Kit-ching, *Anglo-Chinese diplomacy 1906–1920 . . .*, Hong Kong University Press, 1978, p. 102.

Chapter 4: China in wartime, 1914–6

1. Daniele Varè, unpublished diary, 13 February 1913.
2. Varè, unpublished diary, 6 October 1913.
3. Ellen N. LaMotte, *Peking Dust*, New York, 1920, pp. 24–5, 27. The American Concession in Shanghai was merged with the British in 1863 to form the International Settlement and America had no other concessions or 'spheres of influence' but pursued an 'open-door policy' by which it was hoped that Americans could trade and invest all over China without restriction to a particular 'sphere'.
4. Jordan Papers, FO 350/12.
5. quoted in Julia Boyd, *A Dance with the Dragon*, London, 2012, p. 84.
6. Jordan Papers, 2 October, 1914, FO 350/12 and Boyd, p. 85.
7. Charles Drage, *Servants of the Dragon Throne: being the lives of Edward and Cecil Bowra*, London, Peter Dawnay, 1966, pp. 260–1.
8. Croly, p. 300, *et seq.*
9. 9 October, 1914, Jordan Papers, FO 350/12.
10. 24 November, 1914, Jordan Papers, FO 350/12.
11. Lansing, p. 369.
12. Reinsch, p. 161.
13. Varè, pp. 140–1. The Legation Quarter in Peking had its own military protection in the form of squadrons of guards stationed in all the larger legations.
14. National Archives, FO 228/1919.
15. P.D. Coates, *The China Consuls*, Hong Kong, Oxford University Press, 1986, p. 410.
16. John Swire & Sons Ltd archive at SOAS: J. Swire letter 10 December 1914, G.T. Edkins letter 15 April 1915
17. A.H. Rasmussen, *China Trader*, London, Constable, 1954, pp. 159, 166–7.
18. Jordan Papers, FO 350/12.

19. Cyril Cannon, *Public Success, Private Sorrow: the life and times of Charles Henry Brewett Taylor (1857–1938) China Customs Commissioner and pioneer translator*, Hong Kong University Press, 2009, pp. 132, 142.
20. Jordan Papers FO 350/12.
21. LaMotte, pp. 192–3.
22. LaMotte, pp. 153–68.
23. LaMotte, pp. 66–70.
24. H.G.W. Woodhead, *A Journalist in China*, London, Hurst and Blackett, 1934, pp. 68–9.
25. Bickers, p. 58.
26. Bickers, p. 35.
27. J.B. Powell, *My Twenty-five Years in China*, New York, Macmillan, 1945, pp. 54–5.
28. Lo Huimin, p. 399.
29. Jordan Papers, FO 350/13.
30. Bickers, p. 30.
31. Bickers, p. 43–4.
32. Bickers, p. 47–8.
33. Donna Brunero, *Britain's Imperial Cornerstone in China: the Imperial Maritime Customs service 1854–1949*, London, 2006, p. 20.
34. Jordan Papers, FO 350/15.
35. Jordan Papers, FO 350/12.
36. Powell, pp. 12–13.
37. F.T. Cheng, *East and West: episodes in a sixty-year journey*, London, Hutchinson, 1951, p. 118.
38. Emily Hahn, *The Soong Sisters*, London, Robert Hale, 1942, p. 69.
39. Mai-mai Sze, *Echo of a Cry*, London, Jonathan Cape, 1947, p. 21–2.
40. Susan Chan Egan, *A Latterday Confucian: reminiscences of William Hung*, Harvard University Press, 1987, p. 46.
41. Chae-jin Lee, *Zhou Enlai: the early years*, Stanford University Press, 1994, pp. 68–9.
42. Alexander Pantsov with Steven I. Levine, *Mao: the real story*, New York, Simon and Schuster 2012, p. 44.
43. Lo Huimin, p. 405.
44. Jerome Ch'en, *Yuan Shih-k'ai*, London, Allen and Unwin, 1961, pp. 217, 227.
45. Meyrick Hewlett, *Forty Years in China*, London, Macmillan, 1944, pp. 92–108.

Chapter 5: The Chinese Labour Corps: Yellow 'eathens are 'elping out in France

1. Daryl Klein, *With the Chinks*, London 1919 (reprinted by Naval and Military Press and the Imperial War Museum, n.d.), p. 147.
2. Chen Ta, *Chinese Migrations*, Washington, Bulletin of the US Bureau of Labor Statistics, 1928, p. 19.
3. Quoted in Mark O'Neill, *The Chinese Labour Corps: the forgotten Chinese labourers of the First World War*, Beijing, Penguin China, 2014, p. 6.
4. http://hansard.millbanksystems.com/commons/1916/jul/24/statement-by-prime-minister #S5CV0084PO
5. David Olusoga, *The World's War*, London, Head of Zeus, 2014, p. 69.
6. Xu Guoqi, *Strangers on the Western Front: Chinese workers in the Great War*, Harvard University Press, 2011, p. 28.
7. Chen Ta, p. 128.
8. Olusoga, pp. 312–13.
9. Xu, *Strangers*, p. 49.
10. Xu, *Strangers*, p. 128.

11. Xu, *Strangers*, p. 128.
12. Chen Ta, pp. 207–10.
13. Xu, *Strangers*, p. 50.
14. Xu, *Strangers*, pp. 45–6.
15. Klein, pp. 151, 147.
16. Klein, pp. 151, 147.
17. Glen Peterson, 'Sans nom, sans visage et top-secret …' in Li Ma, *Les Travailleurs chinois en France dans la Première Guerre Mondiale*, Paris, CNRS Editions, 2012, pp. 111–25. There is some doubt over the deaths from cold as Peterson notes, pp. 128–9.
18. Peter Johnson, *Quarantined: life and death at William Head Station 1872–1959*, Victoria, Heritage House, 2013, p. 147.
19. Johnson, pp. 150–3.
20. Chen Ta, p. 145.
21. Chen Ta, p. 148.
22. Xu, *Strangers*, p. 90.
23. *War Memoirs*, Boston, 1935, p. 235.
24. Johnson, p. 154.
25. 'GSO', *G.H.Q (Montreuil-sur-mer)*, London, 1920, p. 156.
26. Xu, *Strangers*, p. 108.
27. Xu, *Strangers*, p. 113.
28. Chen Ta, p. 211.
29. Chen, p. 156.
30. Leeds University Library Special Collections, Liddle/WW1/G.S.Dent, Major W.A., DL0181.
31. Klein, p. 152, 186–8, Xu, *Strangers*, pp. 137–9.
32. Xu, *Strangers*, pp. 144–5.
33. Chen Ta, p. 147.
34. Pantsov, p. 65.
35. Klein, p. 145–7.
36. The Qingming festival in spring when families gather to sweep family graves and make offerings of food, paper money and incense, has recently been declared a public holiday in China.
37. Dominek Dendooven, 'Les T'chings': mythe et realite a propose du CLC dans la region du front en Flandre occidentale' in Li Ma, pp. 459–73.
38. Marianne Bastid-Bruguière, 'Le retour en Chine des travailleurs chinois de la Grande Guerre: quel héritage?' in Li Ma, p. 491.
39. Mark O'Neill, *From the Tsar's Railway to the Red Army*, Melbourne, Penguin, 2014 and Alexander G. Larin, 'Chinese in Russia: an historical perspective' in Gregor Benton and Frank N. Pieke, *The Chinese in Europe*, Basingstoke, Macmillan, 1998.
40. Brian Fawcett, 'The CLC in France 1917–1921' in *Journal of the Royal Asiatic Society Hong Kong Branch*, vol. 40, 2000, pp. 61–2. Hui Yuhe's tombstone is depicted in Li Ma, pl. XIX.

Chapter 6: Spies and Suspicions

1. National Archives, FO 228/1919.
2. Woodhead, p. 65.
3. William Jennings Bryan 1860–1925, US Congressman, Secretary of State 1912–1914, anti-evolutionist who elsewhere described England as having bestowed an 'inestimable boon' on India in the English language.
4. Woodhead, pp. 65–6.
5. Nish, p. 182–3.

6. Woodhead, p. 66.
7. National Archives, FO 228/1919.
8. National Archives, FO 371/2913.
9. Woodhead, pp. 70–3.
10. National Archives, FO 228/1919.
11. Nish, pp. 184–5.
12. National Archives FO 350/12.
13. Lo Huimin, p. 661.
14. Frances Wood, *No Dogs and Not Many Chinese: Treaty Port life in China 1843–1943*, London, John Murray, 1998, pp. 175–7.
15. Woodhead, pp. 69–70.
16. P.D. Coates, *The China Consuls*, Hong Kong, Oxford University Press, 1988, pp. 405, 252.
17. Lo Huimin, p. 406.
18. Woodhead, p. 74.
19. Lo Huimin, p. 377.
20. National Archives, CAB 24/146.
21. This and subsequent references are taken from Hugh Trevor-Roper, *Hermit of Peking: the hidden life of Sir Edmund Backhouse*, London, Eland, 1993, pp. 162–87.

Chapter 7: A crucial year of chaos and decisions: 1917
1. A. Scott Berg, *Wilson*, London, New York, Simon and Schuster, 2013, p. 421.
2. Reinsch, p. 168.
3. LaMotte, pp. 139–40, 183–4.
4. Xu Guoqi, *China and the Great War*, Cambridge University Press, 2005, p. 145.
5. Reports to the Cabinet, National Archives, CAB 24/146, 22 and 24 February 1917.
6. Powell, pp. 33–4.
7. National Archives, FO 371/2658.
8. Xu, *China and the Great War*, p. 239.
9. Lo Huimin, p. 661.
10. Xu, *China and the Great War*, pp. 242–3.
11. 7 September 1917, National Archives, FO 371/2913.
12. 16 July, National Archives, FO 371/2913
13. 9 July, National Archives, FO 371/2913.
14. St. John Perse, pp. 263, 313.
15. Family sources via Christopher Arnander.
16. 16 July, National Archives, FO 371/2913.
17. His-cheng Ch'i, *Warlord Politics in China*, Stanford University Press, 1976, p. 6.
18. Hewlett, pp. 92–108.
19. Xu, *China and the Great War*, p. 172. On tax, Chu, p. 39.
20. Cabinet Minutes 4 April 1917, National Archives, CAB 24/146.
21. Margaret Macmillan, *The Peacemakers: six months that changed the world*, London, John Murray, 2001, p. 320.
22. National Archives, FO371/2913.
23. Paul Mantoux, *Les Délibérations du Conseil des Quatre*, Paris, CNRS, 1955, vol. 1, p. 330 [Frances Wood translation].
24. Bruce A. Elleman, *Wilson and China*, Armonk, M.E. Sharpe, 2002, p. 226.
25. Tyler, pp. 261–3.
26. National Archives, CAB 24/146, 14 November 1917.
27. National Archives, FO 371/2913, 20 October 1917.
28. National Archives, Jordan Papers, FO 350/16, February and June 1918.

29. Lo Huimin, pp. 549, 661.
30. National Archives, FO 371/2913.
31. National Archives FO 371/2913.
32. 5–8 September 1917, National Archives FO 371/2913.
33. Xu, *China and the Great War*, p. 199.

Chapter 8: After the war, the disappointment
1. Reinsch, pp. 317, 342.
2. National Archives, Jordan Papers FO 350/16.
3. Xu, *Strangers*, p. 229.
4. Macmillan, p. 315.
5. Lo Huimin, p. 659.
6. Xu, *China and the Great War*, p. 259.
7. http://avalon.law.yale.edu/20th-_century/wilson14asp
8. Georges Clemenceau, *Grandeur and Misery of Victory*, London, 1930, p. 140.
9. Xu, *China and the Great War*, p. 209.
10. Harry Hussey, *My Pleasures and Palaces: from Sun Yat-sen to Mao Tse-tung*, New York, 1968, p. 157.
11. Chu, p. 14.
12. Hussey, pp. 247–8.
13. Chu, p. 10–11.
14. Yuan-tseng Chen, *Return to the Middle Kingdom: one family, three revolutionaries and the birth of modern China*, New York, Union Square Press, 2008, pp. 84–5.
15. Conversation with Dr. Zaki Kour, see also F. Seymour-Cocks, *The Secret Treaties and Understandings*, London, Union of Democratic Control [1918].
16. Berg, p. 579.
17. Nish, pp. 214–5.
18. Elleman, pp. 42–3.
19. Harold Nicolson, *Peacemaking 1919*, [1933], London, Methuen, 1964, pp. 18, 72, 103.
20. Nicolson, p. 153.
21. Macmillan, p. 308.

Chapter 9: Anatomy of a Betrayal: the interpreter's account
1. A Japanese diplomat and historian writing on 1 August 1919, quoted in Elleman, p. 53.
2. Lo Huimin, p. 661.
3. Macmillan, p. 324.
4. Lloyd George, vol. 1, p. 154.
5. Thomas Edward LaFargue, *China and the War*, Stanford University Press, 1937, p. 197.
6. Chen, p. 86.
7. Mark Levich, *Panthéon de la Guerre: reconfiguring a panorama of the Great War*, Columbia, University of Missouri Press and National World War 1 Museum, 2006.

Chapter 10: China's reaction
1. The square as it is today was created by removing buildings in front of the Tianan gate in the 1950s.
2. Rana Mitter, *A Bitter Revolution: China's struggle with the modern world*, Oxford University Press, 2004, p. 9.
3. Gao Wenqian, *Zhou Enlai: the last perfect revolutionary*, New York, Public Affairs, 2007, pp. 39, 42, and Howard L. Boorman, *Biographical Dictionary of Republican China*, New York, Columbia University Press, 1967, p. 392.

4. Lee, p. 164 and http://chine.information.com/guide/etudiants-ouvriers-chinois-en-france_2604html

5. Lu Xun, *The Real Story of Ah-Q and other tales of China*, translated by Julia Lovell, London, Penguin, 2009, p. xix.

6. Ch'i, p. 22.

7. Ch'i, p. 2.

8. http://hansard.millbanksystems.com/commons/1940/jul/18/transit-of-war-materials-china

9. See Iris Chang, *The Rape of Nanking*, New York, Penguin, 1997, and John E. Woods, *The Good Man of Nanking: the diaries of John Rabe*, New York, Knopf, 1998.

10. Cao Bingyan. The Search for Allies: Chinese alliance behaviour from 1930 to the end of World War II, 2009, http://lpu.edu/CHIS/History/GraduateDegree/MADMS/Theses/files

11. *Financial Times*, 29 January 2010.

12. https://iiss.org/events/archive2015-f463/july-636f/fullerton-lecture-fu-yong-d260

Index